TRUST AND DISTRUST IN SINO-AMERICAN RELATIONS

TRUST AND DISTRUST IN SINO-AMERICAN RELATIONS

Challenge and Opportunity

Steve Chan

Rapid Communications in Conflict and Security Series
General Editor: Geoffrey R.H. Burn

CAMBRIA
PRESS

Amherst, New York

Requests for permission should be directed to:
permissions@cambriapress.com, or mailed to:
Cambria Press
University Corporate Centre,
100 Corporate Parkway, Suite 128
Amherst, New York 14226, U.S.A.

Library of Congress Cataloging-in-Publication Data on file.

ISBN: 9781604979978

良藥苦口 忠言逆耳
Good medicine is nauseous to the taste;
candid advice is unpleasant to the ear

TABLE OF CONTENTS

Chapter 1: Introduction 1

Chapter 2: Gauging Another State's Trustworthiness 47

Chapter 3: A Weak Form of Trust Reflecting External
Compulsion 97

Chapter 4: A Semi-Strong Form of Trust Motivated by
Reputational Considerations 135

Chapter 5: A Strong Form of Trust Grounded in Appropriateness
and Unthinkability 183

Chapter 6: Conclusion 209

Postscript 253

Index 257

Rapid Communications in Conflict and Security 263

About the Author 265

TRUST AND DISTRUST IN SINO-AMERICAN RELATIONS

Chapter 1

Introduction

In 2012, two eminent scholars published a much-cited monograph commenting on the "strategic distrust" that has characterized Sino-American relations.[1] Kenneth Lieberthal and Jisi Wang are not only well-known scholars but they have also played influential roles in official circles in Washington and Beijing respectively. In publishing their work reflecting their respective government's concerns about and perceptions of the other country's policies, these authors expressed the belief that a more sound understanding of the other side could contribute to better management of their mutual distrust. They "believe that each side can better manage the issue of strategic distrust if its leaders have confidence that they have an accurate picture of the way the other leadership thinks on the issues that produce this distrust."[2]

A distrust of another state, however, does not necessarily have to reflect misunderstanding or misperception. It can instead be based on sound reasons and legitimate concerns about the other side's motivations. Logically, a more accurate understanding of the other leadership's thinking does not rule out the possibility of increasing one's skepticisms about its intentions and thus deepen one's distrust. A more accurate understanding of the other side can even be used to more effectively exploit its vulnerabilities. In *Addressing U.S.-China Strategic Distrust*, Lieberthal and Wang report pervasive misgivings held by their respective governments' officials regarding their counterparts. For instance, Chinese officials perceive that the U.S. is trying to encircle China, and conversely, American officials are concerned that China is seeking to eventually displace U.S. leadership in East Asia. Both sides hold these views despite the other's reassurances to the contrary. But are each party's concerns and perceptions unwarranted and if so, how can one tell? Moreover, why have their reciprocal reassurances thus far evidently turned out to be unpersuasive to the other side?

In addition to the possibility of mutual trust and that of mutual distrust, one country can trust the other but the latter does not trust the former in return—hence the possibility of one-sided trust. For instance, one can well imagine that Adolf Hitler knew about his own untrustworthiness and actually believed in Winston Churchill's trustworthiness.[3] He might also have believed that Churchill had understood him accurately and thus knew him to be untrustworthy. In this case, he could expect Churchill to distrust and resist him, and Anglo-German hostility would ensue even though Hitler had thought Churchill could be trusted and even though Churchill had understood Hitler accurately.

It is true that distrust can stem from a lack of sound understanding, and it can have a corrosive effect on a relationship that can otherwise be mutually rewarding. But misplacing one's trust in another leader or state is dangerous, if this target of one's attribution turns out to be a "wolf in sheep's skin." Neville Chamberlain is remembered by history for his naïve faith in Adolf Hitler's trustworthiness. He was taken in by Hitler's reassurances that Germany had only limited territorial and political ambitions. Therefore, not only distrust may be grounded in cogent arguments and valid evidence, but mistaken trust can also exact very high costs. The management of peaceful and stable interstate relations entails more than just the removal of distrust—or even gaining the other side's trust.

One may even question the extent to which trust—a belief in the benign nature of another state—is necessary for interstate cooperation. Arguably, the USSR and the Western countries held deep and abiding concerns about the other side's ulterior motives and long-term ambitions. But these misgivings did not prevent them from cooperating to fight the Axis powers during World War II. More recently, from about 1972 to 1989, the U.S. and China were practically tacit allies that had worked together to oppose the USSR. As these two examples suggest, neither trust nor regime affinity are a prerequisite for states to collaborate in their pursuit of mutual gains. Thus, states can still cooperate even when they entertain serious doubts about the other side's motivations or intentions, a view that differs from the position that "mutual trust is necessary for cooperation."[4] For example, states can negotiate arms limitation deals even while still maintaining a robust capability to ensure a devastating military retaliation. My view is closer to Robert Axelrod's argument that cooperation does not require trust; "there is no need to assume trust between the players: the use of reciprocity can be enough to make defection unproductive."[5] Trust can promote cooperation but cooperation does not necessarily entail trust. Why then should we bother with studying trust? Because cooperation not based on trust (in its strong form as will be explained later) is likely to be fragile and fleeting. This cooperation reflects a marriage of convenience, a temporary convergence of interests—a distinction from a more robust and enduring kind of cooperation based on shared identities as my typology of trust will highlight.

Moreover, whether the other side has a democratic government appears to be neither necessary nor sufficient for interstate cooperation. After all, during the time of close Sino-American strategic collaboration (1972–1989), China was much more authoritarian than today. In the years after World War II, Washington has also not hesitated to support various repressive and authoritarian regimes in Latin America, East Asia, and the Middle East. As another example that touches on a basic source of Sino-American tension, Washington was a staunch supporter of Taiwan under

Chang Kai-shek's rule when it was hardly a democracy but this support has actually waned even though this island has become more democratic over time. As Charles Kupchan has remarked, "... foreign policy behavior —in particular, the practice of strategic restraint—is a more important variable than regime type per se in isolating the causes for peace."[6]

Just as states can cooperate even though they distrust each other, outward signs of cooperation and even formal declarations of goodwill do not mean that the problem of distrust has been resolved. The German-Soviet Non-Aggression Pact of 1939 provides an example. It did not stop Hitler from launching Operation Barbarossa to invade the USSR. And, as shown by events subsequent to the signing of the Sino-Soviet Treaty of Friendship, Alliance and Mutual Assistance in 1950, relations between two close allies can deteriorate and mutual trust can be seriously undermined.

As just mentioned, perceptions of another state can undergo major and abrupt changes. This occurred, for instance, after Richard Nixon's visit to China and the overthrow of the Shah in Iran. In these and other cases, dramatic changes in governmental assessments and academic discourse reflect the improvement or deterioration in official relations, even though the basic character of the other side's regime might not have changed. China was in the "out" group but was quickly reclassified after Nixon's visit as a member of the "in" group opposing the USSR, whereas Iran's status went from a steadfast ally to an international outcast after U.S. diplomats were seized and held as hostages in Tehran. Similarly, imperial Germany was at one time admired by leading Americans (including President Woodrow Wilson) as a model of progress, efficiency, and rule of law, but public image and elite opinion in the U.S. turned negative against this country as World War I approached.[7] Thus, judgments about another country's friendliness or hostility can change rather quickly and sharply, and perceptions of the level of threat that country poses and the amount of trust it deserves can also undergo similar revisions even in the absence of a basic change in its regime character.

This phenomenon points to an inherent uncertainty in conducting interstate relations. Even when one has complete confidence that another state's current leaders are honorable people who are sincere in declaring their good intentions, can one assume that their successors can also be trusted? Indeed, even for the other state's current leaders, can one expect them to continue their present disposition if circumstances change— such as if they were to gain a decisive military or economic advantage? James Fearon calls attention to this problem, suggesting that a state's inability to commit itself credibly to abiding by its promises in the future presents a fundamental obstacle standing in the way of interstate cooperation.[8] This commitment problem points to a basic difficulty in securing trust. How can a state assure its counterpart that it will not change "its color" in the future? And why should its counterpart believe that it will not renege on its promises when it is advantageous for it to do so in the future? Fearon's rationalist approach argues that it will take costly signals in order to persuade others that one can be trusted. The greater the potential costs that one imposes on oneself for undertaking any possible opportunistic behavior, the more credible one's commitment not to engage in such behavior.

Is it easier for a state to lose others' trust in it than for it to build others' trust in it? Given the acuteness of the so-called security dilemma, officials are more likely to commit the mistake of being unwarrantedly pessimistic about the intentions of others than the opposite error of being lulled into complacency by their opposite numbers.[9] To the extent that officials are socialized to share a Hobbesian view of interstate politics, it will probably take more massive and more decisive information to persuade them to believe that their counterparts are trustworthy than the other way around (i.e., it will only take a small amount of even ambiguous evidence to incline them to suspect their counterparts' trustworthiness). Deborah Larson remarks that "people need more evidence to conclude that someone is trustworthy than they need to establish he is not."[10] As a corollary, one may hypothesize that it is easier to lose others' trust than to build or restore it. "A state widely regarded as unreliable like the former

Soviet Union will have to carry out *many* cooperative acts to convince the other side that it can be trusted to keep an agreement. Whereas trust takes a long time to create, it can be destroyed in an instance."[11]

WHY STUDY INTERSTATE TRUST?

It behooves analysts and officials to address interstate trust as a process rather than as an outcome. Trust is not something that is to be gained and can then be forgotten about. It needs to be constantly nurtured. Ronald Reagan and Mikhail Gorbachev succeeded in overcoming decades of distrust between their countries. This trust, however, has been significantly eroded in the years since 1989. Today there is again a profound distrust characterizing the relationship between Washington and Moscow. Tension between them has been exacerbated by many developments, including recent events pertaining to Ukraine's status and the secessionist movement in some parts of that country. Seen in this light, trust is a matter of degree (and not a binary decision of either having it or not having it), and it requires constant updating based on new information. Moreover and as just implied, it is a contingent attribution to be extended or withheld depending on how another state is perceived to have acted— or to have refrained from acting—recently. President Reagan was fond of citing the Russian maxim, "trust but verify" (Доверяй, но проверяй).[12]

Untrustworthy states can be expected to masquerade as the trustworthy type in order to gain the confidence of their prospective victims. They will try to conceal their true character by imitating those that are actually trustworthy. Thus, it is necessary to distinguish the untrustworthy ones from others who are trustworthy so that one will not be victimized by the untrustworthy ones' attempts at strategic deception. The costs of misplacing one's trust in someone like Hitler can be very serious. In the language of statistical analysis, both the dangers of Type 1 and Type 2 errors are present. One should be concerned about committing the mistake of "false positive" (misperceiving an untrustworthy state as trustworthy) as well as making the mistake of "false negative" (a failure to recognize a trustworthy state for what it is).

Naturally, mutual distrust can poison bilateral relations to the extent that it exacerbates and perpetuates a cycle of antagonism, producing a highly combustible strategic climate such that a small spark can ignite a large conflagration. The spiral model of conflict points to such an escalatory process and was exemplified by events leading to World War I.[13] Mutual distrust can thus be a fundamental driver of the dynamics producing war. To the extent that such perceptions are unwarranted, they also deny to the parties involved the benefits that a better relationship would have otherwise brought to them. Thus in addition to the risks of abetting interstate tension and even conflict, unjustified suspicions about others' intentions impose an opportunity cost in the rewards of cooperation foregone.

The reference made to the outbreak of World War I just now describes the deep distrust existing between the two opposing sides of this belligerence (such as between France and Germany, and between Austria-Hungary and Russia). This distrust was a contributing cause to this conflict. But ironically, distrust also played another and perhaps less publicized role among the allies on each side. Russia and France were each worried that their strategic partnership might unravel, and both were concerned about British abandonment. Similarly, Germany was anxious not to lose its ally Austria-Hungary, and the latter was eager to shore up Germany's support. Consequently all these countries sought reassurances from their allies and they also tried to reassure their allies—that is, to demonstrate that they could be *trusted* to keep their commitments. Their collective efforts to bolster their trustworthiness in their allies' eyes created policy rigidities and exacerbated the escalatory dynamic. Thus, efforts to build trust among allies can ironically have a destabilizing effect when seen in a larger context. Trust rather than distrust could be a problem. As a counterfactual example, would Vienna have been as bellicose in its policy toward Belgrade if it had greater doubts about

Berlin's backing, and would St. Petersburg be as ready to order military mobilization if it were more unsure of Paris's intentions?

A country or person's trustworthiness matters when officials grapple with specific issues and situations fraught with the risk of escalation. Do they have confidence in the basic honesty of their counterparts? Are they inclined to believe in the threats or promises made by their fellow diplomats? Are they likely to accept accounts offered by their counterparts, seeking to explain or justify the actual conduct or announced intentions of these counterparts' government, or at least to accord these explanations and justifications the benefit of doubt? Or are they likely to view these communications skeptically and to dismiss them as "hot air" and even deliberate deception? A state that has earned a general reputation for being honest and thus trustworthy is much more likely to have its diplomacy taken seriously than others whose prior behavior has shown them to be unreliable or insincere. Its declared policy is much more likely to be believed, whether it is to do something or to refrain from doing something. Interestingly and contrary to conventional wisdom, John Mearsheimer concludes that leaders and diplomats do not usually lie to their foreign counterparts and that they are instead more disposed to lie to their own citizens, a practice that is more common for democracies than nondemocracies.[14]

That leaders and diplomats tend to lie less to their foreign counterparts than commonly supposed reflects perhaps Anne Sartori's argument that it pays to have a general reputation of being honest in one's diplomacy.[15] An honest country does not make a threat unless it is serious about actually implementing this threat when the stipulated circumstances come to pass. It does not make empty threats, pretending that it will act in a foreign situation when it actually does not intend to do so. This view values a country's honesty or trustworthiness as a matter of general reputation so that others' perceptions are not limited to isolated instances. What it does—or fails to do—on one occasion or toward one actor will have ramifications for other occasions pertaining to other actors.

Sartori claims, for example, that Beijing's failure to invade Taiwan in 1950–1951 as its propaganda had suggested made its subsequent threat to intervene in the Korean War less credible to Washington.[16] Applying the same general logic, some people have opposed reducing Washington's current support of Taiwan on the grounds that other U.S. allies will, as a result, have reason to question the firmness of U.S. commitments to *them*.[17] Reputation can matter even in the absence of clearly or explicitly articulated threats, promises, or quid pro quo bargains. Thus, for example, NATO's (North Atlantic Treaty Organization) attack on Muammar Gaddafi's Libya—a country that had given up its program to develop weapons of mass destruction—would presumably make Iranian and North Korean leaders more reluctant to dismantle their weapons programs out of a fear of being attacked after they have thus disarmed themselves. From their perspective, Gaddafi had obviously misplaced his trust in the mistaken belief that giving up his weapons program would save him from Saddam Hussein's fate. In this view, by denying himself the deterrent benefit afforded by such weapons or even just perceptions that he might have them, he had actually made himself more vulnerable to attack.

Because one can never know for sure the other side's intentions, trusting the other party always means accepting uncertainties and taking risks. To a larger or lesser extent, trust requires a leap of faith. One relies on another's current or past behavior in order to infer its future intentions. Naturally, one's own actions stemming from this diagnosis can influence the other side's future conduct, thus fostering the possibility of self-fulfilling or self-denying prophecies. For instance, if one distrusts the other, actions stemming from one's distrust can in turn incline the other to respond in a manner that confirms this distrust.

Trust, or distrust, plays a critical role in interstate relations because many situations facing officials are inherently ambiguous. The available evidence can lend itself to multiple competing interpretations. Whether an official trusts or distrusts a counterpart can thus predispose him or her to accept one interpretation and reject others. For instance, news of Soviet demilitarization in 1955–1956 was seen by U.S. Secretary of State John Foster Dulles through the prism of "inherent bad faith of the communists."[18] He was inclined to believe that Soviet demilitarization indicated that the USSR was getting weaker rather than nicer—that this decision reflected Moscow's dire economic circumstances rather than a change in its basic motivation. Such an interpretation naturally has policy consequences, making a U.S. decision to reciprocate with similar détente gestures less likely and an inclination to "turn up the heat" more likely. "If the Soviets changed their policy, Dulles inferred that they must have done so out of weakness. This meant that the United States should push the Soviets even harder."[19] This example thus shows how a possible attempt at conciliation may be misconstrued when one is deeply distrusted by the other side. Instead of inviting reciprocation, this attempt can have the counterproductive effect of encouraging a counterpart to adopt even more coercive measures (hence, the possibility of self-denying prophecy). In her study of several turning points in U.S.-Soviet relations during the Cold War, Deborah Larson used "missed opportunities" to describe failed efforts to achieve negotiated settlements on arms control, the status of Berlin, and the unification of Germany, failures that can at least be in part attributed to distrust.[20]

Trust in another actor provides the basis for projecting its future intentions, and it also serves as a prism to assess its current or past conduct. It inclines a person or state to give the other side the benefit of doubt whereas distrust has the opposite effect of imposing a more demanding burden of proof on this counterpart in order for it to demonstrate its sincerity or honesty. When, for example, Korean Airlines Flight 007 was shot down by a Soviet interceptor in September 1983, most people in the West were willing to accept the explanation that this aircraft's violation of Soviet airspace was a mistake and not a deliberate provocation (such as if this flight were on an intelligence mission undertaken in conjunction with the U.S.). Many were outraged by the loss of 269 lives caused by this incident. More recently in July 2014, Malaysian Airlines Flight 17 crashed in Ukraine near its border with Russia, and 283 passengers perished in this tragedy. Western indignation was focused on pro-Russian Ukrainian separatists and even Russians who were suspected of firing the missile that had brought down this aircraft. People in the West were not, however, nearly as outraged when Iran Air Flight 655 was shot down in Iranian airspace by a guided missile fired from *USS Vincennes* in July 1988. This incident caused even more civilian deaths (290), but Westerners were inclined to accept this tragedy as an honest mistake. The U.S. government also regretted the loss of three lives when five U.S. guided bombs hit the Chinese embassy in Belgrade in May 1999, again claiming that it was an honest mistake.

We do not know enough specifics behind these episodes or others like them (such as the 1967 attack on *USS Liberty* by Israeli forces resulting in 34 fatalities) to be definitive about whether they were caused by innocent human or mechanical errors, or conversely, intended as a deliberate provocation. These examples do, however, help to highlight the important role that trust plays in predisposing people's interpretations of and their reactions to situations with limited and imperfect information. Whether they have trust in another country and its leadership can be a critical factor in deciding whether such an event is resolved peacefully or escalates into a major crisis. As a counterfactual thought experiment, how would most Americans interpret and react to news that a U.S. embassy or a U.S. naval vessel in international waters had been attacked by the Chinese air force? Would they accept an explanation from Beijing claiming that this attack was due to an intelligence or communication failure? This is not just a rhetorical question as one can easily imagine simulation exercises intended to elicit responses from people in different countries to such hypothetical scenarios in order to gain some empirical indication of their level of mutual trust or distrust. Parenthetically, this is also a good place to acknowledge that their different willingness to trust U.S. and Chinese officials may very well incline readers to disagree with my interpretation of the various historical episodes to be introduced in the following discussion.

WHAT DOES IT MEAN TO TRUST?

The Merriam-Webster online dictionary defines trust as a "belief in someone or something is reliable, good, honest, effective, etc." It cites confidence, credence, and faith as its synonyms. Significantly, all these adjectives and nouns share one thing in common: they all refer to another person or entity's performance at a future time. As such, to have trust in someone or something is tantamount to believing that this person or entity will act favorably in a given circumstance—or that this party will at least not try to hurt one deliberately. This belief is premised on attributing to the party in question an inherent disposition or capacity. In foreign relations, trust pertains primarily to one's belief about another state's future intentions as opposed to its future capabilities.

The stronger this belief, the more confident one is about the target's future intentions. Trust is thus based on one's subjective assessment about the target. It is distinct from cooperation which refers to actual conduct, specifically working together with another party for some shared benefit. As already indicated, cooperation does not require trust even though trust facilitates it. It can happen when the parties involved have common interests and expect others to reciprocate their behavior (without necessarily believing that others have benign intentions). Trustworthiness/untrustworthiness refers to the collective judgment of observing bystanders about whether a person or entity deserves to be trusted or should be distrusted.

The study of trust has had a rather long tradition in political science, sociology, and social psychology. Trust in government has been a staple question in the study of American public opinion and political behavior at least since the launch of the National Election Studies in the 1950s.[21] Trust has also been a central idea in the field of comparative politics, such as pertaining to different countries' civic cultures.[22] From Edward Banfield's classic study of the fictitious Italian town of Montegrano to Robert Putnam's influential study of regional differences in Italy, it looms large as a key determinant of effective governance, good society, and even a vibrant economy.[23]

In the field of international relations, a lack of trust holds the key to the so-called security dilemma.[24] A trust deficit causes both sides in a game of prisoners' dilemma to choose defection, thus bringing about a worse outcome than had they cooperated. Mutual suspicions also underlie other stylistic representations of international relations such as the spiral model of conflict.[25] As already mentioned, given the inherently ambiguous nature of many situations, whether one is willing to trust another state is critically important in deciding how one forms one's opinion about an event and decides on a response to it. Yet despite the centrality of trust in international relations, there have been relatively few studies that focus on it.[26] However, as shown by several reviews of the relevant literature, there has been recently an increasing level of attention to develop and delineate this concept.[27]

Andrew Kydd defines trust as "a belief that the other side prefers mutual cooperation to exploiting one's own cooperation, while mistrust is a belief that the other side prefers exploiting one's cooperation to returning it."[28] This definition of trust is actor-specific; A may trust B but not C. Russell Hardin sees trust to be more issue-specific: "For us to trust you we must believe your motivations toward us are to serve our interests, broadly conceived, with respect to the issues at stake."[29] It is thus possible for me to trust you to manage my retirement investment but not the care of my children. In Hardin's formulation, trust is seen as "encapsulated interest." To the extent that another person's interests incorporate or encompass my interests, it is in his or her interest to advance mine.[30] Both Kydd and Hardin are concerned with particularistic trust (as opposed to generalized trust which will be discussed shortly).

The nature of particularistic trust is explicated further by Margaret Levi and Laura Stoker: "Trust is relational; it involves an individual making herself vulnerable to another individual, group, or institution that has the capacity to do her harm or to betray her. Trust is seldom unconditional;

it is given to specific individuals or institutions over specific domains."[31] The idea of making oneself vulnerable to potential defection by the other side is consistent with the claim that to trust someone is to give this person the benefit of doubt or to have faith in his or her intentions.

In an interesting emendation of this reasoning, Vincent Keating and Jan Ruzicka argue that the U.S. and USSR/Russia do *not* necessarily have a trusting relationship simply because they have both voluntarily taken on vulnerability to the other side's nuclear forces. Instead of trusting the other side, each state relies on the credible threat of its nuclear retaliation and it has a high degree of confidence that this threat will deter its counterpart from attacking it. This confidence does not reflect their view of the other side's benevolence, but is rather based on their assiduous efforts to ensure the viability of their respective retaliatory force. It should not be conflated with trust which Keating and Ruzicka see as "an ideational structure that *cognitively reduces or eliminates the residual risk and uncertainty* that is part of any decision."[32] Instead of relying on voluntary exposure to the other party's defection as an indication of trusting the latter, they claim that an absence of hedging strategy reveals trust and point to the U.S.-Japan security relationship as an example.

To anticipate the later discussion, a confidence based on deterrence refers to a weak form of trust whereas a confidence in the benevolence or goodwill of the other side refers to a strong form of trust. Aaron Hoffman argues that "the US-Soviet nuclear relationship is an example of cooperative risk-taking without trust."[33] He presents a fiduciary conception according to which "trust refers to an actor's willingness to place its interests under the control of others based on the belief that those actors will honor their obligation to avoid using their discretion in a harmful manner."[34] Thus according to this conception, when a small country spends less on its own defense as a result of its reliance on the military protection of a powerful ally like the U.S., its free-riding behavior actually indicates its trust in the latter.[35]

In addition to emphasizing the other party's preference to advance one's interests, Levi and Stoker also stress its inclination to refrain from doing harm: "Even when there is no call for trust, a person or institution can possess the attributes of trustworthiness, which assure potential trusters that the trusted party will not betray a trust.... The trustworthy will not betray the trust as a consequence of either bad faith or ineptitude."[36] The last sentence indicates that in addition to not having bad intentions, the recipient of one's trust must have the necessary competence to avoid causing harm.

Do you believe that most people (including strangers) can be trusted? This question asks about generalized trust and as such has been at the center of inquiries about a country's social capital.[37] This social capital, based on generalized trust, is taken by social scientists to be vital for promoting and ensuring a vibrant civic culture essential for cooperation among citizens, the development of a liberal participatory democracy, and the general well-being of a society. Francisco Herreros defines generalized trust as "a more or less well-grounded expectation about the preferences of other people,"[38] preferences that are congruent with one's own. In a similar vein, Jan Delhey and Kenneth Newton see generalized trust as "the belief that others will not deliberately or knowingly do us harm, if they can avoid it, and will look after our interests, if this is possible."[39] People in the Nordic countries have consistently shown a higher level of generalized trust than those in South America. Significantly, the level of generalized trust has been in steady decline in the U.S. and mass disaffection has been on the rise in many advanced industrialized countries.[40] As Robert Putnam has remarked, "[e]very year fewer and fewer of us [Americans] aver that 'most people can be trusted.' Every year more and more of us caution that 'you can't be too careful in dealing with people.'"[41] In November 2015, a survey of Americans reported that only 19% of the respondents indicated that they could trust their government always or most of the time, and Republicans and Republican-leaning respondents were more inclined to say that they sometimes or never trust their government than Democratic ones (89% versus 72%). The former were also more likely to say that they were "angry" with their government than the latter (32% versus 12%).[42]

In contrast to particularistic trust, generalized trust is not actor-specific and does not even need to be issue-specific. It is a diffuse sense of confidence that people are generally nice and will not try to take advantage of others. It is not based on a cost-benefit calculation or even the expectation of direct reciprocity. In the rendition given by Eric Uslaner,[43] trust is driven by shared norms and based on moralistic rather than strategic reasoning. It is the result of a person's socialization. As Peter Nannestad has noted,[44] measurement of this generalized trust has been troubled by ambiguities concerning the boundaries of the moral community and of the issue domain that it refers to. Is this community limited to one's neighbors, fellow citizens or co-ethnics, or does it extend to immigrants and foreigners? Does it pertain to the impartiality of the criminal justice system, the integrity of politicians, or the objectivity of the news media?

Brian Rathbun has applied the concept of generalized trust to international relations.[45] He makes the interesting argument that instead of international institutions being created to foster trust, this disposition precedes and motivates the formation of international institutions such as the League of Nations and the United Nations. Generalized trust creates expectations of diffuse reciprocity and reduces concerns about opportunism, and Rathbun sees this orientation rather than U.S. preponderance to have had a stronger influence on those American leaders who favored multilateralism.

In this book, trust refers to a general confidence about another state's future intentions which are seen to be benign or at least not hostile. I will present three forms of trust depending on how the party making this attribution sees the main source influencing the target's future disposition. Are this target's intentions shaped primarily by compelling external circumstances, or motivated by a more general albeit still self-regarding concern for its reputation? Or are these intentions more likely to be based on moralistic rather than strategic reasoning, reflecting the logic of appropriateness rather than the logic of consequences? The three forms of trust just sketched parallel roughly Deborah Larson's discussion of the three meanings that the concept of trust can take on psychologically: predictability, credibility, and good intentions.[46]

One may, for instance, say "You can trust Aunt Betty to complain about the weather as usual." In this weak form, trust refers to a sense that another person or state's behavior is predicable such as exemplified by the proposition that one can expect a declining state to be more conciliatory or a democracy to be more peaceful in its foreign relations. Trust can have a second meaning as in "You can trust Elizabeth to keep her appointment." In this semi-strong form, trust refers to a state's credibility in the sense that one can count on it to implement its pronouncements or to carry out its commitments. This semi-strong form is obviously related to the target's general reputation for being honest and reliable. In its third meaning, trust reflects a confidence in another person or state's basic goodwill. This strong form of trust refers to the expectation that the target has benevolent intentions and will refrain from exploiting one even when given the opportunity to do so—that it "will do what is right" given one's "essential faith" in its character.[47] This form of trust tends to be based on shared identity and strong norms such as those existing among members of a security community like those in the North Atlantic region and the European Union.[48] Some, however, have argued that a common identity is neither necessary nor sufficient for "moralistic trust" based on a general expectation of diffuse reciprocity. Brian Rathbun makes this claim with respect to the thinking of U.S. leaders in their debates about whether their country should join the League of Nations and the North Atlantic Treaty Organization.[49]

WHY FOCUS ON SINO-AMERICAN RELATIONS?

This book takes up the subject of interstate trust and distrust with particular attention to the relationship between the U.S. and China, arguably the two most consequential countries in contemporary international political economy and security matters. Although the term "trust" is often heard in commentaries on Sino-American relations, there has not been any systematic or analytic attention to this crucial concept. Indeed, as already mentioned, the international relations literature has largely ignored this topic (except for a few scholars like Kegley and Raymond, Kydd, Larson, and Rathbun already cited).

Much of the recent discourse on China's rise focuses on the policy implications of this country's increasing capabilities, but Beijing's future intentions deserve equal, if not greater, analytic attention. As Stephen Walt has shown, a country's capabilities tend to be less consequential for interstate relations than how others perceive it will use these capabilities.[50] During the Cold War, most major and minor states aligned themselves with the stronger U.S. in opposition to the weaker USSR because they saw Moscow as being more threatening than Washington. Balance-of-power theory cannot explain this behavior because according to it, these other states should have taken the side of the less powerful USSR. They should have balanced against the strongest one among them rather than jumping on the bandwagon with it. Their behavior can only be explained by their perception that even though it was weaker, the USSR was more menacing to their interests. A perception of threat of course reflects a belief that the target of this attribution is prone to use its power in harmful ways—that is, its future intentions are distrusted. Thus in the absence of further explanation, the fact that China is growing stronger does not in itself suggest whether others should have more or less trust in it (after all, with the USSR's collapse, U.S. power has also risen). Moreover, as just implied, whether Beijing or Washington deserves to be trusted extends beyond just these two countries. Other states are also interested in this question. How these other states assess their respective trustworthiness can be quite informative, because the convergence of most states' judgments reflects a collective wisdom that *tends* to be more right than wrong most of the time.

The last remark in turn touches on learning theory and the important incentives at work in "getting it right" when states try to assess each other's trustworthiness. As Andrew Kydd explains, "although the learning process is noisy and prone to errors of all kinds, beliefs over time and on average are more likely to converge towards reality than to diverge from it.... Mistaken beliefs may arise, whether unjustified trust or unjustified mistrust, but over time they are more likely to be corrected than to remain or be further exaggerated."[51] He notes this tendency "implies that of the conflicts we observe, [only] a relatively small percentage will be driven by mistaken mistrust."[52] Thus, although one may regret that states sometimes distrust each other, it does not logically or empirically follow that this distrust is either unwarranted or the root cause responsible for their conflict. In the parlance of international relations discourse, it is just possible that when a conflict occurs, one or more of the contesting states are in fact the expansionist (and thus the untrustworthy) type rather than the (merely) security-seeking (and thus the trustworthy) type. At the same time, when a government acts contrary to its promises or even its own intentions, this may be an instance of "involuntary defection" due to domestic circumstances beyond its control as described in Robert Putnam's two-level games.[53] This behavior need not suggest betrayal or bad faith.

With Chinese and American officials, scholars, and ordinary citizens interacting more frequently and their knowledge about each other improving, and as China's information environment becomes more open and accessible (the U.S. as a developed democracy already provides observers with an information-rich environment), one would expect the prospects for mistaken distrust to attenuate. Conversely, these developments imply that should a conflict between these two countries occur, it is less likely to be the product of mistaken distrust and hence a tragedy of misunderstanding.[54] If evidence of mutual distrust persists even with more abundant and accurate information provided by protracted contact and multiple encounters in different contexts, it may very well validate offensive realism's pessimism that at least one of the parties and possibly both are in fact expansionist and thus untrustworthy.

It is naturally more difficult to assess another state's intentions than its capabilities. It is even more difficult to predict its future intentions when circumstances change. For instance, will China behave with moderation and restraint when it becomes even more powerful in the future? Will it honor its commitments when it makes further relative gains to the disadvantage of its neighbors? Predicting the future intentions of another state necessarily entails large analytic uncertainties and policy risks because this country's leadership and capabilities will change. Two implications follow from this observation. First, the more benefit of doubt one is inclined to extend to another actor, the more one trusts it. Second, there is something that one can do to change one's trustworthiness in others' eyes (i.e., to affect others' probability assessment that one is the trustworthy type). As remarked earlier, in the face of serious existing distrust, greater effort has to be made to establish one's trust. In the language of the rationalist theory of interstate signaling, this effort has to entail more consequential self-imposed costs in order for it to be seen as credible.

MAIN ARGUMENTS

This book makes six major arguments. First, although one may wish for greater trust in Sino-American relations, the existing mutual distrust is deeply rooted and not entirely unjustified. Establishing mutual trust between these two countries will require a fundamental change in their political culture and identity, something that will require basic revisions in their elite and mass attitudes and entail an arduous and protracted process with uncertain prospects. In the meantime, it would be more reasonable and realistic for leaders of both countries to strive for a common understanding of the basic parameters governing their interactions. Lest this view is seen to be too pessimistic, I should hasten to add that the trust glass is in some respects more half full than half empty such as indicated by the deep economic interdependence that has developed between these two countries. Moreover, compared to the 1950s and 1960s, mutual security suspicions have abated significantly. There has been much progress which gives hope for further improvements in this relationship (even while recognizing that it is also subject to reversal with new leaders and challenges).

Second, trust is not just a bilateral matter so that, for example, Washington's commitment to defend Taiwan necessarily contradicts its pledge to Beijing to reduce and eventually eliminate U.S. arms sales to that island (in its 1982 joint communiqué with China, the U.S. government has stated "that it does not seek to carry out a long-term policy of arms sales to Taiwan, that its arms sales to Taiwan will not exceed, either in qualitative or in quantitative terms, the level of those supplied in recent years since the establishment of diplomatic relations between the United States and China, and that it intends gradually to reduce its sale of arms to Taiwan, leading, over a period of time, to a final resolution"[55]). Thus, an effort to gain trust from one party may very well come at the expense of undercutting it in the eyes of another. Furthermore, reciprocal attempts by rival blocs to bolster their trustworthiness in the eyes of their respective allies could trap them in a competitive process leading to a conflagration that neither side has wanted. As already mentioned, events leading up to World War I exemplify this dynamic of chain-ganging and the general problem of entrapment in alliance politics.[56] A further implication of the multisided nature of interstate trust is that being a far more active global power than China (which remains primarily a regional state focusing on its immediate neighborhood), the U.S. will have a more challenging job of reconciling its various interests and commitments in many different parts of the world so that it will be seen as trustworthy by all the relevant others interacting with it.

Third, trust is built on the basis of equity, parity, empathy, and reciprocity. Elizabeth Economy captures the essence of this concept in noting: "In any relationship, trust is built over time. It requires clarity of intention, predictability of action, shared sensibilities, a willingness to give before one takes, and mutual respect."[57] The Chinese adage "what you dislike to be done to you, don't do to others" (己所不欲勿施於人) also expresses the same idea. Trust is enhanced when one accepts to live by the rules and principles that one wishes to apply to others. Washington would presumably not welcome the prospect of a Chinese version of the Monroe Doctrine in East Asia, and Beijing is inclined to believe that the U.S. has sought to deny China a sphere of influence, something that the U.S. had explicitly asserted in the Western Hemisphere and that it had also tacitly accorded to the USSR (in Eastern and Central Europe) during the Cold War. As another example, stripped of nationalist emotions and the issues of contested sovereignty and self-determination, Taiwan's geostrategic relevance to China is similar to Cuba's relative to the U.S.[58] Perceived discrepant standards of judgment and treatment in such comparable cases can reflect existing distrust and also contribute to exacerbating it.

Fourth, how a state acts in stressful situations, or conversely, how it acts when it is relatively free to behave without constraints (such as when other states are not expected to push back), tends to reveal its true character and hence its trustworthiness. Does a state proclaim its allegiance to free trade only when it enjoys a trade surplus but practices protectionism when it faces economic hard times? As another example, does it infringe on its people's basic civil liberties or violate the rules of war during times of national emergency? The more it is able to resist such temptations, the more one can believe that it is sincere about its expressed values and avowed principles. This phenomenon indicates that it is strongly committed to these values and principles even when confronted with challenging circumstances, and that it is not just a fair-weather proponent giving lip service to them. Alternatively, does a state treat its own citizens such as political dissidents and minority groups shabbily? Does it betray its allies or spy on them? Does it run roughshod over small, weak neighbors with whom it happens to have political differences?[59] Here again, a country's conduct toward third parties, especially those that are weak, needy, unpopular, or in distress, provides a basis for inferring its trustworthiness. If, for example, it treats its own people and its allies poorly, foreigners and competitors would not likely expect to be treated any better. Naturally, as a country becomes more powerful, others are less able to restrain it and they would have to rely more on its own self-restraint (such as resulting from its domestic politics and professed principles) to stop it from acting opportunistically and wantonly. U.S. officials are concerned that with China's increasing economic clout and military capabilities, Beijing has become more assertive in its territorial contests in the East and South China Seas. Chinese leaders are similarly aware of the historical record of repeated U.S. interventions in the Caribbean and Central America, and are clearly wary of Washington's agenda to promote regime change abroad (often in the name of humanitarian intervention) at a time of its unipolar preeminence.

Fifth, democracies' more transparent policy processes help to disclose their preferences and motivations. This transparency makes it more difficult for them to disguise or conceal their true intentions.[60] In contrast to autocracies' decision processes which are shrouded in secrecy, democracies' domestic policy debates provide a rich source of information for foreigners. This democratic openness, however, can reveal a democracy's sincerity not only when it believes another state to be trustworthy but also when it views the latter with deep suspicion. The latter situation was exemplified when in March 2015 forty-seven Republican senators addressed an open letter to Iranian leaders, stating that any nuclear deal that they might reach with President Barack Obama would only be an executive agreement and as such it could be rescinded by a future U.S. administration. This communication had the intent and effect of undermining the prospect that such a deal would come to fruition. It also heightened doubts in the minds of foreign audiences about the U.S. president's ability to actually "deliver"—that is, to gain domestic approval for—any arrangement agreed to by the negotiators in view of the strong domestic opposition to this deal. The senators' communication can be expected to have repercussions on U.S. reputation beyond just Iran, because the negotiation in question was a multinational effort involving the Europeans, Russians, and Chinese, engendering suspicions in their countries about the authority or sincerity of U.S. negotiators.

Executive-legislative politics can affect foreign trust in another way. Shortly after President Jimmy Carter recognized Beijing as the sole legal government of China, Congress passed the Taiwan Relations Act pledging U.S. support for that island. From the Chinese perspective, this and other similar episodes can appear to be a "good cop, bad cop" charade whereby promises made by one part of the U.S. government can be nullified by another part, and whereby a chief executive's real or contrived domestic constraints can be used to extract additional Chinese concessions. In this respect, a democracy's supposed smaller "win set"— that a democratic leader is supposed to face stronger political constraints imposed by many domestic veto groups—provides a strategic lever to gain a bargaining advantage over an authoritarian counterpart.[61] The existence of such veto groups, however, also raises the question whether a democratic chief executive can actually be trusted to gain domestic ratification (ratification used here not necessarily in its formal legal sense but rather referring more generally to domestic political acceptance) for a deal that has been reached with a foreign counterpart. This chief executive's supposed domestic constraints can be a negotiation advantage as just remarked—but only to a point. Foreign counterparts may walk away from negotiation if they believe that this person has been seriously weakened in domestic politics.

Sixth and finally, strategic restraint holds the key to building mutual trust. Although some macro conditions, such as compatible social orders and shared cultural heritage, can ease this process, they are neither necessary nor sufficient for this process to succeed. Moreover, these conditions are not within the capacity of officials to influence and change in the short term. In contrast, strategic restraint is something that they can practice and it can make a more important difference.[62]

This restraint entails accepting limits to one's use of military force, complying with existing treaty obligations and international conventions, and respecting each other's traditional sphere of influence. It also requires states to eschew opportunistic behavior and to recognize their respective sensibilities. Thus, they should try to ease rather than complicate the domestic problems facing the other side as its officials struggle to meet the challenges created by partisan politics, competing economic interests, and nationalistic and even xenophobic public opinion.

Significantly, the practice of strategic restraint necessarily constrains or encumbers the more powerful party to a larger extent than the less powerful party. As the world's only superpower, the U.S. may very well feel that strategic restraint will involve more concessions on its part as it already enjoys a huge advantage in asserting its preponderance all over the world. Conventions that limit a state's policy discretion, including its unilateral exercise of power, may be perceived to hamper it more than other countries, including China. Such conventions of course tend to protect the weaker states from being victimized by the stronger ones as the strong are by definition less in need of such protection. Still, norms of mutual strategic restraint serve not only to limit the currently more powerful countries. Rather, they promote co-binding by all countries. They facilitate greater behavioral predictability by building shared expectations and encouraging mutual adjustments by all sides. Although they can eventually produce the strong form of trust, fostering these norms is initially important for launching cooperation on the basis of reciprocity. With respect to Sino-American relations, these norms also contribute to dampening the dynamic of rivalry and help to ease concerns about possible role reversal stemming from prospective power shifts.[63] Despite their advantages after winning a war, victorious countries have often in the past refrained from exploiting their strength for momentary gains and have instead sought to create more enduring institutions of cooperation in order to pursue the benefits of stability and amity for the long haul.[64] Naturally, possible future power shifts can affect the parties' relative bargaining power and consequently the terms of negotiated norms to be had. Therefore, although an incumbent hegemon may be wary of being hemmed in by the rules and conventions of strategic restraint that limit the unhindered use of its current power, these norms contribute to "locking in" its present or future competitors and to mobilizing the assistance of third parties in this effort.

THE REST OF THE BOOK

Trust and its opposite distrust refer to one's belief or expectation about how another state will act in the future. The conduct in question may involve either an act of omission or an act of commission. One can, for example, trust the other party not to cheat or defect when given a chance. One can also rely on its word that it will provide assistance when needed. In assessing whether the other side deserves to be trusted, one naturally considers a variety of indicators, including both its words and deeds and especially one's own past encounters with this other state.

Chapter 2 asks which indicators would a reasonable official use in order to discern the trustworthiness of another state. What would these indicators tell us about mutual perceptions between China and the U.S.? One can start by studying the publicly declared policies of each side, such as Beijing's announced intention for its "peaceful rise" and "harmonious society" and Washington's agenda for "regime change" and pivot to Asia. One can then consider actual conduct such as a country's force deployment and weapons acquisition. Neither of these sources of information can be conclusive about a country's future intentions, and will therefore have to be complemented by other kinds of evidence (e.g., how well does it treat its racial minorities and political dissidents, and its smaller and much weaker neighbors?). Contemporary Sino-American relationship dates back to at least the Chinese Civil War in which Washington supported the current Beijing government's nemesis, the Kuomintang. This relationship has been tumultuous, inclining both sides to be distrustful. This mutual distrust is not necessarily rooted in misperception, and it has remained even though officials and scholars on both sides have come to understand each other much better than before. This distrust is profound but not unreasonable, even in the absence of anxieties abetted by the so-called Thucydides's Trap engendered by China's relative power gains recently.[65] Long-term efforts to build trust will require these countries to adjust how they define their interests and indeed, their identities from which these interests are derived.[66]

Chapter 3 presents the weak form of trust, arguing that to the extent that Beijing and Washington have confidence in the other side refraining from hostility, they believe that this restraint reflects primarily circumstantial constraints rather than dispositional motivations.[67] That is, both parties tend to attribute this restraint to the extrinsic compulsion faced by the other side rather than its intrinsic goodwill. One can, for instance, believe that nuclear deterrence will keep the other side from attacking, without necessarily attributing to it any benign intention. As another example, U.S. officials can believe that Beijing will assume a cautious and even accommodative posture so long as its military capabilities are still much weaker than those of the U.S. As a third example, some formulations of the democratic peace theory argue that democracies are not inherently more peaceful; rather, democratic institutions of political checks and balances tend to limit a chief executive's discretion to involve his or her country in war.[68] These examples illustrate a rather weak claim on trust because should circumstances change, a state can act out its natural impulses and reveal its true character. Thus according to this formulation, China can become aggressive if it gains a strategic advantage in the future, and a democracy's war proneness can increase when its political power becomes more concentrated.

It is sometimes argued that democratic governments are more trustworthy.[69] But why should this be so? When one lists those countries that have fought most foreign wars and undertaken most military interventions abroad in recent history, most of them are democracies (e.g., the U.S., Britain, France, Israel, and India). Moreover, just as democracies rarely if ever fight each other, autocracies have also generally kept peace among themselves.[70] Chapter 3 explores how a government's democratic character enhances its trustworthiness in others' eyes. Its other topical focus is how states' capabilities are likely to affect others' assessment of their trustworthiness and their own inclination to accept evidence of others' trustworthiness. Although the topic of power shift or power transition has dominated much of recent discourse on Sino-American relations, there is a dearth of discussion on how exactly a state's relative capability and how changes in this capability can be expected to affect others' perceptions of its trustworthiness as well as its own perception of others' trustworthiness. One may want to ask, for example, whether a strong country is more likely to make empty threats than a weak country and if so, is it more likely to be exposed as a bluffer—and whether the probability of this exposure may motivate it to bluff in the first place.

Chapter 4 takes on the semi-strong form of trust. In this version, a counterpart is deemed to be somewhat trustworthy due to its self-restraint rather than direct environmental constraint. Nevertheless, as in the weak form of trust this self-restraint is attributed to the other party's utilitarian calculation about the potential consequences of its actions. Robert Axelrod's formulation of the evolution of cooperation, especially the role played by the shadow of the future in influencing the behavior of even self-regarding egoists, illustrates this semi-strong form of trust.[71] A counterpart is expected to refrain from exploitative or opportunistic behavior out of a belief that the benefits of long-term cooperation will outweigh any momentary gains to be made from defection. This counterpart's expected behavior is still self-regarding even though it eschews a myopic definition of its interests. For instance, it considers how its defection from cooperation may invite retaliation and cause damage to its general reputation for trustworthiness in the eyes of third parties. As another example of the semi-strong form of trust, John Ikenberry has shown how those post–1945 multilateral institutions created by Washington have promoted self-binding as well as mutual binding by the Western countries, thereby fostering reciprocal confidence that all will play nice and by common rules.[72] Naturally, the converse is also pertinent. When a founding member or chief sponsor of an international organization acts unilaterally in violation of the common norms it has propagated, or is perceived to have done so, this behavior is more destructive of trust. Whereas the weak form of trust relies on external forces compelling a counterpart to refrain from opportunistic behavior, the semi-strong form refers to this actor's "enlightened" vision of its own interests as a restraint. Both forms, however, share a common expectation based on this counterpart's calculation of an action's potential costs and benefits, but the boundary conditions separating them are admittedly fuzzy.

Economic interdependence and participation in multilateral institutions are particularly relevant to building this semi-strong form of trust, and Chapter 4 will attend to how self-selection into these relationships indicates an investment in a state's reputation for being trustworthy and also for trusting others. Those that expect international conflict in the future and are hence unwilling to pay the price of such engagement will be reluctant to enter into interstate economic exchanges and join multilateral institutions in the first place. Trusting and trustworthy states are more likely to initiate and accept these external ties, and their participation in these ties reassures others that they have benign intentions. The more costly consequences a state will suffer in the event of such ties being upset, the more credible is its reassurance. Moreover, these types of international engagement can over time socialize the participating officials, thereby altering their values and identities in a way that can promote the strong form of trust based on shared membership in a security community.

In Chapter 5, I turn to the strong form of trust indicating one's confidence that the other party will eschew opportunism for reasons other than cost-benefit calculation. The logic of appropriateness rather than the logic of consequences provides the primary motivation for this kind of expected behavior. The former logic explains an actor's behavior by his or her acceptance of particular roles or norms.[73] This actor follows certain rules of exemplary behavior because this conduct is thought to be natural, rightful and legitimate. It is deemed trustworthy because it has been socialized to hold such beliefs, and to believe that any conduct contrary to the accepted roles or norms is illegitimate, repugnant and wrong. According to this strong form, one trusts the other party because of its self-image and social understanding. Unlike the weak and semi-strong forms of trust, this strong form points to a non-material source for explaining the other side's trustworthiness. Loosely speaking, identity rather than interest is the driver behind this strong form of trust, even though in reality these two are intertwined and mutually constitutive (such as in the emergence of security communities).[74] An actor strives to live up to the rules and expectations prescribed or encapsulated by its identity as a matter of obligation and duty rather than material advantage. The evolution of this strong form of trust is foreshadowed by and indeed premised on the breakdown of a perception of "us versus them" between two countries, and the formation of a common identity or "we feeling."[75] Christopher Hemmer and Peter Katzenstein emphasize the role of mutual identification undergirding the NATO alliance, distinguishing this alliance from the design of others formed by the U.S. in Asia.[76]

Realists are skeptical of the logic of appropriateness in shaping states' behavior although moral principles and ethical scruples do sometimes affect a state's choice of policy. One example occurred during the Cuban Missile Crisis. Robert Kennedy was supposed to have tipped the Executive Committee's deliberations in favor of a naval blockade and against a surprise air strike against Soviet missiles in Cuba because "a sudden attack would be 'a Pearl Harbor in reverse'."[77] The so-called nuclear taboo—the nonuse of nuclear weapons since 1945 by those countries that possess them—provides another possible example.[78] This use has come to be seen as incompatible with one's identity as a "civilized state." In security communities, strong mutual trust is demonstrated by the open, undefended borders such as those among the Western European countries that were erstwhile enemies in bitter wars and between the U.S. and Canada that were once highly suspicious of each other's intentions.[79]

Socialization that changes an actor's behavior due to its evolving self-identity rather than its calculation of self-interests reflects the basic logic of appropriateness,[80] even though identity and interests tend to be interrelated as already mentioned.

Importantly, the strong form of trust does not have to depend on another state's self-restraint. Ted Hopf offers a logic that goes even beyond that of appropriateness.[81] As an illustration of the latter logic, Alex Wendt has claimed that the Bahamas does not expect an invasion by the U.S. because it knows that Washington will restrain itself.[82] Hopf argues "instead, a U.S. invasion of the Bahamas is unthinkable or unimaginable to the Bahamans."[83] That is, "the Bahamans are far past the point of deliberating over U.S. intentions—confidence in U.S. inaction is far more deeply embedded in the identities and discourses of the two states, such that the idea of invasion never comes up as a possibility."[84] Hopf thus introduces the logic of unthinkability and unimaginability that aptly describes the nature of a security community. For members of this community, the idea of resorting to war as a means of settling their disputes has become literally unthinkable and unimaginable. Trust among these states becomes institutionalized, and their relationships take for granted shared expectations of continued amity.

In general, the more devastating consequences a policy entails if one's confidence is misplaced, the greater the amount of trust placed in the other party one's action conveys. Thus, for example, the Anti-Ballistic Missile (ABM) Treaty signed by Moscow and Washington in 1972 (but terminated in 2002 when the U.S. withdrew from it) provided strong mutual assurance that neither side had any intention of initiating a nuclear strike against the other. By limiting each side's missile defense system to just one civilian site, both parties deliberately exposed themselves to the other's full retaliatory force should there be a nuclear conflict. This deliberate exposure in turn offered a costly and thus convincing proof that neither side had any intention of initiating a nuclear strike against the other. Parenthetically, the same logic argues that the termination of this treaty conveys the opposite message.

As will be explained later, the close economic relationship between the U.S. and China today offers somewhat of a parallel to the ABM Treaty by creating valuable "hostages" vulnerable to the other side's retaliation. These two countries trade heavily and China holds a huge amount of U.S. debt.[85] Described by Zachary Karabell as "superfusion,"[86] this intense economic relationship is indicative of a high level of trust. Both sides will suffer very serious economic costs should their political relationship become destabilized. Their existing economic ties are "endogenous" to their political relationship because if their business people had expected political turmoil, they would not have entered into these economic ties in the first place (as this turmoil would have made their business deals unprofitable and even money-losing propositions, especially if these deals entail large, irretrievable investments for the long haul). Consequently, thriving Sino-American trade, investment and financial exchanges indicate the business people's confidence in their countries' current political relationship and also their optimism about the future of this relationship. This level of confidence or optimism in the stability of future relationship points to the so-called "second face of security" whereby domestic economic interests can be expected to self-mobilize or be mobilized to promote policies congenial to enhancing and consolidating bilateral trust.[87]

As shown in the development of security communities, transactions initially undertaken for material reasons can over time foster common identities. Conversely, the extent to which the people of two countries hold exclusive or even antagonistic identities tends to sharpen mutual suspicions and sustain hostile perceptions,[88] halting or limiting the amount of transactions between them. It is instructive to compare inter-Korean relations with relations across the Taiwan Strait. Whereas thriving commerce in the latter case has been decisive in building mutual confidence in recent years, the lack of large economic linkages is among the reasons for the more volatile relationship in the former case. Chapter 6 takes up the aforementioned themes and concludes that although there remains significant distrust in Sino-American relations, there have also been some favorable developments over recent decades so that compared to the 1950s and 1960s, there exist today more propitious conditions for growing mutual trust. Still, this progress is vulnerable to reversal as shown by recent Russo-American relations.

Chapter 6 also summarizes the preceding chapters and offers some substantive prognoses and policy recommendations about Sino-American relations. It concludes that strategic restraint is more important than either compatible social orders or shared cultural heritage in building trust,[89] which involves a protracted process that starts with a convergence of elite interests and values and only subsequently permeates to the general public. While common identification features the culmination of this evolution, strategic restraint presents an initial step to provide for mutual accommodation from which trust can be gradually developed. Authoritarian regimes are as capable of strategic restraint as democracies. Neither regime similarity nor democratic institutions are necessary for building trust. In contrast to macro conditions such as the nature of a country's regime type, social order, or cultural tradition, leaders are more in control of the policies that they decide to pursue. They are in a better position to exercise strategic restraint than to affect those macro conditions just mentioned.

Strategic restraint involves eschewing opportunistic behavior, accepting mutual limits on the use of military force, observing a country's treaty obligations, respecting another country's traditional sphere of influence, and self-binding and co-binding efforts that communicate costly commitments. When a state refrains from self-serving or self-aggrandizing behavior in a particularly permissive situation (when it can act relatively freely without punitive consequences) or in a particularly stressful situation (when it faces tough choices between competing values and objectives), its inaction is revealing. This behavior reassures others as it indicates a decision not to defect when opportunism can be most rewarding.

The timing of states' action and inaction is important. A costly signal undertaken when a state is in a strong bargaining position is likely to be taken more seriously as an indication of its trustworthiness than when this state is faced with difficult domestic and/or foreign circumstances. This is so because a signal is more credible when it is not undertaken under duress but rather in a circumstance when an actor does not have to make concessions (I argue that especially stressful *and* especially permissive situations are likely to be more informative of an actor's character). Naturally, a powerful state is better able to afford concessions. Therefore, this signal has to be costly and difficult to reverse in order for it to be seen as credible.

A conciliatory gesture initiated by a state is more likely to be reciprocated when its counterpart is particularly receptive to this overture, such as when it has a new leader who is not politically or personally committed to previous policies. In general, a politically secure leader is in a stronger position to make concessions to a foreign counterpart and thus to jump start a process of reciprocation to build mutual trust. Conversely, when a leader faces a deep partisan division, strong electoral challenges, and/or a limited tenure, this incumbent official is in a less favorable position to make such concessions, to reciprocate concessions from a foreign counterpart, or to secure domestic ratification for a deal reached with this counterpart. Should China become more democratic, leaders in Beijing will have to contend with more domestic veto players and a more vocal, even critical, mass public. If so, a more democratic China may not be more accommodating.

Historically, costly and often unilateral concessions seeking accommodation have come typically from the weaker side in a relationship (especially when it faces severe domestic and/or foreign challenges, a situation that should dilute and even contravene its attempt at accommodation and conciliation as already mentioned). Ironically, even though the weaker side should want to have more reassurance about the stronger side's trustworthiness, the dominant party has less incentive to give this reassurance simply because it is in a stronger position. A powerful country (or one that is becoming more powerful) has less need to place its faith in others by accepting their word. It is in a better position to undertake unilateral action to remove or at least greatly reduce those uncertainties that a weaker country will have to put up with. By virtue of its power, this country is better able to take matters into its own hands. As the world's two most powerful countries, the U.S. and China have according to this reasoning less need to trust other countries and are also less inclined to trust them (including each other)—even though given their powerful status, other states should be most interested in assessing their respective trustworthiness.

SOME CONCLUDING CLARIFICATIONS AND CAVEATS

The term "trust" conjures up positive traits such as reliability, cooperation, and even virtue, whereas distrust has the opposite connotations. Yet as I have already remarked, interstate cooperation is possible without trust, and interstate distrust is not always unwarranted. Indeed, when seen in some multilateral contexts, efforts to build or demonstrate trust can be a source of instability. Thus, if some weaker states did not have confidence that their powerful allies would come to their rescue, they would not have perhaps challenged and even fought their much stronger adversaries. For example, Egyptian and Syrian leaders would have been much less inclined to start past wars against Israel if they had doubted the USSR's trustworthiness as an ally. Similarly, Pakistani leaders would have been much more reluctant to get into wars against India had they not counted on the U.S. and China to prevent their country from devastating military defeat and even political collapse.[90] In these cases as in the process leading up to the outbreak of World War I, a country's trust in its ally's support (and this ally's efforts to demonstrate its trustworthiness) was a contributing factor to belligerence. Without the belief that a powerful ally will bail them out of severe military and political difficulties, these countries would have been much less likely to undertake risky policies of provocation and confrontation. Similarly, Taiwan would not have held out against a much stronger China and would have been more inclined to come to terms with Beijing due to its much weaker (bilateral) bargaining position had its leaders not expected the U.S. to "have their back." The aforementioned examples also point to the danger of entrapment whereby an ally becomes embroiled in an unwanted confrontation because of its junior partner's reckless behavior, behavior that is encouraged by this ally's perceived commitment in the first place (hence the moral hazard of making alliance commitments). Surely, this risk was evident to U.S. officials when they talked about "leashing Chiang Kai-shek" and, more recently, when they tried to restrain the pro-independence policies of Taiwan President Chen Shui-bian.

Some situations can be especially revealing about how people come to trust others. For example, a *coup d'état* obviously signifies a betrayal of trust on the part of those conspirators who have been entrusted with military authority by their superiors. Yet the success of this plot requires a tremendous amount of trust among these same conspirators in a context where secrecy, speed and coordination are of paramount importance and where failure carries very grave consequences for them personally. The conspirators must trust each other sufficiently in order for them to act even when they cannot be sure of their partners' commitment and thus to protect themselves against the danger of these partners' possible defection. Similarly for those who embark on suicide missions such as the *kamikaze* pilots and terrorist bombers, they must have a very high degree of confidence that their sacrifice would not be in vain (when there is little mechanism to enforce, or even observe, that others will honor their commitments). A strong sense of belonging to the same moralistic community with a shared identity and common cause seems to be an essential factor for people in these situations to overcome distrust.

States do sometimes reverse their policy commitments and may thus appear to be untrustworthy. The U.S. withdrew from the Indochina War, leaving its allies in Saigon and Phnom Penh to fend for themselves. Moscow did the same in Afghanistan as well as when Mikhail Gorbachev decided not to order the Red Army to protect fellow communist regimes in Eastern and Central Europe from popular uprisings. Similarly, Beijing had abandoned its support for the Khmer Rouge and some other communist insurgency groups along its periphery. The U.S. had also switched its diplomatic recognition from Taipei to Beijing, and had abrogated its defense treaty with the former. Recently, Beijing has begun to put increasing pressure on Pyongyang, joining international criticisms and sanctions against its traditional ally. Even though they are unlikely to be described as such in most conventional accounts, these episodes could be seen as a betrayal of trust from the perspective of those states hurt by the policy changes. Such perceptions, however, do not necessarily mean that those states making the policy changes were unwise or immoral.

In the following chapters, I will refer to various incidents that reflect U.S. or Chinese trustworthiness. It is certainly not my intention to provide a scorecard as if judging a boxing match. I do not provide nearly enough information about these incidents to offer a thorough analysis of their circumstances. Depending on their vantage point, some readers may object that I am too critical of the U.S. or China. I would ask them to put on the "veil of ignorance" and consider how they would judge an action if an actor's identity is concealed from them. What if the shoe is on the other foot? They should ask whether it is reasonable to expect the people and leaders of China to develop certain image of the U.S., and whether the American people and their leaders will come to hold certain views about China. After all, it is the other side's perceptions about oneself and not one's own self-image or some objective truth that matter if we are to understand its behavior. Moreover, it should not be surprising that people in different countries are likely to recall different salient episodes in their national history and to reach different interpretations of their past encounters.

Evidence for judging a country's trustworthiness can surely be ambiguous and controversial. This evidence is also asymmetric in the sense that the U.S. offers a much more information-rich environment than China (even though information about Chinese policy processes has become more accessible over time). As a democracy, there are more discordant voices and opposition groups that can challenge and obstruct a U.S. administration's policies. An independent and active media also thrives on exposing policy disagreements and failures in Washington. Thus, it is much easier to observe inconsistencies and even contradictions in U.S. policies than Chinese policies. Moreover, as the global hegemon the U.S. has taken on more foreign responsibilities and made more overseas commitments than China which remains a regional power. Thus there are more occasions when Washington has found its credibility or trustworthiness tested, and the relevant information is also more available.

Finally, for those who have read up to this point, it should have become evident that my analytic style and emphasis are different from the usual practice of Sinologists. Unlike the latter scholars who tend to study China as a case by itself, I try to compare its conduct with that of the U.S. As Adam Przeworski and Henry Teune have argued some time ago,[91] the logic of studying comparative politics (and by implication, international relations also) calls for analysts to substitute the proper names of our cases with the names of the pertinent variables. Moreover, in contrast to the typical analytic style of Sinologists who tend to adopt a descriptive or narrative approach focusing on particular events or leaders in Sino-American relations, I try to embed my study in the general context of international relations research. I will draw on theoretical and empirical generalizations from this research in order to inform my quest for a better understanding of trust in Sino-American relations. At the same time, the ideas and arguments I present for this dyad should have broad relevance for establishing trust and dispelling distrust for other countries.

NOTES

1. Kenneth Lieberthal and Jisi Wang, *Addressing U.S.-China Strategic Distrust* (Washington, DC: John L. Thornton Center, Brookings Institution, 2012).
2. Ibid., 5.
3. Andrew H. Kydd, "Sheep in Sheep's Clothing: Why Security-Seekers Do Not Fight Each Other," *Security Studies* 7, no. 1 (1997): 114–154.
4. Andrew H. Kydd, *Trust and Mistrust in International Relations* (Princeton, NJ: Princeton University Press, 2005), 39.
5. Robert Axelrod, *The Evolution of Cooperation* (New York: Basic Books, 1984), 174.
6. Charles Kupchan, *How Enemies Become Friends: The Sources of Stable Peace* (Princeton, NJ: Princeton University Press, 2010), 407.
7. Ido Oren, "The Subjectivity of the 'Democratic' Peace: Changing U.S. Perceptions of Imperial Germany," *International Security* 20, no. 2 (1995): 147–184, and *Our Enemies & US: America's Rivalries and the Making of Political Science* (Ithaca, NY: Cornell University Press, 2003).
8. James D. Fearon, "Rationalist Explanations for War," *International Organization* 49, no. 3 (1995): 379–414.
9. Robert Jervis, *Perception and Misperception in International Politics* (Princeton, NJ: Princeton University Press, 1976).
10. Deborah W. Larson, "Trust and Missed Opportunities in International Relations," *International Organization* 18, no. 3 (1997), 725.
11. Niklas Luhmann, *Trust and Power* (New York: Wiley, 1979), 28–29 quoted in "Trust and Missed Opportunities" by Larson, 725 (emphasis in original).
12. Ronald Reagan, "Trust but Verify," accessed June 2, 2017, https://www.youtube.com/watch?v=As6y5eI01XE.
13. Robert Jervis, "Cooperation under the Security Dilemma," *World Politics* 30, no. 2 (1978): 167–214; Paul M. Kennedy, *The Rise of Anglo-German Antagonism, 1860–1914* (London: Allen & Unwin, 1982); Barbara W. Tuchman, *The Guns of August* (New York: Dell, 1962); and William R. Thompson, "A Streetcar Named Sarajevo: Catalysts, Multiple Causation Chains, and Rivalry Structures," *International Studies Quarterly* 47, no. 3 (2003): 453–474.

14. John J. Mearsheimer, *Why Leaders Lie: The Truth about Lying in Interna-tional Politics* (Oxford: Oxford University Press, 2011).
15. Anne E. Sartori, *Deterrence by Diplomacy* (Princeton, NJ: Princeton University Press, 2005).
16. Anne E. Sartori, "The Might of the Pen: A Reputation Theory of Communication in International Disputes," *International Organization* 56, no. 1 (2002): 121–149.
17. Shelley Rigger, "Why Giving Up Taiwan Will Not Help US with China." *AEI Asian Outlook* (November 29, 2011), accessed June 2, 2017, www.aei.org/article/foreign-and-defense-policy/regional/asia/why-giving-up-taiwan-will-not-help-us-with-china; and Nancy B. Tucker and Bonnie Glaser, "Should the United States Abandon Taiwan?" *Washington Quarterly* 34, no. 4 (2011): 23–37.
18. Ole R. Holsti, "The Belief System and National Images: A Case Study," *Journal of Conflict Resolution* 6, no. 3 (1962): 244–252.
19. Deborah W. Larson, *Anatomy of Mistrust: U.S.-Soviet Relations during the Cold War* (Ithaca, NY: Cornell University Press, 1997), 46.
20. Larson, "Trust and Missed Opportunities," 703.
21. Margaret Levi and Laura Stoker, "Political Trust and Trustworthiness," *Annual Review of Political Science* 3 (2000): 475–507.
22. Peter Nannestad, "What Have We Learned about Generalized Trust, If Anything?" *Annual Review of Political Science* 11 (2008): 413–436.
23. Edward C. Banfield, *The Moral Basis of a Backward Society* (New York: Free Press, 1958); and Robert D. Putnam, *Making Democracy Work: Civic Traditions in Modern Italy* (Princeton, NJ: Princeton University Press, 1993).
24. John H. Herz, "Idealist Internationalism and the Security Dilemma," *World Politics* 2, no. 2 (1950): 157–180; and Jervis, "Cooperation under the Security Dilemma."
25. Lewis F. Richardson, *Arms and Insecurity* (Pittsburgh: Boxwood Press, 1960).
26. Aaron M. Hoffman, *Building Trust: Overcoming Suspicion in International Conflict* (Albany, NY: State University of New York Press, 2006); Charles W. Kegley, Jr. and Gregory Raymond, *When Trust Breaks Down: Alliance Norms and World Politics* (Columbia: University of South Carolina Press, 1990); Kydd, "Sheep in Sheep's Clothing," "Trust Building, Trust Breaking: The Dilemma of NATO Enlargement," *International Organization* 55, no. 4 (2001): 801–828, and *Trust and Mistrust*; Larson, "Trust and Missed Opportunities," and *Anatomy of Mistrust*; and Brian C. Rathbun,

"Before Hegemony: Generalized Trust and the Creation and Design of International Security Organizations," *International Organization* 65, no. 1 (2011): 243–273, "From Vicious to Virtuous Circle: Moralistic Trust, Diffuse Reciprocity, and the American Security Commitment to Europe," *European Journal of International Relations* 18, no. 2 (2011): 323–344, "The 'Magnificent Fraud': Trust, International Cooperation, and the Hidden Domestic Politics of American Multilateralism after World War II," *International Studies Quarterly* 55, no. 1 (2011): 1–31, and *Trust in International Cooperation: International Security Institutions, Domestic Politics and American Multilateralism* (Cambridge: Cambridge University Press, 2012).

27. Aaron M. Hoffman, "A Conceptualization of Trust in International Relations," *European Journal of International Relations* 8, no. 3 (2002): 375–401; Vincent C. Keating and Jan Ruzicka, "Trusting Relationships in International Politics: No Need to Hedge," *Review of International Studies* 40, no. 4 (2014): 753–770; Torsten Michel, "Trust, Rationality and Vulnerability," in *The Vulnerable Subject: Beyond Rationalism in International Relations*, eds. Amanda R. Beattie and Kate Schick (Houndmills: Palgrave Macmillan, 2013), 86–109; Brian C. Rathbun, "It Takes All Types: Social Psychology, Trust, and the International Relations Paradigm in Our Minds," *International Theory* 1, no. 3 (2009): 345–380; and Jan Ruzicka and Vincent C. Keating, "Going Global: Trust Research and International Relations," *Journal of Trust Research* 5, no. 1 (2015): 8–26.

28. Kydd, *Trust and Mistrust*, 6.

29. Russell Hardin, *Trust* (Cambridge: Polity, 2006), 68.

30. Russell Hardin, *Trust and Trustworthiness* (New York: Russell Sage Foundation, 2002).

31. Levi and Stoker, "Political Trust," 476.

32. Keating and Ruzicka, "Trusting Relationships," 755 (emphasis in original).

33. Hoffman, "A Conceptualization," 384.

34. Ibid., 394.

35. Mancur Olson and Richard Zeckhauser, "An Economic Theory of Alliances," *Review of Economics and Statistics* 48, no. 3 (1966): 266–279.

36. Levi and Stoker, "Political Trust," 476.

37. Putnam, *Making Democracy Work*, and *Bowling Alone: The Collapse and Revival of American Community* (New York: Simon & Schuster, 2000).

38. Francisco Herreros, *The Problems of Forming Social Capital. Why Trust?* (New York: Palgrave Macmillan, 2004), 8.

39. Jan Delhey and Kenneth Newton, "Predicting Cross-National Levels of Social Trust: Global Pattern or Nordic Exceptionalism?" *European Sociological Review* 21, no. 4 (2005), 311.
40. Pippa Norris, ed., *Critical Citizens: Global Support for Democratic Government* (Oxford: Oxford University Press, 1999); Susan J. Pharr and Robert D. Putnam, eds., *Disaffected Democracies: What's Troubling the Trilateral Countries* (Princeton, NJ: Princeton University Press, 2000); and Dietlind Stolle and Marc Hooghe, "Inaccurate, Exceptional, One-sided or Irrelevant? The Debate about the Alleged Decline of Social Capital and Civic Engagement in Western Societies," *British Journal of Political Science* 35, no. 1 (2005): 149–167.
41. Putnam, *Bowling Alone*, 140.
42. Stephen Collinson and Tal Kopan, "Donald Trump Taps into Deep Republican Anger at Government," (November 23, 2015), accessed June 2, 2017, http://www.cnn.com/2015/11/23/politics/voters-distrust-anger-government-pew-poll/index.html.
43. Eric M. Uslaner, *The Moral Foundations of Trust* (Cambridge: Cambridge University Press, 2002).
44. Nannestad, "What Have We Learned."
45. Rathbun, *Trust in International Cooperation.*
46. Larson, "Trust and Missed Opportunities," 714–715.
47. Hoffman, *Building Trust*, 7, 20.
48. Emanuel Adler and Michael Barnett, eds., *Security Communities* (Cambridge: Cambridge University Press, 1998); Karl W. Deutsch, Sidney A. Burrell, Robert A. Kann, Maurice Lee, Jr., Martin Lichtenman, Raymond E. Lindgren, Francis L. Loewenheim, and Richard W. Van Wagenen, *Political Community and the North Atlantic Area: International Organization in the Light of Historical Experience* (New York: Greenwood, 1957); and Hoffman, *Building Trust.*
49. Brian Rathbun, "Before Hegemony," "From Vicious to Virtuous Circle," and "The 'Magnificent Fraud'."
50. Stephen M. Walt, *The Origins of Alliances* (Ithaca, NY: Cornell University Press, 1987).
51. Kydd, *Trust and Mistrust*, 16.
52. Ibid.
53. Robert D. Putnam, "Diplomacy and Domestic Politics: The Logic of Two-Level Games," *International Organization* 42, no. 3 (1988): 427–460.
54. Kydd, *Trust and Mistrust*, 75.

55. "The Joint Communique of the United States of America and the People's Republic of China (the 1982 Communique)," American Institute in Taiwan, accessed June 2, 2017, https://www.ait.org.tw/en/us-joint-communique-1982.html.

56. Thomas J. Christensen and Jack Snyder, "Chain Gangs and Passed Bucks: Predicting Alliance Patterns in Multipolarity," *International Organization* 44, no. 2 (1990): 137–168; Richard N. Rosecrance and Steven E. Miller, eds., *The Next Great War? The Roots of World War and the Risk of U.S.-China Conflict* (Cambridge, MA: The MIT Press, 2015); and Glenn H. Snyder, *Alliance Politics* (Ithaca, NY: Cornell University Press, 1997).

57. Elizabeth Economy, "Xi's Tour Won't Fix the U.S.-China 'Trust Deficit,'" *Foreign Affairs* (February 15, 2012), accessed June 2, 2017, https://www.foreignaffairs.com/articles/united-states/2012-02-15/xis-tour-wont-fix-us-chinese-trust-deficit.

58. Alan M. Wachman, *Why Taiwan? Geostrategic Rationales for China's Territorial Integrity* (Stanford, CA: Stanford University Press, 2007).

59. Kydd, "Sheep in Sheep's Clothing."

60. Kenneth A. Schultz, *Democracy and Coercive Diplomacy* (Cambridge: Cambridge University Press, 2001).

61. Putnam, "Diplomacy and Domestic Politics."

62. Kupchan, *How Enemies Become Friends.*

63. Jeffrey W. Legro, *Rethinking the World: Great Power Strategies and International Order* (Ithaca, NY: Cornell University Press, 2005), and "What China Will Want: The Future Intentions of a Rising Power," *Perspectives on Politics* 5, no. 3 (2007): 515–534.

64. G. John Ikenberry, *After Victory: Institutions, Strategic Restraint and the Rebuilding of Order after Major Wars* (Princeton, NJ: Princeton University Press, 2001).

65. Graham Allison, "The Thucydides Trap: Are the U.S. and China Headed for War?" *The Atlantic* (September 24, 2015), accessed June 2, 2017, www.theatlantic.com/international/archive/2015/09/united-states-china-war-thucydides-trap/406756/.

66. Alexander Wendt, *Social Theory of International Politics* (Cambridge: Cambridge University Press, 1999).

67. Jonathan Mercer, *Reputation and International Politics* (Ithaca, NY: Cornell University Press, 1996).

68. T. Clifton Morgan and Sally H. Campbell, "Domestic Structures, Decisional Uncertainty, and War: So Why Kant Democracies Fight?" *Journal of Conflict Resolution* 35, no. 2 (1991): 187–211; and Bruce Bueno de

Mesquita, Alastair Smith, Randolph M. Siverson, and James D. Morrow, "An Institutional Explanation of Democratic Peace," *American Political Science Review* 93, no. 4 (2003): 791–807.

69. Aaron L. Friedberg, *A Contest for Supremacy: China, America, and the Struggle for Mastery in Asia* (New York: Norton, 2011); and Lieberthal and Wang, *Addressing U.S.-China Strategic Distrust.*

70. Mark Peceny, Caroline Beer, and Shannon Sanchez-Terry, "Dictatorial Peace?" *American Political Science Review* 96, no. 1 (2002): 15–26.

71. Axelrod, *The Evolution.*

72. Ikenberry, *After Victory.*

73. James G. March and Johan P. Olsen, "The Institutional Dynamics of International Political Orders," *International Organization* 52, no. 4 (1998): 943–969, and "The Logic of Appropriateness," Arena-Centre for European Studies, University of Oslo (2014), accessed June 2, 2017, http://www.sv.uio.no/arena/english/research/publications/arena-working-papers/2001-2010/2004/wp04_9.pdf.

74. Adler and Barnett, *Security Communities*; Deutsch et al., *Political Community*; and Richard Merritt, *Symbols of American Community* (New Haven, CT: Yale University Press, 1966).

75. David L. Rousseau, *Identifying Threats and Threatening Identities: The Social Construction of Realism and Liberalism* (Stanford, CA: Stanford University Press, 2006).

76. Christopher Hemmer and Peter J. Katzenstein, "Why Is There No NATO in Asia? Collective Identity, Regionalism, and the Origins of Multilateralism," *International Organization* 56, no. 3 (2002): 575–607.

77. Graham Allison, *Essence of Decision: Explaining the Cuban Missile Crisis* (Boston: Little Brown, 1971), 197.

78. Nina Tannenwald, *The Nuclear Taboo: The United States and the Non-Use of Nuclear Weapons since 1945* (Cambridge: Cambridge University Press, 2007).

79. Kenneth Bourne, *Britain and the Balance of Power in North America, 1815–1908* (Berkeley: University of California Press, 1967).

80. Alastair I. Johnston, *Social States: China in International Institutions, 1980–2000* (Princeton, NJ: Princeton University Press, 2008).

81. Ted Hopf, *Social Construction of International Politics: Identities and Foreign Policies, Moscow, 1955 and 1999* (Ithaca, NY: Cornell University Press, 2002), 292–293.

82. Wendt, *Social Theory*, 360.

83. Hopf, *Social Construction.*

84. Ibid.
85. Steve Chan, "Money Talks: International Credit/Debt as Credible Commitment," *Journal of East Asian Affairs* 26, no. 1 (2012): 77–103; and Daniel W. Drezner, "Bad Debts: Assessing China's Financial Influence in Great Power Politics," *International Security* 34, no. 2 (2009): 7–45.
86. Zachary Karabell, *Superfusion: How China and America Became One Economy and Why the World's Prosperity Depends on It* (New York: Simon & Schuster, 2009).
87. Steven E. Lobell, "The Second Face of Security: Britain's 'Smart' Appeasement Policy towards Japan and Germany," *International Relations of the Asia-Pacific* 7, no. 1 (2007): 73–98.
88. Rousseau, *Identifying Threats*.
89. Kupchan, *How Enemies Become Friends*.
90. Steve Chan, "Major-Power Intervention and War Initiation by the Weak," *International Politics* 47, no. 2 (2010): 163–185; and Russell J. Leng, *Bargaining and Learning in Recurring Crises: The Soviet-American, Egyptian-Israeli, and Indo-Pakistani Rivalries* (Ann Arbor: University of Michigan Press, 2000).
91. Adam Przeworski and Henry Teune, *The Logic of Comparative Social Inquiry* (New York: Wiley, 1970).

CHAPTER 2

GAUGING ANOTHER STATE'S TRUSTWORTHINESS

Trust refers to one's judgments about another person or state's future intentions. Will it abide by its current assurances and declared preferences? Or will it act opportunistically when given a chance? We typically think of trust in a context where the other party may be inclined to behave in ways inimical to our interests. For instance, will an ally abandon its promise to come to one's defense, or will a currently accommodating state become more aggressive when it gains more power? Trust therefore incorporates one's judgments about the honesty, sincerity and reliability of another state's diplomacy,[1] but this concept also includes an assessment of this other state's benign intentions. It pertains particularly to the question of how seriously one should take this other state's current statements as a basis for predicting its future behavior.

If this other state's statements profess an open and unremitting hostility, this information can be taken as prima facie evidence that it should not be trusted and should instead be treated as an adversary in one's planning for the future. This view does not deny the importance of evaluating whether the other party is making empty threats or issuing a serious warning. Its threats and warnings may or may not be credible. When it behaves according to its professed intention—such as to actually carry out its deterrence threat by attacking—one may conclude that it is after all honest, sincere and reliable, but is nevertheless malevolent. Most analyses of trust, however, have been more concerned with the question of how to evaluate another state's declaration of a friendly intention or at least an accommodating disposition. How much credibility should one give to such indication?

A Chinese maxim advises people to listen to another person's words and watch his or her deeds (聽其言 觀其行). In interstate relations, do the other state's words and deeds indicate a friendly or hostile disposition? Do its words and deeds correspond? Although they do not convey exactly the same meaning, international relations scholarship is replete with binary characterizations of states as satisfied or dissatisfied, satiated or expansionist, status-quo oriented or revisionist, and offensively or defensively minded. The clear implication is that some states are greedy, aggressive, and unreliable, whereas others are not. Naturally, those that are greedy, aggressive, and unreliable will often try to disguise their true character by mimicking others that are not. This attempt to deceive creates a masking effect because states belonging to the former type will try to make themselves as indistinguishable from the latter type as possible.

Masking effects can take a second form. When a country's lofty ideals and practical, even realpolitik, considerations are aligned, it is difficult to tell which of these factors is actually driving its foreign policy. When these two sets of factors collide, however, officials have to decide which ones should receive priority. Such situations are stressful for them but are also informative about whether their standard proclamations of policy values are actually honored by their deeds, and should therefore be taken seriously. In the case of the U.S., the treatment of Mohammad Mossadegh, Jacobo Arbenz, Salvador Allende, and, more recently, Mohammed Morsi and Viktor Yanukovych—leaders who were democratically elected but who were for one reason or another repugnant to Washington—provides "critical tests" in the usual sense of social scientific inquiry seeking to determine the relative contribution of several competing variables to an occurrence. Does support for democracy trump realpolitik concerns, or vice versa? As another example, inaction to stop the Rwandan genocide tends to cast doubts on whether U.S. and Western interventions elsewhere (e.g., Libya, Syria, Kosovo) were motivated by humanitarian concerns rather than geostrategic reasons.

As another example and one that comes closer to the core of Sino-American relations, does Washington support Taiwan's *de jure* independence? The answer thus far has clearly been "no," even though the U.S. prefers to see the maintenance of the status quo across the Taiwan Strait —and hence Taiwan's *de facto* independence—for an indefinite future. Opinion surveys of the people on Taiwan have shown repeatedly that a large majority would prefer *de jure* independence—if they can be assured that this preference can be implemented without provoking Beijing to resort to military force to prevent it.[2] In this case, Washington's declared support for democracy and self-determination clearly has limits, and it is subordinated to its larger interest not to destabilize its relations with Beijing. The former values are not the only ones shaping U.S. policy, and not even the most important ones. That both Washington and Beijing have been going against the popular grain of Taiwanese public opinion must be a source of considerable discomfort to both. In both capitals, it is a matter of "y penser toujours, n'en parler jamais"—always think of it but never speak about it, a remark attributed to Leon Gambetta on France's loss of Alsace-Lorraine after the Franco-Prussian War of 1870.

One can follow the customary logic of social science inquiry to study a country's different responses to "most similar cases" in order to address the issue of masking effect. Did Washington support the right of Crimeans for self-determination—or those living in Kashmir, Palestine, and Bangladesh? Its opposition to Russia's annexation of Crimea claimed that all the people in Ukraine should have a say in Crimea's decision to secede (and not just those living in Crimea), and this decision should comply with Ukraine's constitution. This is, of course, a position shared by Beijing with respect to Taiwan's status.

As yet another example, a state's signals to its counterpart may be subject to misinterpretation due to the masking effect. Thus when Nikita Khrushchev decided to pull Soviet troops out of Austria and to undertake limited military demobilization in the 1950s, U.S. officials were faced with competing interpretations. Moscow might be sending a conciliatory message or it might be adopting military retrenchment due to economic distress. Both interpretations seemed plausible. The implication of this illustration is that timing is critical. If Moscow had the former intention in mind, it should have undertaken these actions when its economy was in a better shape. Similarly, Mikhail Gorbachev's concessions to the West —made at a time when the USSR was suffering a sharp decline—naturally inclined some people to ask whether they were made because of Moscow's dire circumstances or because of a transformation in its basic character. Paradoxically, officials are less likely to initiate policy reforms or changes when things are quiet or going well. These reforms and changes tend to instead occur under less favorable circumstances, thus engendering doubts such as those just mentioned. By implication, if one wishes to establish trust in a counterpart's eyes, the time to convey reassurance and conciliation is when one is in a relatively strong bargaining position.

One would not be too much concerned about the future intentions of micro states such as Monaco and Tuvalu because they clearly lack the capabilities to do great harm to others. Intentions matter far more for those states commanding great destructive power. In the extreme case of a unipolar power like the U.S., no other country or combination of countries has sufficient countervailing military capability to check it. This checking will have to come mostly from its self-restraint reflecting its domestic considerations and natural impulses. The stronger a country becomes, the more powerful should be the influence of its internal politics and ideological inclinations in shaping its external intentions. The strength of powerful states enables them to act *relatively* unhindered in their external relations, especially in their immediate neighborhood. How they conduct themselves in situations of unrivalled strength is instructive. But how they do *not* conduct themselves in such situations is even more informative (such as *not* to throw their weight around and *not* to push as hard on a deal as they could have). Inaction sometimes speaks louder than action. The following discussion shows that while regrettable, mutual distrust in Sino-American relations is not unreasonable. By distrust, I mean attributing malevolent intentions to the other party, the opposite of trust.

LISTENING TO THE OTHER'S WORDS

States routinely propagate their policy agendas, communicating their public preferences and intentions that they want the world to believe in. These declarations cannot necessarily be taken at their face value because officials have been known to misrepresent—that is, to say one thing but do something else. Still, these official statements are germane to how others will judge the friendly or hostile disposition of their source. Do these statements reassure others or alarm them? Do they convey an intention to challenge the status quo or to preserve it? Do they legitimize the unilateral use of force? Do they challenge the legitimacy of other ruling elites? Do they honor international agreements and conventions? Can a state's actions be taken to suggest an encroachment on others' traditional spheres of influence? When people claim that a particular country defends or seeks to upend the international order—assigning to it a status-quo or revisionist orientation—they should but often do not actually address these questions by comparing its statements and conduct with those of others.

The public face of Beijing's foreign relations has undergone significant change over time. Panchsheel (in Sanskrit, five virtues), or the Five Principles of Coexistence, was a key cornerstone of China's public diplomacy in the 1950s. Sino-Soviet amity based on a common ideology was another cornerstone of China's diplomacy in those early days. In the mid- and late 1960s, however, struggle against both Soviet revisionism and American imperialism became the hallmark of Chinese foreign policy, with Beijing championing its support for "people's war" in other countries to promote world revolution. After President Richard Nixon's visit to Beijing in 1972, Chinese foreign policy focused on the "anti-hegemony" struggle, seeking to build a grand coalition with other countries to oppose the USSR. Since Deng Xiaoping's pivotal decision to reform the Chinese economy in the late 1970s and especially since the Tiananmen crackdown in 1989, China has pursued economic exchanges with other countries and it has abandoned the rhetoric of class struggle and people's war. It has settled most of its land borders with its neighbors (with India being the one major exception), and it has prioritized domestic economic development as a national goal. As China's economic and military capabilities have risen in recent years, Beijing has launched several "charm offensives" seeking to win over foreign friends. It has propagated ideas such as "peaceful rise" and "harmonious society" to reassure other states. It seeks to convey its commitment to the international status quo by emphasizing the Westphalian principles of state sovereignty and noninterference in other states' domestic affairs.

One can describe in similar broad strokes the evolution of U.S. foreign policy since 1945. Victory in World War II was followed quickly by the disintegration of the wartime alliance between Moscow and its Western allies, and by Washington's enunciation of the Truman Doctrine to provide U.S. aid to those states threatened by communist takeover. In the same year (1947), George Kennan wrote his famous "X article" in *Foreign Affairs*, introducing Washington's official policy of containing communism. In Asia, the outbreak of the Korean War in June 1950— and the subsequent U.S. navy's "neutralization" of the Taiwan Strait and the Chinese counter-intervention in the Korean War—estranged Sino-American relations for the next two decades. Washington built a series of alliances around China, occasionally threatening to support the Kuomintang to retake the Chinese mainland and to use nuclear weapons in

Taiwan's defense. With Washington's support, the Kuomintang government was able to retain China's seat in the United Nations until 1971. In
the 1960s and 1970s, the U.S. also committed vast amounts of resources
to fight the Vietnam War, ostensibly to stop the spread of communist
and especially Chinese influence. The Sino-Soviet split and Nixon's visit
to Beijing introduced a period of Sino-American collaboration to oppose
the USSR. This period, however, was relatively short-lived, as it came
to an end with Beijing's crackdown on domestic dissidence in 1989 and
the end of the Cold War shortly thereafter. Although Washington had
always given verbal support to democracy and capitalism, it tried to
export these ideals to other countries with increasing vigor in the wake
of the USSR's dissolution and its ascendance to a unipolar status. The
push for regime change reached a new height during George W. Bush's
presidency, when he singled out Iraq, Iran, and North Korea as an "axis
of evil." His invasion of Iraq, justified by allegations that Saddam Hussein
had (or was developing) weapons of mass destruction and that Baghdad
had connections with Al Qaeda (later shown to be untrue), exemplified
especially a turn toward more "muscular" U.S. policies and unilateral
assertiveness. Since the USSR's demise, the U.S. has intervened actively
abroad (e.g., in Kuwait, Bosnia, Kosovo, Libya, Haiti, Somalia, although
not Rwanda), often in the name of humanitarian relief and sometimes
without U.N. authorization. More recently, the Obama administration
announced a policy to pivot to Asia, which involves a redeployment
of U.S. military resources from other regions to areas closer to China.
In contrast, the Trump administration has implied a more isolationist
posture in its early pronouncements, although it has not been reticent in
warning North Korea about decisive U.S. action if Pyongyang does not
cease its development of nuclear weapons.

Although the international relations literature is replete with references
to China as a revisionist power and the U.S. as a status-quo power,[3] states
obviously play both offense and defense in their foreign policy.[4] They
can seek to promote and protect some norms while at the same time
challenging others that are less congenial to them. In the 1960s especially,

Beijing professed openly an agenda to overthrow the capitalist world order through its support of armed insurgencies in other countries. Since then, however, its official rhetoric has undergone a decisive change in avowing support for the principle of noninterference in other countries' internal affairs. In contrast, during the Cold War Washington had cast itself in the role of defending the international order (hence, the characterization of its official policy as "containment") and assisting incumbent governments against armed insurrections supported by foreign (communist) sources. It has more recently given a greater emphasis to transforming other countries' political and economic systems, popularly described as the promotion of "regime change" abroad. It has, for example, aided rebel groups seeking to overthrow the incumbent government in Libya and Syria. Thus, there has been a role reversal between China and the U.S. in both their policy declarations and actual conduct pertaining to the key tenets of the Westphalian state system.

Labels such as revisionism and status-quo orientation seek to suggest a state's disagreement with or its support for the ordering principles and basic norms governing international conduct. Yet there has been little scholarly attempt to actually compare Chinese and U.S. statements about and actual conduct concerning matters such as the legitimacy of ruling elites, the rules of warfare, the procedures for making territorial adjustments, and protocols for mutual accommodation of spheres of influence. The current literature tends to rely on rhetorical assertions in assigning these labels rather than on a systematic analysis of the relevant evidence. Whether one agrees or disagrees with the U.S. policy to promote regime change abroad, it is not a commitment to the status quo. Similarly, regardless of one's views on the U.S. Congress's decision to override a presidential veto (in late September 2016) in passing a law that allows families of the victims of the 9/11 terrorist attack to sue the government of Saudi Arabia, or its passage of the 1996 Helms-Burton Act that claims extraterritorial jurisdiction for the U.S. to pursue its sanctions against other countries, such actions obviously challenge the existing international rules. The former legislation is a breach of the doctrine of sovereign immunity and creates a precedent so that, for example, a Pakistani family can now also try to ask for similar legal recourse against the U.S. for the deaths and injuries caused by Washington's drone attacks. Likewise, China's unilateral assertion of its sovereignty over a large area in the South China Sea implies a revisionist motivation. Scholarly discussion on the ostensible revisionist or status-quo orientation of China and the U.S., as on other topics such as the power-transition theory,[5] tends to reflect the participants' soft power to control and frame popular discourse rather than their attention to systematic comparisons of these countries' statements and behavior.

References to a state's supposed revisionist or status-quo orientation are obviously laden with suggestive connotations about this state's policy intentions. This putative orientation communicates to other states with a different political or economic system whether the state in question harbors an agenda to undermine their current system—even if this transformation or conversion is being sought by peaceful means (such as when Americans in favor of engaging China justify their support for this policy by arguing publicly that it will eventually incline the Chinese people to adopt Western attitudes and interests and to reject their current government). An avowed agenda to replace another country's extant political and economic system is unlikely to endear this target country's incumbent officials to this agenda's propagator or to enhance their confidence in the latter's friendliness. Similarly, whether one agrees or disagrees with the U.S. policies to expand NATO membership to include former Soviet-bloc countries or to pivot to Asia, one can perhaps understand Moscow and Beijing's reactions to them by recalling how Washington itself had responded to perceived Soviet attempts to project its influence in the U.S. backyard (such as in Cuba, Nicaragua, and Grenada). As implied earlier, in seeking to judge another state's future intentions, the most easily accessible information is what it says publicly about its intentions.

Making Sense of the Other's Deeds

States naturally do not just rely on others' public statements to judge their future intentions. They reach back to the past, especially past encounters involving themselves, for additional information to make this assessment. Historical memories of especially traumatic episodes have an enduring effect, creating a lasting legacy even long after their occurrence. Given the different international positions and experiences of the U.S. and China in the past century or so, it is not surprising that the Chinese have a surfeit of negative, even bitter, recollections of past encounters that shape their judgment of whether the U.S. has a friendly or hostile disposition toward their country.

Sinologists are all too aware of the role of historical memories in influencing contemporary Chinese policy, as they routinely invoke the "century of national humiliation" in Chinese people's discourse on their country's foreign relations.[6] There is, however, usually little sign of empathy—a willingness to imagine how other countries would have been affected had they experienced events similar to those recalled and emphasized by the Chinese national psyche. How would Americans have judged China's trustworthiness had Beijing intervened in the American Civil War and as a result of this intervention, had perpetuated the Confederacy's secession from the Union? What if Chinese troops had joined the British in sacking Washington D.C. in 1814, looting and burning the Capitol and the White House? How would Americans have reacted if a Chinese army had marched toward Rio Grande shortly after the Declaration of Independence, with an avowed intention to establish a pro-Chinese government in Mexico? Would Washington have countenanced a strong Chinese political and military presence on Cuba, backing Havana's defiance of its colossal neighbor to the north? How would a Beijing-led alliance of states located in the Caribbean and Central America with the ostensible purpose of containing American expansionism and opposing U.S. regional hegemony be received by Washington? These questions point to empathy which is a key characteristic of and contributor to trust.

Rather than just insisting on the correctness of one's self-image, empathy requires that one puts oneself in a counterpart's shoes and imagine how one would have reacted to a situation if the roles are reversed. Empathy is especially effective in promoting trust when top leaders are able to build bonds through personal contact.[7]

John Rawls's well-known metaphor of "veil of ignorance" invites people to imagine how they would go about constructing a just society when they lack specific information on their own personal circumstances (such as their assets, abilities, and position in society).[8] For example, what would they consider to be fair, just or right on the question of slavery if they had an equal chance of ending up being a slave or a slave owner? In this spirit, Benjamin Schwarz remarks:

> Hardliners and moderates, Republicans and Democrats, agree that America is strategically dominant in East Asia and the eastern [sic] Pacific—China's backyard. They further agree that America should retain its dominance there. Thus U.S. military planners define as a threat Beijing's efforts to remedy its own weak position in the face of overwhelming superiority that they acknowledge the Unites States holds right up to the edge of the Asian mainland. This probably reveals more about our ambitions than it does about China's. Imagine if the situation is reversed, and China's air and naval power were a dominant and potentially menacing presence on the coastal shelf of North America. Wouldn't we want to offset that preponderance?[9]

My rhetorical questions just now are intended as a thought experiment with a similar purpose in mind. They ask readers to consider how their opinions may change if they should find themselves in their counterpart's position. To the extent that those counterfactual episodes I mentioned are likely to arouse strong feelings of anger and suspicion of the part of Americans, they point to the deep historical roots of Chinese distrust of the U.S.

Some readers may protest that this discussion is one-sided as it does not provide historical examples that could incline Americans to doubt

China's trustworthiness. This one-sidedness, however, reflects a basic asymmetry in the structure of these countries' past relations. We lack historical parallels in which China had played a similar role or had become similarly involved in a comparable situation to that which the U.S. had appeared in those encounters mentioned earlier pertaining to China. For instance, U.S. gunboats had sailed up and down the Yangtze River before 1949 but there has not been an analogous instance of Chinese soldiers being stationed on U.S. soil and its gunboats patrolling the Mississippi. As another example, while the U.S. had led an economic embargo and political boycott of China (e.g., denying China's seat in the United Nations and at the same time urging allies to refuse diplomatic recognition of the Beijing government) in the early decades of the People's Republic, China had not undertaken analogous policies. This does not mean that China is more trustworthy or was less hostile; only that these countries' conduct has reflected their different power positions. Simply put, the U.S. has loomed much larger in those events highly salient to China's historical memory than vice versa. Compared to Washington's importance in the political economic history of modern China and those of its neighbors, Beijing's profile has been very small in the domestic politics and foreign relations of those countries located in the Western Hemisphere.

This is not to say that other countries, including the U.S., will or should necessarily trust China, or that China has not behaved in ways that can contribute to their distrust. For example, Chinese commercial piracy and export of sensitive missile technology have naturally undermined Beijing's trustworthiness in U.S. eyes. Smaller countries bordering China, like Vietnam, Korea, and Mongolia, have plenty of unpleasant historical experiences to dispose them to distrust China. Recent Chinese behavior, such as Beijing's extensive territorial claims in the South China Sea and its military modernization program, would also naturally alarm its smaller neighbors. These neighbors find themselves in an unbalanced power relationship with China just as has been China's position relative to the U.S. in those episodes or situations mentioned previously.

How seriously is one committed to one's professed principles and avowed values? Inaction can communicate this information when a situation presents difficult choices between lofty ideals and instrumental calculations. Thus, Washington's nonresponse or lethargic response to the genocide in Rwanda and ethnic cleansing in Bosnia was revealing.[10] Similarly, when the U.S. failed to react strongly to the overthrow of democratically elected governments in Bangkok, Cairo, and Kiev, albeit ones that the U.S. had found to be objectionable for one reason or another, its posture was similarly instructive. Naturally, when Washington was actually complicit in organizing and supporting violent coups against such governments (e.g., Salvador Allende, Mohammad Mossadegh), officials in Beijing will understandably be skeptical about the claim that the U.S. distrusts China because it is not a democracy.[11] Rather, this claim is likely to be interpreted by Beijing to say "we cannot trust you until you become more like us."[12]

Other examples of inaction come to mind. Despite realists' expectation that no major state will depend on another state to provide for its defense, Germany, Japan as well as many other developed states have thus far eschewed nuclear weapons. South Korea has similarly refrained from developing these weapons despite the fact that its nemesis across the 38th parallel has done so. Such nonoccurrence of the expected (from the realist perspective) can be interpreted to suggest that these U.S. allies do not see a grave danger of being attacked by other countries and were such a contingency to occur, they have a high level of confidence in the U.S. coming to their assistance. Inaction, even free riding, on the part of these U.S. allies (such as not to acquire their own nuclear weapons and not to spend adequately on their own defense) demonstrates their trust in the U.S. honoring its defense commitments to them.

As another example, several Southeast Asian countries have territorial contests over different parts of the South China Sea, putting them in opposition to China's sovereignty claim over the same area. Their current posture indicates that they agree to disagree—that is, they would rather continue their dispute with China and postpone a settlement until a later time. Why would the smaller claimant states want to wait rather than to settle now if conventional wisdom argues that China is likely to grow stronger and thus to improve its bargaining position in the future? One plausible reason could very well be that they have confidence that the U.S. would support them and that this U.S. support would offset any possible increase in Chinese power (another plausible reason could be the relevant leaders' anticipation of serious domestic opposition to any prospective settlement). Thus, an acceptance of protracted contest implies a vote of confidence in the U.S. by, for example, the Philippines and Vietnam. Similarly, for Taiwan to hold out against China's unification overtures despite an increasingly unfavorable cross-Strait power balance is not unrelated to its officials' expectation that the U.S. would protect their country.

The examples provided in the preceding two paragraphs are significant because they point to convergent attitudes on the part of policy elites in different countries and different contexts. As mentioned earlier, majority opinion tends to be right over time and this opinion shows that foreigners find the U.S. to be generally trustworthy. It is also important to note that these examples point to what states had done—or not done—rather than just their policy declarations. That is, they refer to actual behavior rather than publicly professed intentions. As such, this evidence should be taken more seriously as indicators of how other countries perceive a state's trustworthiness, in this case, the U.S. It is also worthwhile to note that just as South Korea's decision not to seek its own nuclear weapons is indicative of its trust in Washington's security commitment, the converse can be true. North Korea's pursuit of these weapons can be interpreted as an expression that Pyongyang is not confident of Beijing's backing in a possible military crisis. Had North Koreans thought that China's nuclear deterrence would extend to protecting them—such as if China would respond to an attack on Pyongyang as equivalent to an attack on Beijing —North Korea would have much less incentive to pursue its own nuclear weapons. This was of course the rationale given by Charles de Gaulle for developing France's independent *force de frappe* because he doubted that Washington's nuclear umbrella would extend to his country.

During the Nixon administration, Moscow had approached Washington to find out how the U.S. would react if the USSR were to initiate a preventive strike against Chinese nuclear facilities at Lop Nor. Washington reacted coolly to this overture, and Moscow dropped the idea. One can very well imagine that had the U.S. supported and even joined this Soviet initiative, history would have turned out very differently. The U.S. decision not to start a preventive war against China, or if you will, to "strangle the [Chinese nuclear] baby in the cradle,"[13] was significant as it could have acted with relative impunity because Beijing at that time lacked the necessary strategic forces to retaliate in kind. Here is then another example of U.S. trustworthiness, demonstrated by its self-restraint or inaction on an occasion when it enjoyed a vast military superiority and when its potential target had only a limited military capability to respond and was experiencing significant domestic disarray and international isolation.

The aforementioned episode also presents an example of a possible preventive war in which a state deliberately attacks another when it is not in imminent danger of being attacked. This attack is motivated by a desire to prevent a perceived threat to it in some distant and indefinite future. Operation Iraqi Freedom was justified at least in part with this reasoning (that the U.S. could not afford to allow Saddam Hussein to acquire weapons of mass destruction). Washington had considered launching preventive attacks against Soviet, Chinese and North Korean targets on several occasions.[14] In some cases the idea of initiating an unprovoked attack was rejected early on in the decision process, but in other cases the attack plans came very close, even within hours, to being implemented—such as those targeting Soviet missile installations on Cuba in 1962 and North Korean nuclear sites in 1994.[15] More recently, Washington has explicitly declined to rule out military action against Iran's nuclear program. Naturally, when a state is known to have started or even just considered starting a preventive war, its reputation for trustworthiness suffers.

In 1997–1998, the Asian financial crisis caused deep economic distress in several countries which devalued their currencies in order to make their exports more attractive. This devaluation could have caused other countries to respond in kind, thus creating a race to the bottom. Beijing, however, refrained from this action which would have had the effect of nullifying or reducing the competitive disadvantage faced by China's exporters as a result of its neighbors' currency devaluations.[16] This self-restraint did not escape the attention of its neighbors. It enhanced goodwill and even trust. In contrast, the U.S. used the Asian financial crisis to press for changes that were widely seen to advance its own interests, such as in its insistence that South Korea must open and deregulate its financial market as a condition for it to receive assistance from the International Monetary Fund.[17]

As another example, China continued to purchase U.S. debts during the Great Recession that started in 2008. It injected liquidity to global financial markets instead of engaging in the panic selling of the massive amount of U.S. loans it already owned. Such behavior is not consistent with the view that it was a revisionist power bent on challenging the international financial order and creating havoc to it in order to demand changes more congenial to its interests. Beijing's actual behavior on this occasion of great financial stress to the U.S. and the European economies suggested that it had acted more like a responsible stakeholder.[18] As will be discussed later, this behavior can surely be motivated by China's self-interest as a massive sell-off of U.S. debt instruments would have caused devastating losses to the investments already made by China as well as serious damages to the world economy (to which China's export-dependent economy has become highly vulnerable). Of course, one does not expect a "responsible stakeholder" to be *only* motivated by altruism (I will discuss later whether a country may become more committed to the existing global order as it gains a larger stake in this order). Finally, when Beijing allowed market forces to lower the value of its currency in August 2015, China was the last follower rather the first mover in a series of currency devaluations starting in Europe and Japan. One is reminded of Susan Strange's words written almost thirty years ago when she commented on the privileged role enjoyed by the U.S. and its currency in the world economy:

> In most countries, whether the balance-of-payments is in surplus or deficit indicates the strength or weakness of its financial position. With the United States, the exact converse can be true. Indeed, to run a persistent deficit for a quarter of century with impunity indicates not American weakness, but American power in the system. To decide on one August [1971] morning that dollars can no longer be converted into gold was a progression from exorbitant privilege to super-exorbitant privilege; the U.S. government was exercising the unconstrained right to print money that others could not (save at unacceptable cost) refuse to accept in payment.[19]

The previous discussion illustrates how others may gauge one's trustworthiness by judging whether one has acted opportunistically when one is presented with favorable circumstances. Does one take advantage of others' vulnerability? The timing of China's military seizure of the Crescent group of islands in the Paracel archipelago in 1974 was widely perceived to have been designed to take advantage of Saigon's distractions and weaknesses as well as the then ongoing process of U.S. disengagement from the Vietnam War. This sudden attack serves as a cautionary reminder that Beijing is capable of taking offensive actions when it finds circumstances to be propitious for such undertaking. This precedent elevates distrust among those Southeast Asian countries that have ongoing territorial disputes with Beijing in the South China Sea.

American action in the Korean War has plausibly had a similar effect on Chinese perceptions of U.S. opportunism.[20] Washington had justified its initial intervention in the name of collective action to oppose Pyongyang's aggression against Seoul. Having gained the military upper hand, General Douglas MacArthur crossed the 38th parallel with the declared goal of unifying the entire peninsula under a pro-U.S. regime. There was even vocal support in some U.S. quarters to press on beyond the Yalu to "roll back" communism in China. U.S. intervention in the Korean War also caused consternation because just a few months before the outbreak of this conflict, Secretary of State Dean Acheson had left Korea outside the U.S. defense perimeter in a speech given at the National Press Club on January 12, 1950.

Parenthetically, the U.S.-led intervention in this conflict was sanctioned by the United Nations but this U.N. authorization was possible only because the USSR was boycotting its proceedings. Moscow was absent because it had wanted to protest against the Beijing government being denied its U.N. seat as Washington and its allies had successfully insisted that the Kuomintang government on Taiwan was the legitimate representative of China (all of China, including the mainland as U.S. officials had denounced the Beijing government as an illegitimate puppet regime controlled by Moscow and had characterized it as a "passing phenomenon").

Another example of unintended miscommunication or change of mind comes from a meeting between Saddam Hussein and U.S. Ambassador to Iraq April Glaspie prior to the latter country's invasion and annexation of Kuwait. Glaspie had told Hussein in December 1990 that "we [the U.S.] have no opinion on the Arab-Arab conflicts, like your border disagreement with Kuwait."[21] In the subsequent U.S.-led war (Operation Desert Storm in 1991) to liberate Kuwait, the destruction of the Iraqi military became another declared U.S. objective.

The aforementioned episodes pertain to pushing one's advantages and expanding one's objectives when one senses a strategic opportunity. They speak to the concern whether a state can be trusted with increased power. In contrast to the earlier example of Washington switching its objective from repulsing North Korea's invasion to destroying its regime and reunifying Korea under a friendly regime, Beijing has chosen unilateral ceasefire and voluntary withdrawal of its troops back to the lines of

actual control existing before the start of a military conflict. It took this
course of action after seizing large chunks of its adversary's territory
in the Sino-Indian and Sino-Vietnamese wars.[22] President George H.
Bush had also halted U.S. troops from advancing into Iraq after evicting
the latter's armed forces from Kuwait.[23] In contrast, his son President
George W. Bush was widely seen to have undertaken a "bait and switch"
strategy, using Saddam Hussein's alleged weapons of mass destruction
and his ostensible connections with Al Qaeda as a pretext to invade Iraq
and overthrow its regime.[24]

U.S. officials and scholars are concerned about how increasing Chinese
power can affect Chinese intentions in the future, inclining Beijing to
become more assertive, even aggressive. In their comments on Sino-
American relations, these same officials and scholars have paid less
attention to similar concerns that the Chinese have about increasing
U.S. power. They have not applied the logic underlying their concerns
about increased Chinese power to the U.S. itself which has become the
world's undisputed hegemon after the USSR's collapse. This discrepancy
implies that relative power gains or losses are not the only factor or
even the most decisive one influencing states' policy agenda and their
trustworthiness even though this variable tends to be the main and often
even the exclusive focus when it comes to analyzing the consequences
of China's rise.

In his thoughtful analysis of trust and distrust during the Cold War,
Andrew Kydd shows that much of the existing evidence suggests that
the U.S. was the trusting type seeking security protection whereas the
USSR was the untrustworthy type inclined to expand and defect when
given the opportunity.[25] Events since the mid-1980s, however, appear to
indicate a role reversal. If for nothing else, the USSR's demise and its loss
of its Eastern and Central European allies augmented further the power
advantages enjoyed by the U.S. and its Western European partners. As
a consequence, they should become less fearful of Russia's capabilities
and should act accordingly if they are the security-seeking type. Their

military campaign against Serbia, invasion of Iraq and Afghanistan, and expansion of NATO's membership contradict this expectation. The geographic proximity of these episodes, involving the military forces of extra-regional powers, to Russia should naturally arouse Moscow's security concerns and elevate its suspicions about the Western countries' intentions. Ceteris paribus, the closer are such episodes to a country's homeland, the more plausible that its responses—such as Ukraine in Russia's case (and Cuba for the U.S. and Korea and Taiwan for China)—are motivated by impulses to seek security rather than expansion.

Russia presents an especially pertinent analogue for China, and its recent experience can be highly informative for Beijing's officials to gauge U.S. and more generally, Western intentions. In ending the Cold War, Moscow had withdrawn its troops from Eastern and Central Europe, and it had accepted the dismantlement of the Warsaw Pact and communist rule in its satellite countries and even the dissolution of the USSR itself. It had also introduced multiparty election and a capitalist economy in Russia. It had even accepted and cooperated with the U.S. in facilitating Washington's military access to and bases in former Soviet republics located in Central Asia. By any measure, these moves point to significant gestures of accommodation and reassurance that have largely gone unreciprocated by the West.[26] Russian officials have argued that as a condition for Moscow's consent to Germany's reunification, Western countries had agreed not to expand NATO to include the former Soviet-bloc countries. Whether there was indeed such an agreement, this expansion could not have contributed to Moscow's trust in Western intentions.[27] It could hardly be indifferent to the Western countries' attempts to, for example, pull Ukraine into their orbit, just as Washington can be expected to protest vigorously if Mexico were to turn into a Russian or Chinese ally. American officials have often expressed their concern that China has an agenda to displace the U.S. in East Asia, but recent Western actions in Russia's near abroad can certainly be construed to indicate even more strongly this intention and an agenda to deny Moscow its traditional sphere of influence.[28]

From Moscow's perspective, NATO expansion represents a major change in Western and especially U.S. attitudes. During the Cold War, Washington had tacitly conceded Central and Eastern Europe as a Soviet sphere of influence. It had, for example, refrained from giving tangible support to those groups that had challenged Soviet political domination and resisted Moscow's armed intervention (e.g., in Budapest and Prague). From Beijing's perspective, this historical background is also pertinent because, contrary Washington's tacit recognition of a Soviet sphere of influence during the Cold War, it has declined to be as accommodative to China.[29] U.S. forces are arrayed within close distance of China's borders, and many of China's neighbors are U.S. allies (formally or informally). Even in the case of China's lone formal ally, North Korea, the U.S. has been interested in promoting a regime change in Pyongyang. These observations are important because when major powers have agreed to demarcate the geostrategic boundaries of their competition, they have historically been better able to manage their differences and prevent conflicts among them from escalating into large wars.[30]

ARMAMENT AND ALLIANCE BEHAVIOR AS INFORMATIVE INDICATORS

Whether a state trusts another is in part shaped by whether it perceives the other state trusts it. A state's armament and alliance behavior can be particularly pertinent to others' judgments of its trustworthiness. The International Institute for Strategic Studies has estimated that the U.S. spent about $581.0 billion on defense in 2014,[31] whereas the Stockholm International Peace Research Institute put this figure at $610.0 billion.[32] Depending on which source one chooses, the U.S. had spent 3.0% or 3.5% of its gross domestic product on its military. These two sources put China's defense expenditures in the same year at $129.4 billion (2% of its GDP) and $216.0 billion (2.1% of its GDP) respectively. The IISS made considerably lower estimates for China's military spending and its gross domestic product than SIPRI, although both sources came up with rather similar figures for this country's defense burden (military expenditures as a percent of GDP). Consulting the World Bank as a third data source yields comparable figures for the U.S. defense burden at 3.5% and China's at 2.1% for 2014.[33] Both in absolute and relative terms, the U.S. has allocated considerably more resources to military purposes than China.

This asymmetry reflects in part the U.S. status as a global power which has interests and commitments in many places in the world. In contrast, China is just a regional power with a smaller array of security concerns. This consideration, however, is offset by the fact that the U.S. has a much safer home region where it is preponderant. Being flanked by two oceans and bordering only two friendly and weak neighbors, it faces a far more benign geostrategic environment in its immediate neighborhood than China which has more immediate neighbors than any other country in the world. Like Germany before the two world wars, China shares a congested neighborhood with several other major and potentially hostile powers as its close neighbors. The U.S. dominance of the globe's commons —sea, air, and space—is supreme,[34] and it has an extensive network of alliances covering every part of the world, including China's immediate neighborhood. Objectively speaking, the U.S. should feel much safer than China in the defense of its homeland and in its security environment more generally (thus, it is hard to imagine any U.S. military planner would want to exchange his or her position with a Chinese counterpart).

Parenthetically, whether U.S. military preeminence contributes to regional peace, stability and trust is a worthwhile topic for careful analysis. It is plausible to argue that this phenomenon has had such an effect in Europe, Latin America, and the Asia Pacific, although this argument does not appear to hold up nearly as well in the Middle East or South Asia. So it becomes relevant to ask whether there are intervening factors that can account for such discrepant outcomes. While this proposition aligns with the reasoning behind the hegemonic stability theory and the power-transition theory,[35] it contradicts and challenges traditional balance-of-power thinking.[36]

There are still other ways of contextualizing a country's defense spending. Ceteris paribus, the more neighbors—especially powerful and potentially hostile neighbors—a country has, the more it can be expected to feel a need to arm itself (the number of neighbors indicates the potential for territorial disputes which are the most likely cause for interstate war).[37] Similarly, the more this country has suffered military invasion and foreign occupation in the past, the more likely would be its felt need to spend on defense. Naturally, when a country enjoys a vast military superiority over its neighbors and indeed all potential competitors *combined*, it should feel more relaxed about its security situation and should thus feel less of a need to continue to outspend other countries by a huge margin. The U.S. accounted for 49% of the world's total military spending in 1995 and 46% in 2006.[38] More recently, this figure has declined to about 37% of the global total but this amount still exceeded the combined military spending of the next highest seven countries.

Seen in this light, the motivation behind U.S. military spending would appear highly suspicious to Beijing, lowering its judgment of U.S. trust-worthiness. The size of this spending seems to be much larger than needed just for self-defense, especially after the U.S. had become the world's only superpower in the wake of the USSR's demise.[39] One can also understand the converse. From Washington's perspective, China is so much larger and more powerful than most of its neighbors. Therefore, it seems hardly reasonable that any country would want to replicate what Japan did in the 1930s and 1940s—that is, to attempt a physical conquest of Chinese territories. If so, the large recent increases in Chinese military spending would also appear suspicious to Washington.

Beyond the size of a country's military expenditures, the nature of its armament acquisition and its force deployment can be informative about its intentions.[40] Long-range stealth bombers, rapid-deployment forces, and aircraft carrier battle groups are designed more for the purpose of force projection than homeland defense. The U.S. has emphasized such weapons systems, and has deployed its forces in many forward positions in Europe, the Middle East, and the Asia Pacific on a permanent basis. This military posture is distinct from that of an "offshore balancer," one that will only intervene in the event that another power is poised to seize hegemony in another vital region. NATO's expansion and U.S. military forays in the Balkans, Central Asia, and the Middle East in the wake of the USSR's collapse would again appear to indicate an offensive rather than defensive agenda. This conduct would further incline Beijing to distrust Washington.

In contrast, despite recent improvements in its armaments and fighting capabilities, China's military deployment and doctrine continue to be focused on the primary mission of obstructing and hampering U.S. operations in a contingency involving Taiwan. They seek to extend China's coastal defense and deny U.S. access to this coastal zone. Washington sees this development to be intended to undermine its military preeminence in the Asia Pacific and to compromise its commitment to defend its formal or informal allies (of course, Beijing can make the same argument about U.S. pressure on Pyongyang having the same effect on *its* commitment to this ally). It is perhaps not unreasonable for U.S. officials to surmise that Beijing harbors the long-term ambition of dislodging the U.S. as the premier power in China's home region, just as the U.S. had done in evicting British influence and establishing its own regional hegemony in the Western Hemisphere over a century ago. It is, however, a far stretch to project China's current military capabilities and force dispositions to that possible future development.

Significantly, Beijing has refrained from acting in one important respect as the U.S. and the USSR have behaved previously. Despite its recent rise, it has not waged an ideological competition with Washington, nor has it sought to create a rival alliance. In contrast to the USSR, China has thus far not mounted any attempt that can be construed to challenge U.S. interests or displace its influence in those regions that have been historically important to Washington, such as Europe, Latin America, and the Middle East. It has not recruited and sustained anti-U.S. allies in these regions as the USSR had done in Cuba, Ethiopia, Syria, and Egypt. Beijing has reportedly turned down Pakistani overtures for a formal alliance. Although it does not completely agree with Washington's policies toward Iran and North Korea, it has nevertheless collaborated in multinational efforts to curtail these countries' development of nuclear weapons. Finally, in the case of China's lone formal ally, North Korea, Beijing has long withdrawn its armed forces from that country after the Korean War ended. In contrast, U.S. forces have remained in South Korea. Except for its possession of a few nuclear warheads, Pyongyang is much weaker than Seoul by almost any measure of national power. North Korea is of course located at China's doorstep but far from the U.S.

Naturally, the U.S. claims that its military presence in South Korea and Japan serves a powerful deterrent against possible North Korean aggression, but it is plausible to imagine that Pyongyang and Beijing are unlikely to share the same perception (just as Americans were not inclined to accept the USSR's public rationale for stationing its missiles in Cuba as an attempt to deter the U.S. after the aborted invasion at the Bay of Pigs). As I will discuss later, the U.S. military presence in South Korea and Japan has been characterized as a "cork in the bottle" that has the effect of discouraging these countries from pursuing an independent military force with nuclear weapons and according to this view, the U.S. military role should therefore reassure China. In this interpretation, Washington's alliances with Seoul and Tokyo serve as *pacta de contrahendo* to restrain South Korean and Japanese militarism.[41] Whether Beijing will find this interpretation credible will depend in part on, for example, whether Washington invokes its treaty commitment to Japan in supporting the latter country's maritime dispute with China in the East China Sea and whether it has sought to apply its military assets located in Japan and South Korea for "contingencies surrounding Taiwan."

The U.S. has also kept its military presence in Germany even though World War II had come to an end seventy years ago. If the danger emanating from an expansionist USSR had once posed a threat necessitating this U.S. military presence, this threat has long since passed at least as far as Western Europe is concerned. The continued existence and even expansion of NATO thus naturally arouse concerns about its intended purpose from Beijing and especially Moscow's perspective. It is also pertinent to note that U.S. alliances in the Asia Pacific, including its military pact with Japan, long predated China's recent rise. That is, these alliances were constructed at a time when Beijing clearly lacked any capability to pose a military threat to its maritime neighbors such as Japan and the Philippines. Thus, from Beijing's perspective the purposes of these U.S. alliances do not appear to be limited to just defensive ones.

Invoking the veil of ignorance whereby one judges a conduct not by its perpetrator's identity, there appear to be good reasons for China to distrust the U.S. and for the U.S. to also have strong misgivings about future Chinese intentions. Charles Maier remarks that "The United States supports a whole structure of formal and less formal commitments to the security of the states in the western Pacific. Their proximity to China means that Beijing perceives an asymmetry of claims. After all, China has no equivalent set of commitments in the Caribbean or Western Europe. That each side will perceive an excessive ambition on the part of the other is inevitable: it is not a misperception, but an inevitable conclusion."[42] In predicting China's inevitable "unpeaceful rise," John Mearsheimer argues that this country will follow the path of other rising powers before it, including presumably the precedent set by the U.S. in establishing its own position as a regional hegemon.[43]

TREATMENT OF WEAK NEIGHBORS
AND DOMESTIC MINORITIES

For powerful states like China and especially the U.S., it is more difficult for others to restrain them by the threat of counterforce. Their counterparts will instead have to rely more on the leaders of these powerful countries to restrain themselves from any excessive and wanton use of the force in their possession. Whether the leaders of such states can be trusted will be judged in part by how they have behaved toward their weak neighbors and their domestic political and racial/ethnic minorities. Those who have shown tolerance, even magnanimity, toward dissident or minority groups will be accorded greater trust than others who are mean and even oppressive toward these groups.

What logic lies behind the idea that a country's treatment of its own people, especially its political dissidents and racial/ethnic minorities, can reflect its trustworthiness abroad? The pertinent inference is similar to the so-called cultural explanation of the democratic peace phenomenon.[44] This phenomenon points to the fact that democratic governments rarely if ever fight each other. The cultural explanation seeking to account for this phenomenon refers to the domestic culture of democracies. People who grow up in democracies are socialized to embrace certain values and attitudes, such as tolerance of political differences and acceptance of diversity. They learn to respect others with different opinions or traits and to compromise with them in politics rather than treating them harshly. They take seriously the protection of minority rights, whether these minorities refer to political or racial/ethnic groups. To the extent that democratic leaders internalize these values and attitudes, they are likely to extend this orientation to their interactions with foreign governments. By the same logic, authoritarian leaders who abuse the human rights of their own citizens and crush their domestic opposition are likely to duplicate this behavior in their foreign relations. Finally, the civic culture of a democracy embodies and promotes mutual trust among its citizens, a phenomenon that inclines democratic leaders to be more trusting of other countries and this disposition is in turn likely to be reciprocated by their foreign counterparts. Naturally, whether a regime is democratic or authoritarian, how it treats its own citizens reflects the extent to which its actual deeds correspond to its professed principles.

The U.S. has a long history of military intervention in the Caribbean and Central America, such as those mounted against Cuba, Panama, Nicaragua, Guatemala, El Salvador, Haiti, the Dominican Republic,

Grenada, and Colombia. These interventions against regimes that Washington deemed to be politically objectionable raise doubts about how it will use its overwhelming power when it finds itself in other comparable situations of hugely asymmetric relations. The U.S. has presented different reasons for undertaking its interventions in Latin America, such as to protect human rights, restore democracy, or depose Moscow's client regimes, but none of the target countries could be construed to pose a serious national security threat to it. Moreover, quite a few of these interventions predated the Cold War or more recent U.S. policies to advance the cause of democracy and human rights abroad. As for its internal social and political conditions, the U.S. rate of incarceration is especially informative. With about 5% of the world's people, Americans account for nearly 25% of the world's prison population, and African Americans constitute a disproportionately large segment of those incarcerated. Large and persistent inequalities in other aspects of the lives of different ethnic and racial groups in the U.S. would also engender foreigners' concerns about whether they will be accorded any better treatment than the discriminated groups (such as dramatized by several recent incidents of police brutality against racial minorities). The enslavement of African Americans, the mistreatment of Native Americans (and the many broken treaties with them), the internment of U.S. citizens of Japanese descent during World War II, and the legal exclusion of Asian immigrants in the past are also not reassuring.

China features a long record of persecuting suspected political dissidents and discriminating against people of non-Han origin or those with "bad" class background. The government's various political rectification campaigns and especially the so-called Cultural Revolution have claimed millions of victims. In the aftermath of the so-called Great Leap Forward movement, millions died of hunger and malnutrition. In 1989, the government used force to suppress demonstrators assembled at the Tiananmen Square, resulting in hundreds if not thousands of death. These casualty figures far outnumbered the deaths and injuries caused by official suppression in the U.S., such as at Kent State and

Selma. Ethnic relations in Tibet and Xinjiang continue to be poor, with many indigenous people in these regions feeling resentful about being denied their cultural tradition and political autonomy. The scale of officially-sanctioned violence directed against China's own citizens has been so horrendous during the Maoist years that those living abroad would be justifiably concerned about their treatment should they come under Chinese political sway. This concern is especially palpable for residents of Taiwan should that island be reunited one day with the mainland. That the Hong Kong authorities have recently been able to end the "Occupy Central" protest movement peacefully obviously has important implications for the people of Taiwan. Beijing's inaction in this case—namely its avoidance of direct intervention, most particularly any involvement by the People's Liberation Army stationed in Hong Kong —is also highly relevant. As already mentioned, severe and pervasive mistreatment of a country's own citizens suggests to foreigners that they will probably not be accorded any more decent treatment. Thus, a government's abuse of domestic human rights seriously undermines its reputation for trustworthiness abroad. Rampant official corruption and graft have the same effect of damaging a country's trustworthiness in foreigners' eyes.

China has fought wars but unlike the U.S., all these armed conflicts have occurred at its borders. Moreover, Beijing has generally eschewed using force against its weakest neighbors. When it has fought, it has instead taken on the strongest adversaries such as the U.S. in Korea, India, Vietnam, and the USSR (in armed clashes over the demarcation of the Ussuri River). When negotiating border settlements with its smaller and weaker neighbors (e.g., Nepal, Laos, Burma, Mongolia), Beijing has usually adopted an accommodating posture and avoided the use of force.[45] It has often settled its borders with these neighbors on terms that are generally more favorable to them. Whether this pattern will continue as China becomes more powerful is an important question, as its ongoing territorial disputes in the South China Sea involve other claimants that are much smaller and weaker than China. Will it depart from its historical pattern of behavior and resort to the overt use of armed coercion against, say, the Philippines? Put in another way, does Beijing's past behavior indicate self-restraint in the use of force when interacting with its smaller and weaker neighbors, or does it reflect its inadequate capabilities in the past? The U.S. has not refrained from applying its overwhelming power when invading its small neighbors repeatedly in the past.

According to the logic presented here, as China becomes more powerful, it should feel more confident and less insecure—and therefore less inclined to pursue forceful, assertive, and even aggressive policies toward its smaller and weaker neighbors. To the extent that it shows this behavioral pattern, it will be seen as more trustworthy. Conversely, to the extent that it becomes more intolerant and coercive in its dealings with these neighbors even as it gains more power over them, it will be seen as less trustworthy.

In this respect, Beijing's policy toward Taipei should be especially informative. Its bellicosity during the 1950s and 1960s can be reasonably understood in the context of circumstances prevailing then, such as the Kuomintang's declared intention (however unrealistic) to invade the mainland and the U.S. military presence on the island and its formal alliance with Taiwan. There was, in other words, more reason for Beijing to feel insecure and to react forcefully at that time. With the abrogation of the U.S.-Taiwan defense treaty, Taipei's increasing economic integration with China and its current leaders' pledge not to declare *de jure* independence, and especially China's vast improvement of its military capabilities, Beijing should now feel more confident about its bargaining position. The logic presented here would therefore argue that if it is trustworthy, its policy toward Taipei should become less bellicose and more accommodating. Whether its policy evolves in this direction should be informative about whether it has basically benign intentions. Such a change will be especially compelling if other states judge the Taiwan issue to be a matter of China's internal affairs. This is so because such judgment should lessen the international constraint faced by Beijing to resort to military force and if Beijing nevertheless refrains from using force in this more permissive circumstance, one may infer that it is even less inclined to use force in disputes where the other party is another recognized state (i.e., in situations where the international repercussions of using force would be more severe). In this light, the first ever meeting of leaders representing the two sides of the Taiwan Strait, held between Xi Jinping and Ma Ying-jeou in Singapore in November 2015, represents a major albeit symbolic breakthrough of improved relations.[46] The conduct of U.S-Cuban relations in a Trump administration would provide a contrasting case.

The aforestated logic also argues that because the U.S. cannot be conceivably threatened by its smaller Caribbean and Central American neighbors, Washington's repeated past military invasions of and interventions against them harms its trustworthiness in foreigners' eyes. Parenthetically, whether some smaller countries will make preemptive concessions to their much more powerful neighbor in order to avoid being victimized by the latter country's resort to force is an interesting empirical question. If this mechanism operates sometimes, it raises another interesting question.

Why, for example, had Grenada and Panama not chosen this course of action to avoid being invaded by the U.S. and if they had pursued such action, why was it insufficient to stop this U.S. invasion? Washington's use of military force against these countries is therefore enigmatic if it is reasonable to expect that these countries' leaders would want to appease the U.S. in order to avoid being attacked. This puzzle extends to Slobodan Milosevic and Saddam Hussein. One could only surmise that they either did not believe that the U.S. threat to attack was serious (i.e., they made the mistake of thinking that the U.S. threat was a bluff) or did not think that the U.S. was appeasable (i.e., Washington was really seeking their political and even physical demise and would not stop its campaign short of this objective) and even if a deal were to be negotiated, they did not trust that Washington would fulfill its terms. If Washington were to renege, who would have the power to compel the U.S. to abide by this agreement?

This question in turn hints at the difficulties encountered in negotiations with Iran and North Korea about their respective nuclear programs. Naturally, Tehran and Pyongyang would be concerned about the enforceability of any prospective deal—such as those provisions pertaining to the lifting of sanctions directed against them and even more importantly, immunizing them against a possible subsequent military attack—once they have given up nuclear weapons. Ironically, the one member of the "axis of evil" that was attacked by the U.S. actually turned out not to have nuclear weapons, whereas of the other two that have not been attacked one actually has these weapons and the other was likely to be developing them. If Washington's intent was to discourage nuclear proliferation, this pattern conveys the opposite message—not having nuclear weapons may make a country vulnerable to attack whereas having these weapons may actually deter it.

To this analytic mix one can add the fate of Muammar Gaddafi who had in 2003 agreed to eliminate all of his country's chemical, biological and nuclear stockpiles for weapons program and who had invited international agencies to monitor and facilitate this dismantlement. In March 2011 NATO forces intervened militarily in Libya's civil war, helping the rebels to overthrow his regime. He was killed in October. Obviously his decision to get rid of his country's material for developing weapons of mass destruction did not protect his government or himself, and his demise would presumably serve as a poignant reminder to Iranian and North Korean leaders as they face international pressure to disarm. In the vernacular of international signaling, Gaddafi's disarmament decision was a costly commitment and should therefore be credible, but it was nevertheless ineffective in gaining U.S. and NATO's trust.

PROMISES KEPT OR NOT, AND OTHER MEMORABLE INCIDENTS

A state's trustworthiness is most easily checked by whether its deeds correspond to its words. Has it done what it has said it would do, and not done what it has said it would not do? Whether one agrees or disagrees with the U.S. decision to finally disengage from the Indochina War, this decision cannot be argued to reinforce its reputation as a trustworthy ally (for South Vietnam as well as Laos and Cambodia). Similarly, regardless of one's agreement or disagreement with President Jimmy Carter's decision to switch diplomatic recognition from Taipei to Beijing, this decision and the concomitant unilateral abrogation of the U.S. defense treaty with Taiwan are again likely to undermine confidence in the U.S. being a reliable and steadfast ally. Washington's reversal of its declared policy to assume a neutral position in the Chinese Civil War after the Korean War broke out and indeed, its intervention in the latter conflict after announcing Korea to be located outside the U.S. defense perimeter would presumably have similar effects in Beijing's eyes. These episodes affected China directly or its closest neighbors. Their effects are likely to be more pronounced and enduring than events happening elsewhere.

There have been other incidents in Sino-American relations with a deleterious effect on Beijing's perception of Washington's trustworthiness and also on its perception of how much Washington trusts it. One of the events that had rocked Sino-American relations was Taiwan President Lee Teng-hui's visit to the U.S. in 1995, ostensibly to speak at an alumni meeting in Ithaca, New York. Officials in the Clinton administration had repeatedly assured their Chinese counterparts that the U.S. government would not issue a visa to Lee in order to avoid giving the appearance of contradicting Washington's official recognition of Beijing as the sole legal government of China. Within days of its latest assurances, however, Washington reversed itself and its decision to allow Lee to visit the U.S. shocked the Chinese officials.[47] This U.S. action and Lee's speech at Cornell University were the proximate cause for the subsequent Taiwan Strait crisis in 1995–1996.

Washington's arms sales to Taiwan have also been a chronic irritant in Sino-American relations. In 1992, President George H. Bush authorized the sale of F-16 fighters to Taiwan even though the U.S. had previously pledged to cut such sales over time.[48] In the Chinese eyes, this and other similar transactions violated both the spirit and letter of Washington's public pledges to Beijing. Perhaps the most searing event in recent Chinese memory was the U.S. bombing of China's embassy in Belgrade, an incident in which three Chinese citizens were killed. Washington claimed that this bombing, carried out as part of NATO's air campaign against Yugoslavia in 1999, was an accident. Beijing and some Western media such as the *Observer* and the *Guardian* were, however, not persuaded.[49] Beijing's unwillingness to give Washington the benefit of doubt in this case was in itself a sign that it did not trust the U.S.

This unwillingness was reciprocated by Washington in an incident involving the Chinese freighter *Yinhe* in August 1993. The U.S. suspected that this vessel was carrying dangerous chemicals to the Middle East, specifically thiodiglycol and thionyl chloride which are ingredients for making poison gas. This ship was harassed en route by the U.S. navy notwithstanding Chairman Jiang Zemin's personal assurance to U.S. Ambassador J. Stapleton Roy that no contraband was on board. This ship was finally boarded and inspected at Dumman, Saudi Arabia, and this search failed to discover any of the suspected material.[50] Some would argue that Jiang's reassurances in the *Yinhe* incident were not credible to U.S. officials because prior Chinese statements such as those about Beijing's export of missile technologies to Iran and Pakistan were misleading. This case thus shows the importance of having a reputation for honesty in order to gain another country's trust. Even though in the larger scheme of Sino-American relations the *Yinhe* affair was a relatively minor incident (although it did raise skepticisms about Washington's much publicized commitment to "the freedom of navigation"), it nevertheless indicated to Beijing that it was not trusted by Washington despite the personal involvement of China's top leader. At the same time and as already mentioned, Chinese officials were also not inclined to accept President

William J. Clinton's word that the bombing of their Belgrade embassy was an accident.

Although not directly involving China, several well-known episodes in U.S. foreign policy would undermine Washington's credibility both at home and abroad. In the U–2 affair, the Eisenhower administration lied about the nature and mission of the spy plane, seeking to use the National Aeronautics and Space Agency as a cover until Moscow disclosed that the plane's pilot Francis Gary Powers was alive and in Soviet custody.[51] The Kennedy administration had its own trials and tribulations. It had, for example, tried to conceal the Central Intelligence Agency's role in organizing, planning and executing the Bay of Pigs invasion.[52] To his subsequent chagrin, U.S. Ambassador to the United Nations Adlai Stevenson had publicly denied U.S. complicity in the bombing raids against Cuba, even though the U.S. had been deeply involved in all aspects of this operation. As another example of a highly controversial chapter in U.S. foreign policy, the Johnson administration alleged that two U.S. destroyers were attacked by North Vietnamese torpedo boats on the nights of August 2 and August 4, 1964. These allegations were used to gain congressional approval of the Gulf of Tonkin Resolution which became the legal basis for subsequent U.S. military involvement in and escalation of the Vietnam War. Various investigations have, however, later concluded that the U.S. navy had been supporting covert South Vietnamese raids against North Vietnam at that time and that at least the second alleged attack had never occurred.[53] The Nixon administration had its own share of controversies. It ended with the president being disgraced by the Watergate scandal, including his administration's attempts to use the Central Intelligence Agency to cover up the criminal involvement of various high-ranking officials in this episode.[54] It led to Nixon's decision to resign rather than be impeached. The seizure of U.S. hostages by the radicals in Tehran presented the greatest political challenge to the Carter administration, which lobbied the Europeans to join its economic sanction against Iran and assured the world that the U.S. would not take any military action until diplomacy had failed to gain the hostages' release. These moves were later seen by U.S. allies as a smokescreen for the military rescue operation that Washington had already decided to undertake.[55] The Reagan administration was in its turn rocked by the Iran-contra scandal, involving high-level officials' attempts to circumvent the arms embargo against Iran and to use the proceeds of weapons sales to Tehran to provide covert funding to Nicaragua's rightist elements fighting the Sandinista government.[56] The foreign policy of President George W. Bush was marked by his administration's rush to war against Iraq.[57] The reasons given for this invasion—that Saddam Hussein had weapons of mass destruction and connections with Al Qaeda—have now been widely discredited. These reasons were propagated by the U.S. president, vice president, and other high-ranking officials like secretaries of defense and state (such as when Colin Powell testified publicly at the United Nations). Arguably, on many of these and similar occasions the American people and their legislators were more the intended audience than foreign leaders.

Episodes such as those just mentioned damage a country's trustworthiness. Many of them involve covert operations so that those responsible have a reasonable expectation that these operations would remain classified secrets and thus be kept from public knowledge. As such, these officials can expect to get away with their deceptions. How they conduct themselves in such permissive circumstances is therefore more telling about their honesty and integrity. When they are exposed as liars, their credibility suffers both at home and abroad. For the same reason (that the perpetrators have good reason to expect that their misdeeds will never be exposed), abuses of prisoners held at Abu Ghraib and revelations disclosed by Edward Snowden on Washington's massive domestic surveillance programs are especially devastating to U.S. reputation. By the same logic, pervasive official corruption in China has a similar negative effect on its reputation. By definition, graft is hidden from the public view and undertaken by those who do not expect to be caught for their dishonesty.

This discussion underscores the vital role played by an independent press and investigative journalism. These institutions serve as a critical watchdog that checks official wrongdoing and duplicity. The U.S. enjoys a huge asset in this respect because of its media freedom and political transparency. Foreigners can trust the U.S. more because an independent press and partisan competition can be expected to expose dishonest officials and because they know this risk, U.S. politicians should be more likely deterred from such behavior in the first place.

It is much easier to register and recall episodes such as those just introduced for the U.S. than China, reflecting two basic asymmetries between these countries. The U.S. has been an active global power with a much more extensive array of foreign involvements than China whose international profile has been heretofore largely characterized by a regional focus on Asia and whose activities have been limited in the first quarter century of the People's Republic's existence as a result of its self-imposed isolation as well as U.S.-led international boycott. As a consequence, there are simply many more instances from which one can draw some inference about U.S. trustworthiness than about Chinese trustworthiness. The available data base is much larger for the former than for the latter. Moreover and as a consequence of Washington's multiple interests and roles in many external relationships, it is much more challenging for it to finesse its foreign policies without appearing to be inconsistent or even contradictory. Thus, for instance, it is difficult for it to honor its pledge to support Taipei without at the same time appearing to have reneged on its recognition of Beijing as the sole legal government of China and its public acknowledgment that Taiwan is part of China.

In addition to such understandable attempts to have "one's cake and eat it too," the U.S. provides an information-rich environment. For reasons already mentioned, there is an information asymmetry that affects attempts to compare it to China. As a democracy and given its active media and vigorous political opposition, criticisms and exposés that reflect poorly on an administration's credibility are much more available for the U.S. than China. When, for example, Syria's Bashar al-Assad attacked his opponents with chlorine gas and thus crossed the "red line" laid down by President Barack Obama, the U.S. press and Republican critics can be counted on to call attention to Washington's inaction. In contrast, the absence of an independent and free press makes such critical voices much less likely to be heard in China. As an authoritarian government, Beijing has a much greater degree of control over the dissemination of information. Democratic transparency can be a double-edged sword. It can communicate resolve when politicians of different stripes unite behind a common policy (an advantage in communicating resolve to foreign audiences that an authoritarian government lacks as it does not have a credible opposition). But when there is discord, it can also convey political vacillation and a policy's fragility. Moreover, democratic transparency can show when a country is trustworthy *and* when it is untrustworthy. Beijing's policy processes are much less accessible to foreign China-watchers and domestic critics alike.

Finally and ironically, to the extent that public opinion in a democracy is pacific or favors isolationism, its leaders may feel a greater need to engage in threat inflation in order to mobilize support for military action abroad. John Mearsheimer's study on lying in international politics concludes that whereas leaders lie to their foreign counterparts much less than commonly assumed, democratic leaders are more likely to lie to their own citizens.[58] Franklin D. Roosevelt's disingenuous allegation of an unprovoked attack on U.S. destroyer *USS Greer* by a German submarine in 1941 in the run-up to the U.S. entry to World War II and Lyndon B. Johnson's similar allegation of U.S. destroyer *USS Maddox* being attacked by North Vietnamese torpedo boats in 1964 as a justification for the passage of the Gulf of Tonkin Resolution to escalate the Vietnam War come to mind as instances of "fearmongering."[59] John F. Kennedy's propagation of a "missile gap" in his 1958 Senate reelection campaign suggests another example. The public justifications given by George W. Bush and his senior advisors for invading Iraq—about Saddam Hussein's weapons of mass destruction and his connections with Al Qaeda—provide still another more recent example. This tendency for threat inflation in order to overcome a skeptical and reluctant public's reservations about foreign military involvement or to attack political opponents for being "soft" or negligent in dealing with foreign adversaries interacts with the overwhelming power of the U.S. and the global reach of its self-perceived interests, leading Mearsheimer to conclude,

> ... because the United States is so powerful and so heavily engaged around the globe, its leaders often confront situations where there are strong incentives to lie either to other states or to the American people. This is a matter of serious concern, since international lying can have serious negative consequences, especially for democracies like the United States.[60]

CONCLUDING REMARKS

This discussion suggests that Sino-American distrust does not necessarily reflect misunderstanding and that both countries have a reasonable basis for not trusting the other. It is of course possible that mutual distrust may be perpetuated by entrenched bureaucratic interests, partisan politics, mental habits, and/or ideological rigidity. But as indicated earlier, one would expect people to learn from their experiences and distrust should be dispelled if those views based on it prove themselves to be consistently wrong. That is, one would expect people's opinions to eventually converge on reality rather than to continue to reflect their imagination. As interactions between Chinese and U.S. officials, scholars, and ordinary people increase over time and their knowledge about and understanding of each other improve, misperceptions are more likely to be challenged and misunderstanding corrected. That a trust deficit has persisted in Sino-American relations suggests at least the possibility that these countries' mutual suspicions are not entirely groundless or unreasonable.

Given a long history replete with instances that arouse reciprocal suspicions, building mutual trust will involve a long and arduous process.

Moreover, given most officials' socialization experience that inculcates in them a Hobbesian worldview, they are naturally inclined to question their counterparts' motivations and intentions. Given this inclination, it will only take a relatively small amount of evidence to confirm their belief that another state is not trustworthy whereas massive amounts of data will be required to cause them to change their predisposition and to conclude that another state can be trusted.

As I will discuss in more detail later, the more pervasive and entrenched is the extent of mutual suspicions, the more significant will reassurance gestures have to be in order to establish trust. Rationalist theorists, such as James Fearon,[61] have argued that in order to be credible, reassurance signals will have to entail heavy self-imposed costs so that the state undertaking such gestures will suffer a serious penalty should it turn out to be unreliable or insincere. In this way, this state attempting reassurance will be able to distinguish or "separate" itself from others that are untrustworthy. Knowing that they are untrustworthy, the latter type of states will be unwilling to impose on themselves similar costly consequences for acting opportunistically. Only those states that are inclined to eschew opportunism will knowingly accept such costs. As a corollary of this proposition, reassurance gestures without heavy self-imposed costs will be dismissed by the other side as "empty talk."

It is perhaps human nature that makes it much easier for us to recall instances when a person or state has acted in an untrustworthy manner. We do not typically remember instances when a state professes that it has no intention of doing something, and point to its subsequent inaction as a confirmation of its trustworthiness. Historians and political scientists do not usually emphasize enough the importance of such nonoccurrence. As a consequence, we are likely to overlook, for instance, the fact that Washington has refrained from trying to overthrow the government in Havana since the end of the Cuban Missile Crisis. The U.S. was rumored to have made a pledge to this effect in 1962 as part of the bargain to dismantle the Soviet missiles on that island. In addition to the aforementioned cognitive tendency, analysts and officials alike are more inclined to credit their own country's policies when trying to explain why certain possible adverse events did not occur. When explaining such nonoccurrence (e.g., when an adversary did not commit military aggression), people tend to attribute it to the other side's circumstances (e.g., crediting this nonoccurrence to one's own deterrence policy) rather than to the other side's natural (peaceful) disposition.[62] An obvious example would be the nonoccurrence of a Chinese invasion of Taiwan. This phenomenon is more likely to be attributed to China's lack of the necessary capabilities or the effects of U.S. military deterrence rather than Beijing's disposition to refrain from using military force except as a last resort.

As just mentioned, when judging another country's trustworthiness, it is much easier to recall those occasions when it has failed to honor its promises or when it has been exposed to have tried bluffing or deception unsuccessfully. One tends to remember when officials have clearly, publicly, and repeatedly staked out their own personal reputation and also their country's reputation to do something and then to have failed to follow through on their announced intention. Washington's abandonment of South Vietnam comes to mind. Saying so does not impugn the wisdom of its eventual decision to extricate itself from the Vietnam War. One may, however, question the wisdom of Washington making its commitment to Saigon in the first place. It is also reasonable to ask about the ramifications of such betrayal of trust in the eyes of third parties, whether friends, foes or neutrals. Moreover, it is pertinent to call attention to the error of circular reasoning such as when one publicizes a particular contest as a test of one's resolve and thus willfully commits his/her country's reputation to its outcome. Having done so, one turns around and justifies persisting in a policy course—even when it has been proven to be wanting—in the name of defending this reputation. In this formulation, a country's commitment to an ally becomes a national interest in itself—rather than the converse of deciding this commitment on the basis of national interest.[63]

Naturally, when a country declares a particular issue to be a matter of national priority or a "core national interest" and says so publicly and repeatedly, it becomes more difficult for it to deescalate a crisis or extricate itself if and when there is a confrontation. Indeed, with each round of confrontation its reputational stake escalates. For Beijing, domestic audience costs has risen over time with increased elite competition and public opinion playing a greater role in the conduct of China's foreign relations. The perceived political cost of having to back down (or to be perceived as having done so) in a situation involving Taiwan, for example, can thus make a dispute highly combustible. Beijing has staked its domestic and international reputation to the cause of national reunification with this island. It has undertaken several much-publicized campaigns involving mass mobilizations and military displays to demonstrate its commitment to this cause. It has pulled back in each prior encounter in order to avert a military showdown with the U.S. Having thus suffered successive reputational setback in these prior encounters, one may infer that it will be more reluctant to repeat this experience again. But should it initiate another confrontation, one would surmise that it must have in the intervening period become more optimistic about how this next confrontation will turn out and/or more resolved or committed to its announced policy course.[64]

When all the parties in a conflict believe that their reputation for trustworthiness is engaged and that they will suffer grievously if they were to be seen abandoning their commitments to their respective allies (or their pledges to their respective domestic constituents), we have some of the main ingredients leading to the tragic collision producing World War I.[65] France felt that if it should fail to support Russia, it would lose that country as an ally. Russia in turn felt that it could not afford to abandon its junior partner, Serbia.[66] For its part Germany was beholden to Austria-Hungary, and was resolved to support it to the point of issuing the infamous "blank check" to Vienna. The collective efforts by these countries to shore up their alliance commitments elevated tension and accelerated the momentum toward war. This observation in turn indicates that a rigid, even blind, attempt to demonstrate one's steadfastness, or trustworthiness, as an ally can be a recipe for disaster.

Trust in interstate relations involves multiple parties. A's efforts to enhance its trustworthiness in B's eyes may very well exacerbate its conflict with C. Thus returning to a point made in Chapter 1, building and keeping trust is not the only thing in the interest of promoting interstate peace and stability. The examples introduced earlier also remind us of Thomas Schelling's insight that all countries in a dispute are likely to feel that they have their prestige and reputation for firmness and trustworthiness at stake. If peace and stability are to be kept, a country must help its counterparts to decouple *their* prestige and reputation from a dispute, and hope that "if we cannot afford to back down [out of a concern for our reputational costs] we must hope that [they] can, and if necessary, help [them to do so]."[67]

NOTES

1. Sartori, *Deterrence by Diplomacy*.
2. Kuan-yuan Wang, "Taiwan Public Opinion on Cross-Strait Security Issues: Implications for US Foreign Policy," *Strategic Studies Quarterly* 7, no. 2 (2013): 93–113.
3. For exceptions, see Robert Jervis, "Unipolarity: A Structural Perspective," *World Politics* 61, no. 1 (2009): 188–213; and Alastair I. Johnston, "Is China a Status Quo Power?" *International Security* 7, no. 4 (2003): 5–56.
4. Timothy W. Crawford, *Pivotal Deterrence: Third-Party Statecraft and the Pursuit of Peace* (Ithaca, NY: Cornell University Press, 2003).
5. Steve Chan, "The Power-Transition Discourse and China's Rise," in *Encyclopedia of Empirical International Relations Theory*, ed. William R. Thompson (New York: Oxford University Press, forthcoming).
6. Peter H. Gries, *China's New Nationalism: Pride, Politics and Diplomacy* (Berkeley: University of California Press, 2004); and Zheng Wang, *Never Forget National Humiliation: Historical Memory in Chinese Politics and Foreign Relations* (New York: Columbia University Press, 2012).
7. Ken Booth and Nicholas J. Wheeler, *The Security Dilemma: Fear, Cooperation and Trust in World Politics* (Houndmills: Palgrave Macmillan, 2008); Naomi Head, "Transforming Conflict: Trust, Empathy, and Dialogue," *International Journal of Peace Studies* 17, no. 2 (2013): 33–56; and Nicholas J. Wheeler, "Investigating Diplomatic Transformations," *International Affairs* 89, no. 2 (2013): 477–496.
8. John Rawls, *A Theory of Justice* (Cambridge, MA: Harvard University Press, 1971).
9. Benjamin Schwarz, "Comment: Managing China's Rise," *The Atlantic Monthly* (June 2015), accessed June 2, 2017, http://www.theatlantic.com/magazine/archive/2005/06/managing-chinas-rise/303972/, 27.
10. Samantha Power, *"A Problem from Hell:" America and the Age of Genocide* (New York: Basic Books, 2013).
11. Lieberthal and Wang, *Addressing U.S.-China Strategic Distrust*.
12. Oren, *Our Enemies & US*.
13. William Burr and Jeffrey Richelson, "Whether to 'Strangle the Baby in the Cradle:' The United States and the Chinese Nuclear Program, 1960–64," *International Security* 25, no. 3 (2000/2001): 54–99.

14. Ibid.; Richard N. Lebow, "Windows of Opportunity: Do States Jump Through Them?" *International Security* 9, no. 1 (1984): 147–186; Karl P. Mueller, Jason J. Castillo, Forrest E. Morgan, Negeen Pegahi, and Brian Rosen, *Striking First: Preemptive and Preventive Attack in U.S. National Security Policy* (Santa Monica, CA: Rand, 2006); and Scott A. Silverstone, *Preventive War and American Democracy* (London: Routledge, 2007).

15. Jack S. Levy, "Preventive War and Democratic Politics," *International Studies Quarterly* 52, no. 1 (2008): 1–24; and Marc Trachtenberg, "Preventive War and U.S. Foreign Policy," *Security Studies* 16, no. 1 (2007): 1–31.

16. Johnston, *Social States*, 135.

17. Jonathan Kirshner, *American Power after the Financial Crisis* (Ithaca, NY: Cornell University Press, 2014).

18. Carla Norrlof and Simon Reich, "American and Chinese Leadership during the Global Financial Crisis: Testing Kindleberger's Stabilization Functions," *International Area Studies Review* (March 2015): 1–24.

19. Susan Strange, "The Persistent Myth of Lost Hegemony," *International Organization* 41, no. 4 (1987): 568–569.

20. Allen S. Whiting, *China Crosses the Yalu: The Decision to Enter the Korean War* (New York: Macmillan, 1960).

21. "Gulf War," accessed June 2, 2017, https://en.wikipedia.org/wiki/Gulf_War.

22. Robert S. Ross, *The Indochina Triangle: China's Vietnam Policy 1975–1979* (New York: Columbia University Press, 1988); and Allen S. Whiting, *The Chinese Calculus of Deterrence: India and Indo-China* (Ann Arbor: University of Michigan Press, 1975).

23. Bob Woodward, *The Commanders* (New York: Simon & Schuster, 1991).

24. Chaim Kaufman, "Threat Inflation and the Failure of the Marketplace of Ideas: The Selling of the Iraq War," *International Security* 29, no. 1 (2004): 5–48, and "Selling the Market Short: The Marketplace of Ideas and the Iraq War," *International Security* 29, no. 4 (2005): 196–207; and John J. Mearsheimer and Stephen M. Walt, "An Unnecessary War," *Foreign Policy* (January–February 2003): 50–59.

25. Kydd, *Trust and Mistrust.*

26. William C. Wohlforth, ed., *Cold War Endgame: Oral History, Analysis, Debates* (University Park: Pennsylvania State University Press, 2013).

27. Amitai Etzioni, "Spheres of Influence: A Reconceptualization," *Fletcher Forum of International Affairs* 29, no. 2 (2015): 117–132; John L. Gaddis, "History, Grand Strategy and NATO Enlargement," *Survival* 40, no. 1 (1998): 145–151; Mark Kramer, "The Myth of a No–NATO-Enlarge-

ment Pledge to Russia," *The Washington Quarterly* 32, no. 2 (2009): 39–61; and Mary E. Sarotte, "A Broken Promise? What the West Really Told Moscow about NATO Expansion," *Foreign Affairs* 93, no. 5 (2014): 90–98.

28. Suzanne Massie, "Opinion: US Intervention in Ukraine Arrogant, Heavy-Handed," Sputnik International (May 5, 2014), accessed June 2, 2017, http://sputniknews.com/world/20140516/189865599.html; Michael McFaul, Stephen Sestanovich, and John J. Mearsheimer, "Faulty Powers: Who Started the Ukraine Crisis?" *Foreign Affairs* 93, no. 6 (2014): 167–178; and John J. Mearsheimer, "Why the Ukraine Crisis Is the West's Fault," *Foreign Affairs* 93, no. 5 (2014): 77–89.

29. Evan Resnick, "The Perils of Containing China," (2013) RSIS Commentary 069/2013 distributed electronically by getresponse@getresponse.com on behalf of RSIS Publications [rsispublication@ntu.edu.sg], Nanyang Technological University, Singapore.

30. Etzioni, "Spheres of Influence;" and Charles W. Kegley, Jr. and Gregory Raymond, *A Multipolar Peace? Great-Power Politics in the Twenty-first Century* (New York: St. Martin's, 1994).

31. International Institute for Strategic Studies, *The Military Balance, 2015* (London: Routledge, 2015).

32. Sam Perlo-Freeman, Aude Fleurant, Pieter D. Wezeman, and Siemon T. Wezeman, "Trends in World Military Expenditure, 2014 (Table 1: The 15 Countries with the Highest Military Expenditure in 2014)," Stockholm International Peace Research Institute (April 2015), accessed June 2, 2017, http://books.sipri.org/product_info?c_product_id=496. Somewhat different figures from these sources are cited in "List of Countries by Military Expenditures," accessed June 2, 2017, https://en.wikipedia.org/wiki/List_of_countries_by_military_expenditures. These discrepancies, however, should not alter the basic argument being made here.

33. "Military Expenditure (% of GDP), 1988-2015," World Bank, accessed June 2, 2017, http://data.worldbank.org/indicator/MS.MIL.XPND.GD.ZS.

34. Barry R. Posen, "Command of the Commons: The Military Foundation of U.S. Hegemony," *International Security* 28, no. 1 (2003): 5–46.

35. Charles P. Kindleberger, *The World in Depression, 1929–1939* (Berkeley: University of California Press, 1986); and A.F.K. Organski and Jacek Kugler, *The War Ledger* (Chicago: University of Chicago Press, 1980).

36. Kenneth N. Waltz, *Theory of International Politics* (Reading, MA: Addison-Wesley, 1979).

37. John A. Vasquez, *The War Puzzle* (New York: Cambridge University Press, 1993), and *The War Puzzle Revisited* (New York: Cambridge University Press, 2009).

38. Dinah Walker, "Trends in U.S. Military Spending," Council on Foreign Relations (July 15, 2014), accessed June 2, 2017, www.cfr.org/defense-budget/trends-us-miitary-spending/p28855; and "Largest Military Expenditures, 2006," Infoplease (2007), accessed June 2, 2017, www.infoplease.com/ipa/A0904504.html.

39. Keir A. Lieber and Daryl G. Press, "The End of MAD: The Nuclear Dimension of U.S. Primacy," *International Security* 30, no. 4 (2006): 7–44.

40. Charles L. Glaser, "Realists as Optimists: Cooperation as Self-Help," *International Security* 19, no. 3 (1994/95): 50–90.

41. Paul Schroeder, "Alliances, 1815–1945: Weapons of Power and Tools of Management," in *Historical Dimensions of National Security Problems*, ed. Klaus Knorr (Lawrence: University Press of Kansas, 1976), 227–262.

42. Charles Maier, "Thucydides, Alliance Politics, and Great Power Conflict," in *The Next Great War? The Roots of World War I and the Risk of U.S.-China Conflict*, eds. Richard N. Rosecrance and Steven E. Miller (Cambridge, MA: The MIT Press, 2015), 98.

43. John J. Mearsheimer, "China's Unpeaceful Rise," *Current History* 105, no. 690 (2006): 160–162.

44. Zev Maoz and Bruce Russett, "Normative and Structural Causes of Democratic Peace, 1946–1986," *American Political Science Review* 87, no. 3 (1993): 624–638.

45. Taylor M. Fravel, *Strong Border, Secure Nation: Cooperation and Order in China's Territorial Disputes* (Princeton, NJ: Princeton University Press, 2008).

46. For related discussion, see Scott L. Kastner and Chad Rector, "National Unification and Mistrust: Bargaining Power and the Prospects for a PRC/Taiwan Agreement," *Security Study* 17, no. 1 (2008): 39–71; and Nien-Chung Chang Liao, "Comparing Inter-Korean and Cross-Taiwan Strait Trust-Building: The Limits of Reassurance," *Asian Survey* 54, no. 6 (2014): 1037–1058, and "Building Trust across the Taiwan Strait: A Strategy of Reassurance," *Issues & Studies* 48, no. 3 (2012): 105–145.

47. John W. Garver, *Face Off: China, the United States and Taiwan's Democratization* (Seattle: University of Washington Press, 1997); and Andrew J. Nathan and Andrew Scobell, *China's Search for Security* (New York: Columbia University Press, 2012), 107–108.

48. Robert S. Ross, "The 1995–96 Taiwan Strait Confrontation: Coercion, Credibility and the Use of Force," *International Security* 25, no. 2 (2000): 87–123.

49. See, for example, "US Media Overlook Expose on Chinese Embassy Bombing," Fairness and Accuracy in Reporting (October 22, 1999), accessed June 2, 2017, http://fair.org/take-action/action-alerts/u-s-media-overlook-expose-on-chinese-embassy-bombing/; and John Sweeney, Jens Holsoe, and Ed Vulliamy, "NATO Bombed Chinese Deliberately," *The Guardian* (October 16, 1999), accessed June 2, 2017, http://www.theguardian.com/world/1999/oct/17/balkans.

50. Kai He, *China's Crisis Behavior: Political Survival and Foreign Policy after the Cold War* (Cambridge: Cambridge University Press, 2016).

51. Rose McDermott, "The U–2 Crisis," in *Risk-Taking in International Politics: Prospect Theory in American Foreign Policy*, ed. Rose McDermott (Ann Arbor: University of Michigan Press, 1988), 107–134; and David Wise and Thomas B. Roe, *The U–2 Affair* (New York: Random House, 1962).

52. Peter Wyden, *Bay of Pigs: The Untold Story* (New York: Simon & Schuster, 1979).

53. Daniel C. Hallin, *The "Uncensored" War* (Oxford: Oxford University Press, 1986); Edwin E. Moise, *Tonkin Gulf and the Escalation of the Vietnam War* (Chapel Hill: University of North Carolina Press, 1996); and Tom Wells, *The War Within: America's Battle over Vietnam* (Berkeley: University of California Press, 1994).

54. Carl Bernstein and Bob Woodward, *All the President's Men* (New York: Simon & Schuster, 1974); and Bob Woodward and Carl Bernstein, *The Final Days* (New York: Simon & Schuster, 1976).

55. Steve Smith, "The Hostage Rescue Mission," in *Foreign Policy Implementation*, eds. Steve Smith and Michael Clark (London: Unwin Hyman, 1985), 16–17.

56. Malcolm Byrne, *Iran-Contra: Reagan's Scandal and the Unchecked Abuse of Presidential Power* (Lawrence: University Press of Kansas, 2014).

57. Bob Woodward, *Plan of Attack* (New York: Simon & Schuster, 2004).

58. Mearsheimer, *Why Leaders Lie.*

59. Ibid., 46–49.

60. Ibid., 13.

61. Fearon, "Rationalist Explanations," and "Signaling Foreign Policy Interests: Tying Hands versus Sinking Costs," *Journal of Conflict Resolution* 41, no. 1 (1997): 68–90.

62. Mercer, *Reputation and International Politics.*

63. William Kaufman, "The Requirements of Deterrence," in *Military Policy and National Security,* ed. William Kaufman (Princeton, NJ: Princeton University Press, 1956), 12–38.

64. Steve Chan, *China's Troubled Waters: Maritime Disputes in Theoretical Perspective* (Cambridge: Cambridge University Press, 2016).

65. Rosecrance and Miller, *The Next Great War.*

66. Jack S. Levy and William Mulligan, "Shifting Power, Preventive Logic, and the Response of the Target: Germany, Russia, and the First World War," *Journal of Strategic Studies* (forthcoming) doi:10.1080/01402390.2016.1242421.

67. Thomas C. Schelling, *Arms and Influence* (New Haven, CT: Yale University Press, 1966), 125.

Chapter 3

A Weak Form of Trust Reflecting External Compulsion

In this chapter, I discuss the weak form of trust. In this form, one believes that another state will refrain from unfriendly acts because it is compelled by its circumstances. This may be due, for example, to a state's inferior capabilities in interstate relations or to its divisive domestic politics. A state's restraint stemming from such constraints reflects a lack of ability rather than necessarily a lack of motivation. Thus, a state may be expected to accept its subordinate position and to adopt an accommodating posture so long as it is relatively weak. But should it gain in strength, it may switch to a more assertive and even aggressive stance which is more compatible with its natural inclination. Similarly, domestic discord and turmoil may sap a state's energy and focus its attention on internal matters, even while its leadership espouses a revolutionary ideology in its external relations. Domestic disarray can thus cause its temporary incapacity but does not alter its fundamental character or basic motivation. When such a state is able to reestablish its domestic order and authority, it may be able to actually implement its avowed foreign policy agenda. Trust in the weak form thus rests on a flimsy foundation and is subject to being revised when circumstances change. One is counting on circumstances to restrain the other party from acting in hostile ways, and trust is operating only in the limited and hence weak sense that one is expecting it to behave "rationally" given its circumstances.

Benjamin Most and Harvey Starr's concepts of "willingness" and "opportunity" help to illuminate this discussion.[1] Foreign policy action requires both conditions. Another state may have an unfriendly disposition ("willingness"), but it will not be able act on this disposition because of its current circumstances (its lack of "opportunity"). Thus it does not pose a present danger. But if circumstances change (i.e., when "opportunity" presents itself), it may be able to act on this disposition—and indeed, its intentions may very well change with its changing circumstances. One thus needs to adjust one's assessment of how much it can be trusted when circumstances change.

Shifts in states' relative capabilities present an obvious and important source of change that can arouse suspicions about the trustworthiness of those gaining power. As an example, Washington may be confident that Beijing is unlikely to use force against Taiwan today. The threat of U.S. military intervention may deter China from attacking Taiwan now. But will Beijing change its policy calculation and disposition in the future as it continues to improve its military capabilities relative to both the U.S. and Taiwan? To introduce another example posing a counterfactual question from Beijing's perspective, would the U.S. have invaded Iraq and Afghanistan and attacked Serbia had the USSR not collapsed? Did the elevation of the U.S. to a position of overwhelming global preponderance incline Washington to behave with more unilateral assertiveness and to adopt more "muscular" policies? More generally, how are power shifts among countries supposed to affect their willingness to trust others?

In addition to power shifts, I will take up in this chapter the question of how interstate trust can be affected by a country's domestic distribution of influence and interests. Does a state's chief executive enjoy great autonomy and discretion in foreign policy, or does this individual have to face powerful veto groups? How influential are those groups that have a stake in maintaining international peace and economic openness, and conversely, how influential are their domestic opponents (such as large state enterprises and the military-industrial complex) that stand to benefit from international tension and economic closure? How are an authoritarian state's officials likely to be affected when public opinion and elite competition begin to play a larger role in the formulation and conduct of their foreign policy? In short, how would/should outsiders adjust their assessments of a state's trustworthiness according to these domestic conditions and their change over time?

POWER SHIFTS AND INTERSTATE TRUST

Although there is by now a large literature on China's rise and also one on other states that have preceded it as earlier rising powers (e.g., Germany, the U.S., Britain, and even Athens at different times in history), there has been surprisingly little attention to the question of how Beijing will intend to use its newly gained power. Most existing studies make the facile assumption that with its power gains, Beijing will become more assertive and insistent in its demands. Its demands can even involve revising the basic rules of the international order that has supposedly been fostered and sustained mainly by Washington. Relatively few scholars argue that despite its recent power gains, "China is too bogged down in the security challenge within and around its borders to threaten the West unless the West weakens itself to the point of creating a power vacuum," and that "vulnerability remains the key driver of China's foreign policy."[2] Similarly, the proposition that as China grows stronger, Beijing will gain a greater stake in the existing order—the one that has enabled its rapid rise—continues to be a minority view. This latter proposition suggests that China's rise necessarily gives Beijing a greater stake in the stability of the existing international system. Parenthetically, Nathan and Scobell's aforementioned remark about the West weakening itself seems prescient in view of President Donald Trump's recent statements on trade, climate change, and the NATO alliance, statements that communicate changing U.S. policies that are likely to divide the West and cause Europe and China to draw closer.

Should others trust China more because it now has a greater stake in the existing order, or should they trust it less because it now has more power to alter it? Conversely, one may also ask whether China's recent ascent means by definition that the U.S. now has a diminished stake in defending the existing international order and hence an increased incentive to seek its revision in order to arrest or reverse its relative decline (such as suggested by some of President Donald Trump's pronouncements). This latter question, however, is rarely asked by scholars who tend to resort to different logic in analyzing China and the U.S. (focusing on China's power gains but not the still overwhelming U.S. preponderance as a possible destabilizing source for international order, while pointing to the large existing U.S. stake in this system but not China's increased stake in it as a stabilizing force).

Most international relations scholars in the West take for granted that the U.S. is a status-quo power because it has to a large measure created and supported the current international order. Some go even so far as to assert that a global hegemon is *by definition* a status-quo power because it has the largest vested interest in the maintenance of this order.[3] This same logic would argue that China's rise should also give Beijing a greater interest in maintaining the same order.

Western analysts do not typically consider the possibility that a hegemon, especially as it gains even more preponderant power (such as for the U.S. in the wake of the USSR's collapse), will be inclined to revise the existing rules and norms of international order to favor its interests even more (or to exempt itself from these rules and norms such as when the U.S. attacked Iraq and Serbia without United Nations authorization). Significantly, whether a state should emphasize containment of another rising power (and thus to focus on opposing the latter's increased capabilities) or whether it should emphasize engagement with this rising power (and thus to shape its interests and enhance its stake in maintaining the current order) has been very much at the core of the U.S. policy debate on how to manage Sino-American relations.

China is typically cast by most international relations scholars in the West as a revisionist power because as an upstart, it is assumed to be dissatisfied with the current international order that it has not had a role in shaping. This order is also assumed to work against an emergent power because its rules and norms are supposed to be rigged against this latecomer. This assumption is made even when a latecomer is seen to have made rapid and great strides in improving its international status— a development that in turn raises the question why should this latecomer not become more satisfied given the tremendous progress that it has made. Contrary to the typical attribution of an incumbent hegemon's motivation which focuses on its *stake* in the existing international order and not its *ability* to alter it, the reasoning applied to a rising latecomer is reversed so that its motivation is seen to be driven by its increasing ability to challenge the existing international order and not by its increasing stake in preserving the order that has enabled its ascent thus far.

Besides this discrepancy, why would a rising latecomer want to cause international instability when the ongoing trends seem to augur the continuation of its ascendance? Why would Germany want to wage a war against Britain when it had already overtaken this rival, and when waiting could enable it to achieve mastery of Europe in due course? Despite its popularity, the power-transition theory does not take up these questions.[4] Instead of seeking to displace a declining Britain, Wilhelmine Germany was more concerned about preventing an emergent threat coming from a rising Russia.[5] I will return to this theme later.

Should a country's trustworthiness be made to depend largely on its stake in an existing order, or on its ability to change this order? It seems that both factors play a role and in an interactive fashion as suggested by Most and Starr's (1989) discussion on "willingness" and "opportunity." For instance, a powerful state suffering relative decline would presumably have a smaller stake in the existing international order and thus feel less committed to defend it, as Donald Trump's recent pronouncements appear to suggest. For states like imperial Germany, their officials may even decide to start a preventive war if they sense an inevitable decline and implacable hostility from a rising challenger. It is an empirical question whether a larger (or large) vested stake in the current international order will necessarily mean a greater commitment to maintain it. It is also an empirical question whether a stronger ability to alter the international order will necessarily mean a greater incentive to do so—or not to do so. Since officials are forward-looking, the evaluation of another state's trustworthiness will reflect their expectations of its prospective stake and ability in addition to its current stake and ability.

Prospect theory presents one basis for such forecasting.[6] States that have made recent gains and that expect to continue these gains should be more risk averse. As states acquire a larger stake in the international order, they should be less inclined to initiate policies that seek to upend or destabilize it. Increasing stake and additional gains to be expected in the future will according to this logic make rising states more committed to the status quo. Conversely, states that find themselves in a domain of loss are more likely to be risk acceptant. Suffering a relative or absolute loss of their power and prestige, they can be expected to undertake more audacious policies in an attempt to reverse their setback. Prospect theory thus predicts that rising powers should be conservative powers that are more interested in keeping what they have acquired than taking risks to make further expansion. In contrast, declining powers are more likely to be motivated to "gamble for recovery." It makes this prediction based on the gains and losses that a state has experienced and is expecting to experience if current trends continue. Experimental research based on people's decision-making has produced voluminous evidence supporting prospect theory's propositions.

In light of this prognosis based on prospect theory, a rising state's professed interest in keeping peace and maintaining stability gains more credibility. Rationalist theory tends to converge with this expectation. It suggests that if a rising state expects to make further gains in the future, it is likely to moderate its demands to be compensated for its improved status. That is, its demands to be accommodated, such as to bring its international status in line with its increased capabilities, are likely to be modest and incremental.[7] But if its growth stalls or becomes even reversed (thus when it finds itself in the domain of actual or prospective loss), it will no longer be willing to accept delayed gratification and will instead insist on full and immediate accommodation of its interests commensurate with its recently gained capabilities. Thus according to this claim, a (formerly) rising state that has stopped growing or one for which the growth momentum has slowed is a more dangerous state. Such inflection points are likely occasions for clashes among the great powers to occur. These are especially dangerous times when multiple states are experiencing these turning points concurrently—and when those whose future augurs a precipitous decline encounter others whose growth is beginning a sharply upward trajectory.[8]

How do states' relative capability and power shifts among them affect trust? A strong state, especially a unipolar power such as the U.S., is more able to reduce uncertainties that other weaker states will necessarily have to tolerate. A really powerful state simply does not have to put up with the many risks that the weaker ones will have to accept—simply because it has the wherewithal to take matters into its own hands rather than relying on others' words. Accordingly, "greater power and lower costs for fighting raise the minimum trust threshold [the threshold that another state must meet in order to convince a powerful counterpart that it can be trusted], so that even small doubts that another country is untrustworthy may be enough to tip the United States over the edge into a conflict."[9] Thus, for example, in matters of strategic defense and nuclear proliferation Paris and Berlin are more likely to accept international agreements fraught with risks than Washington. Rather than relying on international inspection, the U.S. has the ability to invade Iraq to remove whatever doubt that it has about Saddam Hussein acquiring weapons of mass destruction. During the Clinton administration, it also came very close to initiating an attack on North Korea's nuclear facilities. It has thus far refused to rule out this option in seeking to deter Iran from acquiring nuclear weapons. Ceteris paribus, really powerful states rely less on trust in the conduct of their foreign policy.

As another illustration, the George W. Bush administration not only refused to join the International Criminal Court (ICC) but also actively lobbied all countries to sign a bilateral agreement with the U.S. (the so-called nonsurrender agreement), seeking their promise to exempt any U.S. personnel accused of committing war crimes from this court's jurisdiction. Washington put heavy pressure on other states to sign these bilateral agreements even though the ICC treaty provides important provisions that should allay Washington's concerns about politically motivated prosecution of its citizens for alleged war crimes and even though there is only a small chance that the contingency these agreements are intended to prevent will ever come to pass. This discussion leads to the hypothesis that a strong country is likely to be less trusting than a weaker one. An overwhelmingly powerful country has the option of undertaking unilateral action whereas its weaker counterparts do not. It does not have to take other states' promises or their professed good intentions at face value whereas those that are truly weak have no alternative but to do so—and might as well make a virtue out of necessity.

A corollary of this proposition comes easily to mind. The stronger a country becomes, the less it will be inclined to trust others. The logic introduced earlier suggests that given its greater power, a rising state will not have to put up with some of the uncertainties that it has tolerated previously even if only reluctantly. It is now in a better position to demand more tangible evidence of another state's trustworthiness. This phenomenon reflects the Italian adage: *fidarsi è bene, non fidarsi è meglio* (to trust is good, not to trust is better). The proposition that a country becoming stronger is less disposed to trust others and the one presented in the previous paragraph suggesting that powerful countries are generally less trusting introduce a paradox in the following sense.

A truly powerful country or one that is getting to be very strong is in a better position to recover from a mistake should it misplace its confidence in a counterpart that turns out to be actually untrustworthy. If the U.S. were to make a mistake in trusting Iranian leaders' promise to discontinue Tehran's nuclear program, the negative consequences should be much less severe for it than for Iran's immediate neighbors. Thus, misplaced trust is much more costly for weak countries than strong ones. The high costs of misplaced trust should incline a weaker country to be more distrustful. For example, it might have made sense for China to be highly distrustful of Taiwan's intentions when this island had a formal defense pact with the U.S. and when China was much weaker than it is now. Now that the U.S. has terminated this defense pact with Taiwan and that China has become much stronger, Beijing should feel more confident about Taipei's intentions (such as it will not use military force to retake the mainland with U.S. support and it will not seek formal independence). Yet according to the proposition introduced earlier, a major gain in relative capability will actually make Beijing less trusting because it can now more afford to take matters into its own hands. Thus, to repeat, even though a more powerful country can more afford to be optimistic about others' intentions, it is likely to become in fact less trusting (by raising the bar that another state must meet in order for it to be trusted).

Significantly, the closer two countries approach power parity, the more important will be their mutual trust in stabilizing their relationship. When their capabilities become approximately equal, this balance is more precarious and mutual trust is more important in preventing minor incidents from setting off a larger conflagration. Moreover, the more equalized the bilateral power balance, the more assurances each side will need in order to alleviate its concern that its counterpart will defect by seeking a quick "break out" to establish its superiority. Both sides are likely to insist on more stringent verification of any security arrangement. When the relationship between two states is characterized by a great power asymmetry (as in, say, U.S.-Haitian relations), the strong does not need to trust the weak and whether the weak trusts the strong does not matter so far as systemic peace is concerned. But when the relationship pertains to great powers, especially when power shifts are occurring rapidly to close their capability gap (such as in Sino-American relations), mutual trust becomes more critical for systemic peace. The dynamics of large and rapid power shifts among major states can engender a variety of psychological pathologies such as fear, anxiety, arrogance, and over-confidence, conditions that are likely to in turn abet the danger of war as highlighted by the power-cycle theory and the literature on preventive war.[10]

The discussion thus far introduces additional theoretical and policy questions. From the perspective of a rising power like China, how can it communicate convincingly to other states—its weaker neighbors, its potential regional rivals, and the established hegemon—that it will continue to have benign intentions toward them even when it becomes more powerful than now? How can it reassure other states that it will not use its prospective power recklessly and wantonly, and that it does not have unlimited ambitions but would instead act with moderation and due regard for the interests, rights, and even privileges of those that have come before it and that have a vested stake in the current international order, especially those pertaining to the incumbent hegemon? Naturally, a rising state is aware that if the other states are deeply suspiciously about how it will use its increased power in the future, these counterparts will not wait for that development to occur—they will take action now to prevent it from happening such as by adopting collective containment and even choosing a preventive war.

These are not idle questions because the most dangerous time for a rapidly rising state like China is when it is still much weaker than the incumbent hegemon even though it is closing the capability gap separating them. This is the time when the preventive motivation may apply to the stronger but declining power such as when Wilhelmine Germany confronted the prospect of an emergent Russian colossus in 1914. If this state believes that the unfavorable trends altering relative national power will continue and that its counterpart cannot be appeased, then waging a preventive war becomes a feasible and even attractive option. It can initiate this conflict to forestall a future challenge from the rising state when it still enjoys a military advantage.[11] The argument that a currently dominant power but one that is suffering relative decline can start a preventive war corresponds with the logic of prospect theory discussed earlier.

In the context of large power shifts, establishing one's trust in the eyes of other states is important for both the rising and established powers. A rising power should be motivated to reassure the established powers in order to avoid being victimized by a preventive war launched by the latter and in order to avoid arousing its neighbors to form a countervailing coalition against it. For their part, the established powers also have good reasons to reassure rising powers so that, for example, their actions will not precipitate an armament race that fosters a climate of distrust and abets the dynamics of rivalry. When such actions produced a clash of arms as in World War I, the most directly involved antagonists— Germany, Austria-Hungary, Russia, France, and Britain—were all worse off because it. The U.S., a relative outsider, emerged from this conflict as the new world power.

At any given time there are likely to be several established powers and also several rising powers. In the years preceding World War I, Britain faced multiple challengers. Germany, Russia, Japan, and the U.S. were all encroaching on Britain's interests and competing with it for influence in various parts of the world. London decided to appease the U.S., conciliate with Russia (and France, another established but declining power, after confronting it at Fashoda in 1898), and join Japan in an alliance in order to concentrate its diminishing resources and its policy attention on Germany which is closer by. Besides China, there are today other emergent or re-emergent powers such as Brazil, India, Russia, Japan, and Germany. Parenthetically, it is an interesting phenomenon that whereas Russia is often included in the ranks of rising or re-emergent powers (the so-called BRIC group), Germany and Japan are typically not considered as such despite their amazing recovery from the devastation of World War II. This phenomenon suggests that the characterization or categorization of a country as a rising power is based less on its supposed power gains and more on its perceived friendly disposition. In the wake of the USSR's collapse, U.S. power has clearly risen. Yet few people have described it as a rising power even though it has been able to establish an unprecedented position of global preeminence.

Naturally, a country can assume the role of an established power in one relationship but that of a rising power in another. Thus, for example, Wilhelmine Germany was in the former role when it was bent on starting a preventive war against Czarist Russia in 1914, but it was also an upstart when posing a challenge to Britain's naval supremacy in the years leading to that conflict. The dynamics among rising and declining powers involve more than just a bilateral rivalry, a contest for global supremacy as the power-transition theory depicts.

On the eve of World War I, imperial Germany, Russia, Austria-Hungary, and Japan were all much more concerned about affairs in their immediate neighborhood than elsewhere in the world. China today is also very much a regional power that lacks global reach. Jack Levy offers a key insight in this regard: one needs to consider the interactions between the global system and the key regional subsystem.[12] It was Europe's conflict dynamics that led to both world wars. The European region (or subsystem) was primarily responsible for these global (or systemic) conflagrations and not the other way around. Germany was more interested in securing its dominance in Europe than seeking to displace Britain's global hegemony. Today's China is also primarily a regional power. The power-transition theory mischaracterizes Beijing's regional aspirations as a worldwide ambition to dislodge Washington's global hegemony. In this view, a key empirical question is how regional rivalries (such as in the case of Sino-American competition in the Asia Pacific) can have global ramifications. In contrast, a more pertinent question during the Cold War would be how the worldwide competition between the U.S. and the USSR had affected regional dynamics in the Middle East, South Asia, and the Horn of Africa—that is, how the Soviet-American rivalry had abetted, for example, the Arab-Israeli conflict, the Indo-Pakistani conflict, and the Ethiopian-Somali conflict.

One may further hypothesize that the speed of power shifts should affect relations among states. Rapid and sudden changes are likely to be destabilizing, whereas if these changes unfold slowly over a protracted period the states involved will have a better chance to work out their status adjustments and make reciprocal accommodations. The necessary accommodations not only entail the established powers to recognize the sensibilities and preferences of the rising states but also require the latter to acknowledge the former's existing roles and interests.[13] A gradual process of incremental changes is more promising for building mutual trust. Conversely, various institutional and psychological rigidities (such as those that impede a declining state's process to downsize its role and expectations in international relations) tend to exacerbate tension and anxiety when multiple states concurrently experience sharp and abrupt changes in their power. It stands to reason that the faster and more sudden states experience large relative gains and losses in their power, the more acute is the commitment problem highlighted by James Fearon.[14]

National power affects a state's trustworthiness in another important way, one that can perhaps help in part explain some episodes introduced in the last chapter concerning U.S. loss of credibility. Just like a poker player with an enormous stack of chips, an overwhelmingly powerful country can afford to bluff. Weaker, sometimes much weaker, states are leery of challenging its threats because should they make the wrong call (i.e., mistaking its serious threat as a bluff), they will suffer devastating consequences. Realizing that others will thus likely be deterred from calling its bluffs, this powerful state will be more tempted to make empty threats (or deceptive statements in the hope of getting away with them). When they are unchallenged, these empty threats will produce the desired results without causing any reputational damage (because these threats will never be exposed as bluffs). They produce victory on the cheap. Even when challenged and exposed as empty gestures, the loss of credibility may not have serious consequences because in the case of the world's premier power, there is no substitute to it. The U.S. did suffer a setback in Vietnam and Syria's al-Assad might have gotten away with the use of chemical weapons despite Washington's deterrence threats. But the U.S. remains as the indispensable global power so that most other countries have little alternative to accommodating it.

Two corollaries follow from this discussion. First, as a country becomes stronger it is more likely to bluff. Second and related, as a country becomes stronger the value of being seen as trustworthy tends to decline. Thus, to some extent power and trustworthiness are inversely related. When a country is very powerful, it does not need to put its trust in others. Moreover, when it is very powerful, it can more afford a loss of trust in others' eyes.

Note, however, that as stated these hypotheses refer to monadic tendencies, that is, how changes in a state's power can alter its general disposition regardless of the other party that it is dealing with. When we consider the power of its counterpart, yet another (dyadic) proposition comes to mind. As mentioned earlier, when the power balance between two states becomes more equalized, mutual trust is more important in stabilizing their relationship. At the same time, a show of resolve becomes now a more decisive factor in determining the outcome of a contest between two approximately equal states. If this proposition is valid— more importantly, if the officials of the pertinent states believe that it is valid—they are more likely to exaggerate their resolve. Naturally, when this exaggeration is taken as a bluff, there is a greater danger for their dispute to escalate to a showdown. Thus, for two equally matched contestants, their reputation for honesty in the practice of diplomacy becomes more important. Do they believe that the other side means what it says and will follow its words with deeds?

The last remark in turn begs the question when countries are more likely to misrepresent. Besides the influence of a country's relative power on its proclivity to bluff as discussed previously, it seems reasonable to hypothesize that the size of a state's stake in a dispute is another important factor. When it has a small stake, it is unlikely to bluff for the simple reason that others will naturally doubt its resolve to actually run the risk of a major confrontation over an issue that it has objectively speaking only a minor interest. Thus, it is hard to imagine that Beijing will make any empty threats regarding, say, conflicts on Cyprus or in Bosnia. Conversely, when a state has an obvious and large stake in an issue, it does not need to bluff because its core interests should be evident to all parties. One obvious example is when a country declares that it will fight to defend its homeland. In most circumstances, this statement is unlikely to be dismissed by others as insincere. For China, the status of Tibet and Taiwan falls into this category. When states have a middle amount of stake in a dispute, they are more likely to bluff and their trustworthiness may therefore be more directly engaged.[15] In these intermediate cases, states may deliberately exaggerate their stake and fake their resolve in order to gain a stronger bargaining position. From Beijing's perspective, the status of Taiwan is likely to belong to this class for Washington.

Parenthetically, we obviously cannot simply accept states' own declarations of their stake in various disputes because as just mentioned, officials can deliberately misrepresent it. As a general heuristic, however, the geographic location of a dispute can be informative about the relative stakes that the parties have in it. Ceteris paribus, the closer is this location to a disputant, the larger is its stake and hence the stronger should be its resolve.[16] For example, the U.S. should have a larger stake, stronger resolve, and more intense preference about Cuba's status than the USSR in 1962. China should be in a similar situation pertaining to Taiwan's status, and Russia pertaining to Ukraine's when compared to the U.S. In predicting the outcome of interstate confrontations, one needs to consider not only which side has greater capabilities but also which side has a larger stake and hence a stronger resolve. The latter two factors may diminish and even nullify the influence of the former variable as attested by the results of the Vietnam and Korean Wars.

Two hypotheses follow from this discussion. First, as the U.S. extends its global reach farther and farther from its home base, its threats and commitments will encounter increasing skepticism in the eyes of its allies and adversaries alike as this physical distance increases (naturally, this physical distance also tends to correspond with cultural and psychological distance; that is, how closely does a country engaging in extended deterrence identify with its protégé?). These threats and commitments will require increasing amounts of tangible effort, such as "sunk costs" and "tied hands,"[17] to make them credible abroad. Naturally, the more threats and commitments U.S. foreign policy accumulates, the greater the chances that some of them will encounter challenges, especially those in the "far abroad."

Second, when a weaker state takes a stand in a confrontation against a much stronger one like the U.S., it is probably not bluffing. That is, it probably means what it says. Most weak states will be intimidated by the prospect of fighting the U.S. Most would have "folded" long before a dispute with the U.S. escalates to the point of military clashes. Only those with the greatest perceived stake and the strongest resolve will accept this challenge and "select" themselves into such a fight (as just mentioned, others with less perceived stake or weaker resolve would have already opted out of these confrontations). Because they are highly motivated and committed to their cause, these opponents (e.g., North Korea, North Vietnam, ISIL—the Islamic State of Iraq and the Levant) are the toughest ones for Washington to deter and if it comes to a fight, to prevail militarily despite the contestants' lopsided capabilities. Thus, North Vietnam's pledge to resist the U.S. in the Vietnam War and China's threat to intervene in the Korean War should in retrospect be taken more seriously than they were at the time when they were made. These last two examples depart from the concept of trustworthiness in the sense of having confidence in another country's benign intentions in the future. But they do pertain to the question of whether and when a state is likely to be honest—that its deeds will probably correspond to its words.

DOMESTIC POLITICS AND INTERSTATE TRUST

In addition to power shifts at the interstate level, a state's domestic circumstances can present another source of environmental constraint. Intra-elite discord and an isolationist public, for example, can limit a chief executive's policy discretion. Britain and France's reactions to Germany's resurgence during the interwar years were belated and inadequate due to their difficulty in forging a national consensus,[18] and despite President Franklin D. Roosevelt's well-known personal preference to intervene more actively against Germany and Japan he was hamstrung by a skeptical congress and public.[19] In the former instances, elite incoherence and class cleavages were among the factors causing indecisiveness. In the latter instance, a hawkish president who would have preferred a more bellicose foreign policy was restrained by his country's domestic alignment of influence and interests. Domestic divisions tend to promote the usual default policy—which is inaction. To the extent that interstate trust pivots strongly on the question of whether another state will launch an aggressive campaign, these divisions tend to enhance foreign trust in the weak form being considered here. This weak form, as already explained, does not necessarily expect another state to have benign intentions, but only that it will be immobilized, in this case, by its own domestic divisions. Given these divisions, foreigners can expect this state's own powerful interest groups to mobilize against possible bellicosity directed against it.

It seems reasonable to surmise that ceteris paribus, when a state's decision processes are decentralized and shared by multiple institutions, it faces a greater prospect of political gridlock. The U.S. with its government of checks and balances and competitive parties appears sometimes to exemplify this tendency. But as elite competition intensifies and political authority diffuses, China also becomes more prone to it. By definition, when politics becomes pluralistic, there are more veto groups that can block executive decisions. One straightforward implication is that democracies may actually find it harder to reach accords with foreigners because of this constraint. Democratic leaders may be more hampered than their authoritarian counterparts to launch (domestically) controversial initiatives to reconcile with a foreign adversary or to reciprocate conciliatory gestures from the latter.

Thus, contrary to some expectations, if China democratizes it does not necessarily mean that this country will more easily settle its disputes with other countries. Mass attitudes in China tend to be more nationalistic than elite opinion, and a larger influence for mass attitudes in its policy processes—especially on those occasions when competing elite factions try to mobilize public opinion for their partisan purposes—can actually contribute to a more bellicose foreign policy. The politics of demagoguery and foreign scapegoating can especially have such an effect in transitioning democracies.[20] Domestic cleavages and elite rivalries may have this effect compared to the opposite tendency of restraining leaders in more established democracies. Ceteris paribus, for both democracies and nondemocracies a leader who is more vulnerable to domestic censure or political backlash is less able to conclude a foreign deal than a counterpart who is more politically secure.[21] A strong authoritarian leader can more afford to initiate bold overtures and make foreign compromises such as when Mao Tse-tung invited Richard Nixon to Beijing and Anwar Sadat visited Jerusalem. Naturally, whether a larger influence for public opinion will restrain or abet certain foreign policy tendencies depends on the nature of this public opinion, such as whether it is more bellicose or isolationist compared to elite opinion.

U.S. presidents have been known to postpone politically controversial decisions (such as recognizing communist China, ending the Vietnam War, conciliating with Raúl Castro's Cuba) until their second term in office when they will no longer have to face reelection campaigns. It also stands to reason that the so-called diversionary incentive—the temptation to fabricate and exploit foreign crises for the purpose of distracting public attention from domestic difficulties and overcoming a regime's unpopularity—pertains to politically insecure leaders. Those who are politically secure have less reason to resort to this tactic. Finally, a politically insecure leader has less negotiation room when bargaining with a foreign counterpart and even if this person is able to reach an accord, she or he faces greater obstacles in getting it ratified by important domestic constituents. Presumably, an authoritarian leader will face less risk of having a foreign deal rejected by the regime's domestic opponents.

How is this discussion of domestic politics germane to a state's ability to honor its foreign commitments or at least its officials' ability to implement those policies that they have communicated previously to their foreign counterparts? The idea of "involuntary defection" is pertinent here.[22] As stated already, domestic political divisions can cause indecisiveness. Sometimes the pressures from these divisions can immobilize the policy process and even cause policy makers to reverse their announced intentions. The U.S. decision to issue an entry visa to Taiwan President Lee Teng-hui, mentioned earlier, illustrates the effects of congressional pressure on executive decision-making in the Clinton administration. The passage of the Taiwan Relations Act also reflects at least in part the dissatisfaction of conservative legislators with President Jimmy Carter's decision to derecognize Taipei as the government representing China. In his discussion of two-level games, Robert Putnam has shown that foreign interests can try to lobby sympathetic supporters in another country and that these sympathetic supporters can in turn join foreign lobbying interests in a transnational coalition to promote their joint cause.[23] Taipei has generally maintained a strong relationship with friendly representatives on Capitol Hill, and has sometimes caused dismay and even anger on the part of U.S. executive officials who perceive it to be making end runs around the administration. As another example, large U.S. business firms have taken up a prominent role in opposing Washington's economic sanctions against Beijing due to its poor human rights record. In these examples, both domestic and foreign interest groups can try to influence a state's political processes and if successful, to alter and even thwart an administration's intended policy. Naturally, a democratic country's political processes are more accessible to such influence attempts than those of an authoritarian country.

The prospect of involuntary defection is also certainly higher for a democratic leader. Even if a democracy's chief executive favors a foreign accord personally, his or her personal preference and the accord that has been successfully negotiated with a foreign counterpart may still fail to gain sufficient domestic support. The U.S. Senate's refusal to ratify this country's membership in the League of Nations despite President Woodrow Wilson's insistence comes to mind as an example. And, as mentioned earlier, strong and public objections from a large number of U.S. senators to a possible deal to constrain Iran's development of nuclear arms had the intent and effect of undermining the prospect of this deal being successfully negotiated in the first place. In this respect again, democratic politics has a double-edged quality. It can restrain a president (such as Franklin D. Roosevelt) who favors a more assertive, even belligerent, foreign policy, but it also hampers efforts by a president (such as Barack Obama) who is interested in reaching a deal in order to avoid a resort to arms. The prospect of involuntary defection naturally raises the question of trustworthiness since it casts doubts on whether a chief executive can "deliver" that which he or she has negotiated with a foreign counterpart. When foreigners have serious doubts in this regard, they are reluctant to enter into negotiation in the first place.

Democracies have often been said to have an advantage over nondemocracies when their leaders seek to demonstrate their resolve by committing themselves publicly and repeatedly to a course of action. James Fearon has pointed to domestic audience costs as a causal mechanism in boosting and buttressing democratic leaders' policy credibility or whether they can be trusted to actually carry out their policy declarations.[24] He argues that these leaders will have to pay a heavy domestic political price if they renege on their declared intention. By deliberately committing their personal and their administration's reputation to a declared policy course and thus figuratively tying their hands, they communicate a greater degree of resolve or commitment to their announced policy. Because democratic leaders are more likely to be held accountable by their domestic opposition and political constituents in this way than authoritarian leaders, this difference makes their policy pronouncements more credible. By implication, democratic leaders can also more easily resort to this means to enhance their credibility—or trustworthiness—in the eyes of their foreign counterparts. By purposefully taking on domestic political costs should they fail to follow through on their professed intention, these leaders can increase their stake in a foreign dispute. The consequent audience costs they assume can be used to offset, for example, foreign doubts about their stake or resolve in a dispute located in the "far abroad." In contrast to democratic leaders, authoritarian leaders are less able to resort to this approach of "tying hands" because they face little or no domestic opposition that will punish them for failing to actually honor their pledges. They are also less sensitive and less accountable to public opinion. These conditions make announced intentions coming from authoritarian leaders less credible since they are less likely to pay a steep domestic political price if they fail to follow through. Thus at least in this respect, domestic conditions tend to make efforts by authoritarian leaders to demonstrate their trustworthiness more difficult.

The preceding paragraph claims that democratic officials have an advantage over their authoritarian counterparts in that they can deliberately invoke domestic audience costs in order to make their policy announcements more credible. If this proposition is true, it implies that when democratic officials decline to commit themselves publicly and explicitly to a policy course, their silence is also revealing. Why would they fail to take advantage of domestic audience costs to demonstrate their resolve? This question introduces an obverse corollary to the proposition that democratic officials can more effectively resort to tying their hands as a means of communicating their foreign policy commitment. When they fail to avail themselves of this opportunity—such as when Washington adopts a deliberate posture of strategic ambiguity with respect to military contingencies involving Taiwan—this phenomenon is informative. A highly resolved state will commit itself to act under publicly specified conditions, whereas a less resolved state can be expected to avoid reputational costs and expand its policy wriggle room by obfuscating these conditions.

Several recent studies have questioned the extent to which domestic audience costs have actually played a role in democracies' foreign policy conduct, and others have argued that leaders in some types of authoritarian systems can also be sanctioned by their domestic opponents for foreign policy failures and that they can also resort to methods such as mass demonstrations as a way to communicate their policy resolve.[25] Some of this research, for example, has found that democratic officials often prefer ambiguity to locking themselves to a particular policy course, and that they are usually able to avoid paying a domestic political penalty for making empty threats (i.e., for failing to do what they have said they would do). To the extent that these observations are true, they invalidate the propositions advanced in the preceding two paragraphs.

In addition to domestic audience costs, the pluralistic nature of democratic politics and the existence of many veto groups can be turned into an advantage under some conditions. When a democracy's chief executive enjoys strong support from the legislature and the opposition party, this popularity sends a strong message to foreigners.[26] An authoritarian leader cannot similarly leverage domestic politics to demonstrate his/her country's credibility or resolve. Thus, although democratic politics can sometimes hamper foreign compromises and even produce involuntary defection, it can have an offsetting advantage that makes those foreign commitments backed by a strong national consensus more credible abroad.

Limited tenure and regular alternation of office holders are a hallmark of democracy. How can officials currently in power commit to foreigners and expect their successors who may have different interests and preferences to honor their commitments? Uncertainties about whether future officials will feel bound by the promises or threats made by current officials of course also apply to authoritarian systems, but authoritarian leaders tend to stay in power for longer periods of time and are less likely to face political challenges to their policies. Electoral cycles and popular mood swings are more likely to produce policy instability in democracies.

These conditions can produce involuntary defection (involuntary from the perspective of the chief executive who had initially negotiated the foreign deal). Several Republican candidates in the 2016 U.S. presidential contest had indicated that if elected, they would abrogate the executive agreement President Barack Obama had reached with Iran to curtail the latter country's nuclear program. In his campaign for the Oval Office, Donald Trump had also stated publicly that if elected, he would "cancel" U.S. participation in the Paris accord on climate change and renegotiate the terms of the North American Free Trade Agreement (NAFTA) and the Trans-Pacific Partnership (TPP); he said that he would withdraw from these agreements unless he could obtain more favorable terms for the U.S. Trump had even openly questioned U.S. defense commitments to its NATO allies unless there is a more equal sharing of the cost burden of this alliance. There have been comparable situations such as when Jimmy Carter unilaterally cancelled the U.S. defense treaty with Taiwan without consulting Congress and when George W. Bush walked away from U.S. membership in the International Criminal Court (ICC) and withdrew from the Anti-Ballistic Missile Treaty.

Because power is by definition more concentrated in an authoritarian system and because the "selectorate" for its leaders is smaller than in a democratic system,[27] the tendency for policy cycling should be weaker (a "selectorate" is the group of powerful individuals, institutions, and interests that is responsible for selecting a political leader and keeping him/her in power). Kurt Gaubatz, however, argues that factors such as electoral turnover and popular mood swing need not undermine democracies' ability to make and honor foreign commitments, and he uses the longer duration of alliances consisting of democracies (compared to alliances between autocracies and alliances of mixed dyads) to support his argument (although acknowledging at the same time that how long an alliance has lasted may not be a satisfactory measure of its democratic members' inclination to uphold their treaty obligations).[28] In contrast, Erik Gartzke and Kristian Gleditsch argue that democracies may actually be less reliable allies.[29] There is an inherent tension between the tendency for democratic politics to produce policy cycling and the desire by officials to lock in their successors to the pledges they had made to foreign allies. "Institutionalizing agreements [such as through the legal formality of signing a defense treaty] limits cycling, but only to the extent that it limits [democratic] representation."[30]

Two implications follow from this discussion. First, due to their greater tendency for policy cycling there may be a stronger demand for democracies to enter into formal alliances. Ceteris paribus, democracies should display a greater tendency to enter into defense treaties and security pacts than autocracies. Second and related, these legal instruments are not only intended to reassure foreign allies, but are also used by a democratic regime to bind its own domestic successors and of course their counterparts' successors. These tendencies suggest that the demand for treaties and other kinds of formal agreements will be higher for democracies. As Charles Kegley and Gregory Raymond have remarked, "Alliance agreements would not be committed to writing if there were not a perceived need to reduce apprehension about the reliability of allies in times of crisis. In this sense, treaties represent to some degree an acknowledgment that a verbal promise may not be sufficient to cement mutual obligations."[31]

In some cases, a negotiation counterpart may not be formally recognized or gaining domestic ratification for a deal may be problematic. For instance, Taipei has been asking Beijing to give it more diplomatic space—that is, for Beijing to drop its opposition to Taipei's membership and participation in various international organizations—as a sign of China's goodwill. Even if Beijing was inclined to accede to this demand because it had confidence in the Kuomintang government when it was in power, it still has reason to be concerned about the intentions of its successor controlled by the Democratic Progressive Party, a party known for its pro-independence sympathies. If this DPP administration (which assumed power in May 2016) were to use Taipei's newly gained presence in international forums to assert and advance its claim of *de jure* independence, it would be difficult for Beijing to retract its earlier concessions. The damage would have already been done. The challenges of crafting an enforceable agreement that would protect the parties against voluntary defection by their respective future leaders stand in the way of reaching a current accommodation.

The U.S. senators' open letter to the leaders in Tehran, mentioned earlier, provides another example. Neither Iran nor North Korea has formal diplomatic ties with the U.S. Both have suspicions about whether a future U.S. administration may repudiate an agreement with them after they have already dismantled their nuclear program. The involvement of other states (such as Britain, France, or Japan in addition to Russia and China, for example) provides an additional feature to guard against a possible future defection by either side, as these other countries also commit their credibility to uphold any settlement that has been successfully negotiated with their cooperation. Should a party to the multilateral agreement renege on its commitment, it will suffer a larger reputational loss because this behavior will also be a breach of trust with respect to the other participants. Naturally, the involvement of other major states in these minilateral talks also serves the purpose of bringing more collective pressure to bear on Pyongyang and Tehran to agree to a deal and if these talks should fail, to lay the ground work for a more effective sanction regime against them. Significantly but often overlooked, the involvement of the other signatories also hints at their role to restrain the U.S. from any unwanted action such as withdrawing from this deal or even attacking Iran or North Korea (as it did against Iraq). If President Trump repudiates the Iran deal as he had promised during his campaign, what are the likely responses from the other signatories besides Tehran? What lessons would Pyongyang draw from this contingency about concluding any deal to curtail its nuclear program?

Sometimes, states may resort to other ways of conveying their intentions such as by means of communiqués. This means bypasses the need for domestic legislative ratification but its enforceability is also more problematic as in the case of various announcements made by Chinese and American leaders after their summitries. These announcements can be deliberately ambiguous, such as Washington's acknowledgment of the Chinese position that there is but one China and that Taiwan is part of China. In this case, rather than committing the U.S. to a clear position, the wording provides a diplomatic loophole.

The logic of collective action suggests another paradox about democracies' policy processes.[32] Special interest groups with a large stake in a particular issue are more likely to lobby actively and have a disproportionate amount of influence when defense treaties (or for that matter, any policy or legislation) are being negotiated or considered for approval. Only a small number of intensely interested groups participate at the negotiation and ratification stages of the treaty-making process when the pertinent issues have a relatively low salience for the general public. Thus the debate on NATO enlargement, for example, tends to reflect the preferences of those politically mobilized groups (such as associations whose members trace their national origin to Eastern or Central Europe) with concentrated interests rather than the preferences of the general public with more diffused interests. But when the moment comes to actually implement the terms of a defense treaty, a larger number of previously inactive groups become engaged. The preferences of this larger public may very well differ from those special interests that were responsible for the treaty's initial adoption.

According to Gartzke and Gleditsch,[33] this discrepancy tends to make democracies less reliable allies than autocracies. Their analysis result corresponds with Alastair Smith whose study also indicates a negative relationship between democratic regimes and decisions to honor treaty commitments to allies.[34] Similarly, B. Ashley Leeds and Jennifer Gigliotti-Labay find that democratic leaders have a lower rate of fulfilling their alliance commitments when called upon to do so with the outbreak of war (34%) compared to their authoritarian counterparts (57%).[35] In another study, however, Leeds reports that most allies keep their commitments (80%, thus only the remaining 20% break their promises).[36] Moreover, the probability of democracies failing to honor a commitment is 16.5% lower than this probability for autocracies. This latter result contradicts those empirical patterns reported by the other studies just mentioned.

Naturally, a state can alter its intention to meet its foreign obligations as circumstances change. In the lead up to World War II, France failed to fulfill its treaty obligation to Czechoslovakia and Britain did not uphold its guarantee for that country's territorial integrity, although both did later declare war on Germany after it invaded Poland. Adolf Hitler had doubts that either of these democracies would come to the aid of its protégés. The U.S. of course also changed its mind about continuing to support Saigon after years of fighting. The nature and extent of Washington's commitment to the current governments in Iraq and Afghanistan are also a matter of continuing debate.

The discussion thus far has focused on those domestic factors that could limit a chief executive's decision autonomy or discretion, and hence are considerations that could hamper this official's ability to carry out his or her policy preferences or intentions. President Gerald Ford, for example, had asked for additional funding to finance the Vietnam War even during the last days of this conflict but his request was turned down by Congress which had become more assertive with increasing disenchantment with this war and in the wake of the Watergate scandal and criticisms of an "imperial presidency." To the extent that a chief executive is hamstrung by domestic factors from taking a more assertive, even bellicose, approach, a prospective target country may be reassured in the sense suggested by the weak form of trust. Even though this official may have hostile intentions, he or she is constrained by domestic circumstances from acting on these impulses. Domestic conditions, however, can also limit or prevent a state from discharging its international commitments as discussed in the previous paragraph. To the extent that these conditions hinder a democracy's fulfillment of its treaty obligations, they weaken its trustworthiness in its allies' eyes. Thus, domestic constraints can either help or hurt other states' confidence depending on whether they are an ally or adversary. An ally would naturally like to see its counterpart's officials to be able to act without such constraints because these officials are supposed to have a friendly disposition. Conversely, an adversary would like to see its counterpart's officials to be domestically constrained because of these officials' presumed hostile inclinations.

In the next chapter, I will provide a more extended discussion on how economic openness or closure is related to the interests and influence of domestic groups. Generally speaking, economic openness and inter-dependence tend to enhance the interests and influence of outwardly oriented groups that have a vested stake in lowering international tension and promoting interstate cooperation. Conversely, inward-looking groups tend to favor import restrictions, large state enterprises, and autarchy in developing the national economy. The developmental path that a state has undertaken leaves a strong legacy on the relative strength of distrib-utional coalitions with these opposing orientations and preferences. Etel Solingen has shown that states in East Asia and the Middle East have pursued divergent strategies for managing their political economies, with significantly different consequences for the security environment of their respective regions.[37] East Asian elites have generally pivoted to staking their political legitimacy on developing their economies by export expansion, whereas Middle Eastern elites have continued to depend on inefficient public enterprises, a large state bureaucracy, and the politics of foreign scapegoating to justify and sustain their right to rule. These divergent approaches have fostered different coalitional politics inside countries in these two regions, and the dominant coalitions have consolidated their domestic positions over time. The external policies pursued by these dominant coalitions cause foreign reverberations that in turn reinforce their domestic hegemony, engendering a general regional dynamic that is self-sustaining and self-reinforcing.

For example, hardliners who stake their reputation on opposing foreign military or religious foes are met by similar hardliners in other Middle Eastern countries, thus perpetuating reciprocal distrust and animosity. Conversely, the model of export-led growth has spread across East Asian countries, with those who prefer a stable and liberal regional order becoming partners in a tacit transnational coalition. This coalition also becomes more entrenched over time and thus more difficult to dislodge. Given the multilateral nature of economic interdependence and the interlocking interests fostered by globalization, this development helps to promote generalized trust (rather than simply bilateral trust) among those involved. Thus domestic coalitional politics and developmental strategies can engender external consequences. They have generally dampened distrust in East Asia while exacerbating it in the Middle East.

Whether a state controls a large, independent source of revenue and is therefore in a financial position to fund large projects, including the military-industrial complex, is a question that bears directly on the chief executive's decision autonomy and discretion. The necessity of seeking authorization for taxes to operate the government presents a major constraint on this chief executive, forcing him or her to negotiate and compromise with other domestic stakeholders who are in a position to extend or withhold their approval. The greater this necessity, the more restrictive is the domestic political context. When a chief executive is liberated from this constraint, the domestic environment becomes more permissive. Large energy exporters in the Middle East have exemplified this situation although the recent dramatic decline in oil price is increasingly threatening this fiscal autonomy. This feature of the energy-exporting countries does not speak directly to their trustworthiness except, of course, financial independence and wealth are a form of power that inclines those states in this fortunate position to be less trusting of others as hypothesized in the previous section. A state's relative fiscal independence, however, pertains to the current discussion in so far as it removes or at least lessens one of the key domestic constraints that most chief executives face in deciding questions of war and peace.[38] It also shapes the nature of the ruling coalition in such a state, making it more possible and likely for such a state to feature and sustain a large public sector and a powerful military-industrial complex. The dominant groups in such a state are more likely to pursue nationalist and confrontational foreign policy and when interacting with similar groups in control of its neighboring countries, are more likely to foster and perpetuate a regional dynamic of armament competition, internecine conflict, and reciprocal distrust.

CONCLUDING REMARKS

Although power shifts and the differences between the U.S. and Chinese political systems have often been invoked in commentaries on their bilateral relations, the mechanisms that are supposed to affect their ties and especially their mutual distrust have usually been left underspecified. This chapter has presented the pertinent causal paths stemming from these two sources. The extant literature is often quite simplistic in its exposition. For instance, a trust deficit cannot just be attributed to other countries' concerns about the ambitions of a rapidly rising state. It can also reflect the latter's concerns that the established powers may seek to block its ascent and even to contemplate a preventive war. Similarly, accommodation cannot be a one-sided affair entailing just concessions made by the established powers to a latecomer. The latter must also accommodate the former so that there will be a smooth and peaceful transition with due regard for the former's existing interests and prerogatives. There must be mutual sensibilities. Moreover, the trustworthiness of a state depends not just on its power but also on its stake in an existing situation. Existing accounts tend to shuttle the logic of their explanation, emphasizing an established state's stake in the current system as a reason for its status-quo orientation while focusing on a rising state's increased power as a motivation for its supposed revisionism. They therefore overlook the possibility that an incumbent hegemon's overwhelming power can be used to alter the existing rules to further its already substantial advantages, and do not give adequate consideration to a rising state's increasing stake in those rules that have thus far enabled its ascent.

Mutual concerns and even suspicions are not necessarily unnatural or unreasonable. The U.S. is concerned about Chinese ambitions for regional hegemony in Asia. Beijing also distrusts Washington's motives. After all, the U.S. has launched a preventive war against Iraq based on its own public explanation, supported secessionists in former Yugoslavia, and announced an intention to pivot to Asia. Paradoxically, precisely because both countries are great powers, they tend to be less trusting of others and they are also less reliant on others to trust them. Yet as their bilateral power balance becomes less asymmetric, the need for greater mutual trust to stabilize their relationship also becomes greater.

One sometimes hears the argument that if only China were a democracy, a possible power transition involving it and the U.S. should not present a great concern for international stability.[39] It is at least premature to speak of such a transition.[40] Moreover, more intense elite competition and a greater role for public opinion will likely make China's foreign policy less compromising and more nationalistic. A strong and politically secure leader is generally in a better position to make the necessary concessions to his or her foreign counterpart in order to break a deadlock. It is true that the transparency of their decision processes enhances the credibility of democracies' resolve. But this transparency has a double-edged effect so that it can also convey to foreign audiences deeply held suspicions, even animosity, that a democracy may have about another country. An independent press, critical political opponents, and multiple accessible sources of information can expose a democracy's unreliability and dishonesty whereas an authoritarian system is better able to prevent such disclosures. Moreover, the pluralistic nature of democratic politics can restrain leaders from pursuing certain policy courses—sometimes to the detriment of a country's trustworthiness in the eyes of foreigners but on other occasions contributing to its trustworthiness in at least the weak form.

Interstate power balance and a country's domestic politics matter in how a process to build trust can be initiated and then sustained. History and theory both seem to suggest that it is the weaker side that makes the larger or more costly reassurance gesture as Mikhail Gorbachev did in a number of asymmetric settlements starting with major Soviet concessions in the Intermediate-Range Nuclear Force Treaty he signed with Ronald Reagan in 1987.[41] This treaty was followed by a series of other substantial and sometimes unilateral concessions, including the membership of a reunited Germany in the NATO alliance. As for domestic politics, democracies are almost by definition likely to have messier political processes with many veto groups and discordant voices. A democracy's chief executive has to be mindful of securing domestic support for his or her foreign policy initiatives and agreements. Ceteris paribus, this official faces more severe domestic constraints and a smaller "win set" than an authoritarian counterpart. Involuntary defection is more likely to occur as a result. Focusing on the USSR's authoritarian regime rather than its relative weakness, Deborah Larson has noted: "Authoritarian regimes can more easily make unilateral concessions than democratic leaders, who are under pressure to show that they have not 'given away the store.' The difference in their domestic systems can help explain why most U.S.-Soviet agreements arose not through a tit-for-tat process but from a pattern of asymmetric concessions by the Soviets."[42] In a similar vein, Charles Kupchan has remarked, "From Moscow's perspective, Russia for successive years made a series of concessions to the West, including accommodating NATO expansion, reacting with restraint to democratic revolutions in its 'near abroad,' and facilitating strategic access for the United States in Central Asia and Afghanistan."[43] It appears that a combination of being weak and authoritarian has actually contributed to Moscow's accommodative policy that helped to end the Cold War and dissipate U.S.-Russian tension in the early years after the USSR's dissolution.

There are important differences between the USSR and today's China. The USSR in the 1980s and post-Soviet Russia in its earlier years were a rapidly declining power beset by serious challenges both at home and abroad. In contrast, China has been a rapidly rising power that has closed the gap separating it and the U.S. even though it is also undeniable that Beijing faces difficult policy problems (including the management of slower economic growth and severe environmental pollution). Moreover, as Evan Resnick has observed,[44] whereas the USSR was weakly motivated to invade Western Europe and the U.S. was strongly motivated to defend it, the current situation in China's immediate neighborhood is in some respects reversed. China appears strongly motivated in its maritime disputes, in its sovereignty claim over Taiwan, and in protecting its interests on the Korean peninsula, whereas the extent of U.S. commitment is less clear in some of these cases. Ceteris paribus, the closer a dispute is located to a country's homeland, the larger should be its stake and hence the stronger should be its resolve to fight. With respect to Taiwan's status, Washington's official posture has been deliberate strategic ambiguity, declining to specify the conditions under which it will intervene militarily to forestall a Chinese takeover of that island. Although today's Sino-American relations are undoubtedly more stable and robust in some respects compared to Soviet-American relations during the Cold War (such as with respect to the strength of these countries' economic ties to be discussed in the next chapter), in other respects such as the geographic demarcation of their competition China and the U.S. are still trying to reach a tacit understanding. The acrimonious exchanges sparked by

Beijing's announcement of an air-defense self-identification zone in November 2013 exemplify this still ongoing process, indicating a more fluid and ambiguous geostrategic situation in contemporary Asia Pacific compared to Cold War Europe.

NOTES

1. Benjamin A. Most and Harvey Starr, *Inquiry, Logic and International Politics* (Columbia: University of South Carolina Press, 1989).
2. Nathan and Scobell, *China's Search*, xi, xiii.
3. Ronald L. Tammen, Jacek Kugler, Douglas Lemke, Allan C. Stam III, Mark Abdollahian, Carole Alsharabati, Brian Efird, and A.F.K. Organski, *Power Transitions: Strategies for the 21st Century* (New York: Chatham House, 2000), 9.
4. Jacek Kugler and Douglas Lemke, eds., *Parity and War: Evaluations and Extensions of The War Ledger* (Ann Arbor: University of Michigan Press, 1996); Organski and Kugler, *The War Ledger*; and Tammen et al., *Power Transitions*.
5. Dale C. Copeland, *The Origins of Major War* (Ithaca, NY: Cornell University Press, 2000).
6. Daniel Kahneman and Amos Tversky, "Prospect Theory: An Analysis of Decision under Risk," *Econometrica* 47, no. 2 (1979): 263–291; and eds., *Choices, Values and Frames* (Cambridge: Cambridge University Press, 2000).
7. Robert Powell, *In the Shadow of Power: States and Strategies in International Politics* (Princeton, NJ: Princeton University Press, 1999).
8. Charles F. Doran and Wes Parsons, "War and the Cycle of Relative Power," *American Political Science Review* 74, no. 4 (1980): 947–965; and Brock F. Tessman and Steve Chan, "Power Cycles, Risk Propensity, and the Escalation of Great Power Disputes," *Journal of Conflict Resolution* 48, no. 2 (2004): 131–153.
9. Kydd, *Trust and Mistrust*, 249.
10. Copeland, *The Origins*; and Charles F. Doran, "Economics, Philosophy of History, and the 'Single Dynamic' of the Power Cycle Theory: Expectations, Competition, and Statecraft," *International Political Science Review* 24, no. 1 (2003): 13–49.
11. Copeland, *The Origins*; and Levy, "Preventive War."
12. Jack S. Levy, "Power Transition Theory and the Rise of China," in *China's Ascent: Power, Security, and the Future of International Politics*, eds. Robert S. Ross and Zhu Feng (Ithaca, New York: Cornell University Press, 2008), 11–33.

13. Paul, T.V., ed., *Accommodating Rising States* (Cambridge: Cambridge University Press, 2015).
14. Fearon, "Rationalist Explanations."
15. Sartori, *Deterrence by Diplomacy*.
16. Vesna Danilovic, "Conceptual and Selection Bias Issues in Deterrence," *Journal of Conflict Resolution* 45, no. 1 (2001): 97–125.
17. Fearon, "Signaling Foreign Policy Interests."
18. Randall L. Schweller, *Unanswered Threats: Political Constraints on the Balance of Power* (Princeton, NJ: Princeton University Press, 2006).
19. Robert B. Stinnett, *Day of Deceit* (New York: Free Press, 2000); and Jeffrey W. Taliaferro, "Strategy of Innocence or Calculated Provocation? The Roosevelt Administration's Road to World War II," in *The Challenge of Grand Strategy: The Great Powers and the Broken Balance between the Wars*, eds. Jeffrey W. Taliaferro, Norrin M. Ripsman, and Steven E. Lobell (Cambridge: Cambridge University Press, 2012), 193–223.
20. Edward D. Mansfield and Jack Snyder, *Electing to Fight: Why Emerging Democracies Go to War* (Cambridge, MA: The MIT Press, 2005).
21. Paul K. Huth and Todd L. Allee, *The Democratic Peace and Territorial Conflict in the Twentieth Century* (New York: Cambridge University Press, 2002).
22. Putnam," Diplomacy and Domestic Politics."
23. Ibid.
24. James D. Fearon, "Domestic Political Audiences and the Escalation of International Disputes," *American Political Science Review* 88, no. 3 (1994): 577–592, and "Signaling Foreign Policy Interests."
25. Jack Snyder and Erica D. Borghard, "The Cost of Empty Threats: A Penny, Not a Pound," *American Political Science Review* 105, no. 3 (2011): 437–456; Marc Trachtenberg, "Audience Costs: An Historical Analysis," *Security Studies* 21, no. 1 (2011): 3–42; Jessica L. Weeks, "Autocratic Audience Costs: Regime Type and Signaling Resolve," *International Organization* 62, no. 1 (2008): 35–64, and "Strongmen and Straw Men: Authoritarian Regimes and the Initiation of Interstate Conflict," *American Political Science Review* 106, no. 2 (2012): 326–347; and Jessica Chen Weiss, "Authoritarian Signaling, Mass Audiences, and Nationalist Protest in China," *International Organization* 67, no. 1 (2013): 1–35, and *Powerful Patriots: Nationalist Protest in China's Foreign Relations* (Oxford: Oxford University Press, 2014).

26. Schultz, *Democracy and Coercive Diplomacy*, and Lisa L. Martin, *Democratic Commitments: Legislatures and International Cooperation* (Princeton, NJ: Princeton University Press, 2000).
27. Bueno de Mesquita et al., "An Institutional Explanation."
28. Kurt T. Gaubatz, "Democratic States and Commitment in International Relations," *International Organization* 50, no. 1 (1996): 109–139.
29. Erik Gartzke and Kristian S. Gleditsch, "Why Democracies May Actually Be Less Reliable Allies," *American Journal of Political Science* 48, no. 4 (2004): 775–795.
30. Ibid., 777.
31. Kegley and Raymond, *When Trust Breaks Down*, 47.
32. Mancur Olson, Jr., *The Logic of Collective Action: Public Goods and the Theory of Groups* (Cambridge, MA: Harvard University Press, 1965).
33. Gartzke and Gleditsch, "Why Democracies."
34. Alastair Smith, "To Intervene or Not to Intervene: A Biased Decision," *Journal of Conflict Resolution* 40, no. 1 (1996): 16–40.
35. Brett A. Leeds and Jennifer Gigliotti-Labay, "You Can Count on Me? Democracy and Alliance Reliability," presented at the annual meeting of the American Political Science Association, Philadelphia (2003), 17.
36. Brett A. Leeds, "Alliance Reliability in Times of War: Explaining State Decisions to Violate Treaties," *International Organization* 57, no. 4 (2003): 801–827.
37. Etel Solingen, *Regional Orders at Century's Dawn: Global and Domestic Influences on Grand Strategy* (Princeton, NJ: Princeton University Press, 1998), and "Pax Asiatica Versus Belli Levantina: The Foundations of War and Peace in East Asia and the Middle East," *American Political Science Review* 101, no. 4 (2007): 757–780.
38. Patrick J. McDonald, *The Invisible Hand of Peace: Capitalism, the War Machine, and International Relations Theory* (New York: Cambridge University Press, 2009).
39. Friedberg, *A Contest*.
40. Michael Beckley, "China Century? Why America's Edge Will Endure," *International Security* 36, no. 3 (2011/12): 41–78; and Steve Chan, "Is There a Power Transition between the U.S. and China? The Different Faces of Power," *Asian Survey* 45, no. 5 (2005): 687–701, and *China, the U.S., and the Power-Transition Theory: A Critique* (London: Routledge, 2008).
41. Kydd, *Trust and Mistrust*, 221.
42. Larson, "Trust and Missed Opportunities," 713.

43. Kupchan, *How Enemies Become Friends*, 397.
44. Resnick, "The Perils."

CHAPTER 4

A SEMI-STRONG FORM OF TRUST MOTIVATED BY REPUTATIONAL CONSIDERATIONS

In the weak form of trust, one believes that another state will not undertake hostile acts because the expected benefits of these acts are outweighed by their expected costs. This situation occurs when, for example, this other state finds itself facing a much stronger foreign adversary or influential domestic interests opposing the pertinent acts. In the semi-strong form of trust, cost-benefit calculations are still the reason responsible for this other state's restraint but they are based now on a more general consideration of the latter's reputation. A state may refrain from defecting in a prisoners' dilemma game even though it can make an immediate gain at its counterpart's expense. It decides instead to cooperate because defection can cause subsequent retaliation by its counterpart and therefore trigger a series of mutual recriminations that would make it worse off in the long run.[1] If a state's defection is observed by third parties, the pertinent adverse consequences have even wider ramifications. Thus, the reputational damage done to a person who has defaulted on debts extends beyond the institution from which he or she has borrowed. This person will have trouble in the future getting loans from other financial institutions. Similarly, when a country defaults on its debts, it pays a reputational cost so that it will be less able to obtain foreign finances in the future or will have to pay more to access these funds.[2] For a rising state, investing in its reputation for being benign dampens others' incentives to consider a preventive war.

In addition to concerns about the prospective costs of opportunistic behavior, a state can be motivated to invest in its reputation for being nice and optimistic because of the potential gains to be had. In the terminology of Robert Axelrod's famous work showing how even self-regarding egoists can cooperate profitably in a situation of prisoners' dilemma,[3] being nice means never to be the first person to defect from cooperation and being optimistic means that one is always willing to take a chance in cooperating even in the absence of any knowledge about the other side's willingness to reciprocate (i.e., unless contradicted by the other side's behavior, one is always willing to take the initial risk of assuming that this counterpart is also nice and is thus disposed to cooperate rather than defect). Being nice and optimistic enables people to initiate a virtuous cycle of cooperation and equally important, helps them to avoid a series of mutual recriminations that puts both of them in a sub-optimal situation (denying them the gains from cooperation that they would otherwise have been able to acquire).

For a powerful state or one that is gaining power, an investment in its reputation extends beyond bilateral relationships. It helps to fend off other countries' suspicions and to head off a possible countervailing coalition directed against it. Whereas a breach of trust invites retaliation (thus making opportunism self-defeating in the long run as just noted), a reputation for being nice and optimistic encourages diffuse reciprocity.[4] A state that cooperates can foster its trustworthiness in the eyes of other states, inclining them to cooperate in return. Such reciprocal behavior can in the long run produce a positive spiral of trust and cooperation, eventually leading to the formation of a security community based on the strong form of trust.

By definition, reputation refers to how a state's actions will have intertemporal or interspatial consequences. If it tries to appease another, will it embolden the latter to make further demands in the future? If it fails to honor its commitment to an ally, will it lose trust in the eyes of other allies? If it fails to keep its promise to A this time, will B and C believe it next time on some other issue? For reputation to influence decisions and actions, officials must believe that such intertemporal and interspatial consequences exist. A state can acquire a reputation for reliability, honesty, and trustworthiness—as well as their opposites— due to its behavior. This reputation can in turn influence how others will behave toward it. For example, as mentioned earlier, Iranian and North Korean leaders will draw conclusions from the fate of Saddam Hussein and Muammar Gaddafi.

In this chapter, I extend Axelrod's insight on the shadow of the future, and show how states can invest in their reputation for being nice and optimistic by accepting economic interdependence and participating in international organizations. These are two important sources of the semi-strong form of trust. Trust in the narrow sense of strategic or instrumental trust is enhanced by a long process involving many rounds of interactions. This kind of trust reflects calculations of gains and losses based on interest. It is dependent on the expectation of specific reciprocity. If a person does not expect to encounter another again in the future, it is more tempting for him or her to defect as in the one-shot game of prisoners' dilemma. The shadow of the future, based on anticipating the other person's likely future response to one's action in the current round of interaction, operates when both parties expect to meet again.[5] This expectation encourages them to eschew a myopic view of their interests for the sake of protecting their reputation for being benign and cooperative, and it fosters the semi-strong form of trust being discussed in this chapter.

When people believe in the goodwill of complete strangers (i.e., someone whom they do not necessarily expect to meet again and thus to either reciprocate or retaliate against them in the future), this phenomenon indicates moralistic or generalized trust, a basic ingredient for general social well-being and democratic politics.[6] This kind of trust usually although not necessarily reflects identity rather interest, and points to a general faith in the benevolent intentions and reliable character of the trustee. This trust need not, however, be entirely altruistic. Those who are optimistic about strangers' goodwill are rewarded when this confidence turns out to be justified and they are treated similarly by like-minded strangers who have been socialized to hold the same faith, whereas those who exploit these optimists suffer reputational costs when their dishonesty or unreliability is observed by others and causes these others to imitate, thus causing an adverse contagion that is destructive of the very fabric of their society. For example, in a political culture that encourages rampant tax cheating or condones pervasive official corruption, everyone loses (or at least almost everyone except the biggest offenders). Conversely, when people share widely the view that such behavior is wrong and unacceptable and act accordingly, they all benefit from this moralistic community based on generalized trust.

Globalization has had the effect of fostering interlocking networks of commercial and financial interests located in many countries and involving an ever-increasing number of transactions and participants. This development contributes to building interstate trust. Trusting states are more likely to become involved in economic interdependence in the first place. Such involvement shows their disposition to trust others. It also signals that they deserve others' trust. Moreover, rising economic interdependence provides the basis for building further trust among those states involved in this relationship.

Similarly, membership and participation in international organizations tend to both reflect and produce trust. Trusting states—those that are optimistic about the prospects of shared governance and those that are willing to submit themselves to the rules and norms of collective decision-making—are more likely to join these organizations in the first place (the isolationist type will not join and the aggressive type will exit when collective decisions go against them as Germany and Japan did in leaving the League of Nations). The experience of taking part in collective decision-making can in turn have a socialization effect on officials, inclining them to accept and internalize the rules and norms of the relevant international communities. Over time they build a reputation for being trustworthy. They gain the confidence of others for playing nice and according to the rules. This latter perception does not necessarily mean that a trusted state will no longer have different interests from others or that it will eschew the use of its power in seeking bargaining advantages. It does mean, however, that it sees the rules and norms of international organizations to have a binding effect on both itself and others.[7]

Importantly, the pertinent rules and norms reflect the instrumental or strategic calculations of the participating states, and at least not initially their sense of belonging to a common moralistic community as would be in the case of the strong form of trust. Most post–1945 global institutions were the result of bargaining between the U.S. and its Western European partners to promote cooperation even in the face of their differences in power and preferences. Over time, however, socialization can produce internalized values and mutual identification that undergird such a community.

ECONOMIC INTERDEPENDENCE

Like most things in life, economic exchanges among states produce both benefits and costs. Interstate trade, for example, provides efficiency gains, allowing a state to specialize where it enjoys a comparative advantage. Consumers benefit from this trade as they gain access to more affordable goods and a greater variety of goods. At the same time, interstate trade exposes a state to increased vulnerabilities and sensitivities caused by its consequent dependency on foreign markets and suppliers.[8] A state pursuing export specialization produces more of certain goods than its domestic market can absorb, and it becomes reliant on imports to meet other areas of its domestic need. An emphasis on export-dependent growth necessarily causes this orientation, and subjects such a state to possible shocks caused by interruptions of foreign supply and closures of markets abroad. In the event of such shocks, a trade-dependent state faces severe adjustment costs. Small trading states are especially exposed to this danger. Ceteris paribus, the heavier a state is dependent on foreign commerce, the more it is sensitive and vulnerable to external shocks—whether these disturbances are intended or unintended by foreigners. When a small economy becomes entangled in a highly asymmetric commercial or investment relationship with a much larger and more powerful counterpart such as in the case of Taiwan vis-à-vis mainland China (or Mexico vis-à-vis the U.S.), the political implications are especially serious.

Foreign investments, loans, and bank assets also present double-edged swords. They bring obvious benefits but also entail evident risks. Properties and operations located abroad can be expropriated by foreign governments, and loans extended to foreign debtors can be repudiated. Similarly, foreign governments can order their banks to freeze assets owned by the citizens or companies of another state (such as those owned by Iran but held in Western countries), or otherwise refuse to service these clients' transactions (such as those experienced by Russians when they were subjected to recent Western sanctions over Ukraine). When investing abroad or making foreign loans, one runs a host of political risks beyond those typically encountered in the domestic setting. As in the case of foreign trade, these investments and loans can be exploited for political purposes. Sometimes, a state may even order its foreign subsidiaries located in third countries to join a boycott against another state (such as when in 1981–1982 the U.S. sought to apply extraterritorial jurisdiction to its companies chartered in Western Europe, demanding that they decline to fulfill their contracts with the USSR to supply it with technology and equipment for building a natural gas pipeline).

In short, foreign economic exchanges entail important political risks. Albert Hirschman's classic study shows how Nazi Germany had used its trade with the smaller and less developed Balkan states in order to gain political influence over them.[9] Indeed, to the extent that another state stands to gain from any economic exchange, the consequent benefit to it creates a security externality such that this benefit can be used to strengthen its military capabilities. Even though foreign commerce produces an absolute benefit for both sides of a transaction, this security externality worries those realists who are concerned about these states' *relative* power positions.[10] Moreover, to the extent that interactions with powerful foreign economic interests entail an unequal political relationship and distort the weaker state's domestic political economy, they have those lasting adverse effects decried by dependency theorists.[11] One such effect is the cooptation of local elites who align their economic preferences and political identities with their foreign counterparts rather than their own mass public.

This effect of foreign commerce or finance on a state's domestic distribution of interests and influence was discussed in the last chapter. Advocates of U.S. economic engagement of China see these interactions to have a long-term effect on how China's domestic stakeholders perceive their own self-interests and even identities, inclining them to become friendlier to Western values and views. As I have argued earlier, economic openness and interdependence tend to be supported by those interest groups that have a liberal and internationalist outlook, groups that are in turn likely to be the chief beneficiaries of this external orientation. These connections highlight the interactions between domestic interests and foreign orientation as suggested by Robert Putnam's well-known metaphor of two-level games.[12] When domestic interests can be powerful lobbyists for certain policies by a state, their role and influence point to the potential for economic openness and interdependence to create and cultivate such friendly stakeholders in another country. Steven Lobell speaks of the "second face of security," whereby a state can influence another state indirectly by influencing the latter's powerful domestic groups that can in turn be mobilized to lobby their government for favorable policies toward the first state.[13]

How does foreign commerce affect interstate peace and, by implication, possibly trust? Norman Angell's classic albeit ill-timed study has famously claimed that trade interdependence has a pacifying influence on interstate relations.[14] When states have a large vested stake in their ongoing commercial relations, they are less likely to go to war supposedly because they want to avoid the prospective loss of the benefits from these relations. As thus stated, interstate commerce promotes trust in its weak form. Officials are inclined to believe that their counterparts are adverse to starting or escalating a conflict because its expected costs (from commercial loss) will outweigh its expected benefits. When two states' economies are intertwined, they cannot hurt the other without also hurting themselves. Although the debate continues on this liberal proposition claiming that trade promotes peace, most scholarly opinion seems to have sided with its proponents.[15]

My immediate concern in this chapter, however, is not with the effects of expected commercial or financial loss on states' incentives to engage in conflict. As just mentioned, this hypothesized relationship refers to the weak form of trust—the belief on the part of officials in one state that their counterparts in another state will be constrained from undertaking hostile acts because of the prospect of commercial or financial loss that these counterparts will suffer. Rather, I am interested here in how a decision to enter into dense and deep economic relations may contribute to a state's image of trustworthiness, enabling it to communicate and advertise its peaceful intentions. While A's decision to engage in economic interdependence may be motivated by instrumental or utilitarian considerations, this decision conveys to B, C, and D the impression that A is willing to accept the risks and vulnerabilities entailed by this engagement. We infer trust by asking how an untrustworthy type would have behaved.

If officials are aware of the double-edged nature of economic exchanges described earlier, why do they nevertheless allow their country to become engulfed in such relations with competitors? It is one thing to enter into deep and wide foreign commercial engagement and financial entanglement with those states that one does not expect future conflict. It is quite a different matter when it comes to countries that are actual or potential adversaries—such as between China on the one hand, and Taiwan, Japan, and the United States on the other. In 2014 China was the top trade partner for Taiwan and Japan,[16] and for the first nine months of 2015 it overtook Canada to also become the largest trade partner for the U.S. According to the U.S. Department of Commerce, the value of China-U.S. trade was $441.6 billion during January-September 2015, and it was $438.1 billion for Canada-U.S. during the same period.[17] Given natural concerns about the security externality caused by interstate trade, what can explain this phenomenon? There was of course a time in recent history when trade was practically nonexistent between this pair as well as for China-Taiwan and China-Japan. During the earlier years of the Cold War, the U.S. and its allies had imposed an economic embargo on both the USSR and China.[18]

Recall that Levi and Stoker have argued that trust "involves an individual making herself vulnerable to another individual, group, or institution that has the capacity to do her harm or to betray her."[19] This view suggests that when a state enters into intense commercial or financial relations with a potential adversary, it is knowingly exposing itself to the possibility of severe repercussions. Its willingness to accept such vulnerabilities conveys an important signal—that it trusts the other party and that it can also be trusted. Moreover, the more severe will be the potential adverse economic consequences that a political rupture can inflict on a state, the more credible is the message that its external economic exchanges communicate about its benign intentions. As James

Fearon has argued, the more severe the self-imposed costs should a state decide to defect (in this case, if this state undertakes policies that would wreak havoc to interstate commerce and financial markets, thereby causing grave injuries to itself), the more believable is its reassurance to refrain from this action.[20] The untrustworthy states—those that expect relations to deteriorate or those that are actually planning aggression—would not have accepted these costs. North Korea comes to mind as an extreme example of an economically isolated state that distrusts others —and is distrusted by others.

According to this logic, when states accept and even intensify their economic interdependence, they are investing in their reputation for trusting others and also for being trustworthy themselves. When U.S. (or Japanese or Taiwanese) companies invest in China, and when China purchases a large amount of U.S. treasury bills, they are in effect exchanging hostages. Should political relations between them deteriorate seriously, Beijing can seize foreign assets and operations in China and Washington can repudiate its debt owed to the Chinese. Such acts are the rough equivalent of "going nuclear" in the economic realm, and most analysts are likely to dismiss them as practically unthinkable. This very unthinkability, however, reflects the devastatingly harmful repercussions that are likely to ensue from such action—not the least for the party initiating such action. This being the case, economic interdependence provides an important means to overcome the commitment problem highlighted by Fearon's classic work.[21] This problem refers to doubts states have about each other's future intentions. Why should I believe that you (or your political successor) will not turn against me when circumstances change? By giving and taking hostages in the form of economic exchanges, states reassure each other that they do not harbor evil intentions. Current officials also bind their own successors since policies to reverse existing levels of interdependence can be very costly (if not impossible, as we may learn from President Trump's trade and immigration acrimonies with Mexico and other countries).

This line of reasoning argues that economic exchanges do not *just* have the effect of promoting peace. Peacefully inclined states are inclined to enter into these exchanges in the first place. Thus foreign trade, investment, and loans need to be endogenized in the sense that their existence and level need to be explained in the first place. These transactions reflect current expectations of stable future relations. This is so because as already mentioned, if states expect hostility, they would presumably want to avoid intimate economic relations. The more intertwined their economies become, the heavier will be the potential costs should there be a political rupture. This view extends the "primacy of politics" proposition contending that trade follows the flag and that militarized disputes tend to curtail trade. The argument being advanced here agrees that politics drives commerce. It also suggests that ongoing commercial relations reflect current confidence in friendly, stable interstate relations in the future.

Importantly, as two states accumulate more and more shared economic interests over time—thereby altering their respective domestic coalition of interests and influence in the direction described in the last chapter—their stake in friendly, stable relations becomes larger. Over time it also becomes more difficult to reverse or overturn the prevailing consensus in favor of continued cooperation. The dominant domestic coalitions in the respective countries become partners with a common cause in fostering and further increasing economic openness and stable political relations. Thus economic interdependence has a self-sustaining and self-reinforcing effect by promoting and entrenching transnational coalitions of liberal internationalists.[22] This view does not deny that economic interdependence or what has been called globalization creates losers and winners both domestically and internationally. Moreover, the process just described is not inevitable and reversals are possible when those who perceive themselves to be losing their status or income become politically mobilized. The British referendum to leave the European Union and the popularity of Donald Trump' candidacy in rallying antiestablishment voters in the U.S. provide poignant reminders of this possibility.

It is possible to argue that economic exchanges are undertaken primarily by the private sector and therefore are not always under the exclusive control of governments. Thus, a state may not be able to simply turn on or off foreign trade or investment at its discretion. At the same time, the state is in a powerful position to influence interstate commerce and finance.[23] It can promote, hinder, and even ban outright foreign trade and investments. In the first three decades of the People's Republic, China had hardly any trade with the West or investments from the West because of the latter's official economic boycott directed against it. Thus, the state in fact occupies the commanding heights, and a country's extent of economic exchange with another does reflect to a very large measure their political relationship. When states have in the past been able to set aside their animosity and establish mutual trust and stable peace, this process has typically started with political accommodation and is only followed subsequently by increased economic and social integration.[24] Thus the latter tends to be the effect rather than the cause of official rapprochement and elite reconciliation.

This discussion does not deny that powerful multinational corporations are in a position to influence a state's policies. In this context, it is pertinent to note that whereas the state can bar its own firms from trading with or investing in another country when there is scarcely any ongoing economic relationship (such as in the case of the U.S. economic blockade of China in the 1950s and 1960s), it is another matter for it to try to stop or reverse these transactions after thriving economic relations have already been established (such as for China and the U.S. currently). In the latter situation, it will have to overcome objections from domestic interest groups with an existing large stake in ongoing relations.

Sometimes business people deliberately bypass legal bans in order to trade with and invest in a formal or potential enemy. Taiwan's firms and investors did so in the years before Taipei loosened its ban against such economic transactions with mainland China. Why would they want to run the risk of being prosecuted at home for "sleeping with the enemy,"[25] and also the challenge of facing significant legal and political uncertainties abroad such as with respect to the protection of their property rights and the enforcement of their business contracts?[26] One would surmise that they would not wittingly submit themselves to such jeopardy unless they have good reasons to feel optimistic about taking on such risks. One such reason is plausibly their expectation that their business deals will not be upset by political instability between their home and host countries. Long-term political stability is an especially important consideration when making foreign investments or loans that will take many years to mature, and when they involve immobile assets located in a foreign country (such as those that are dedicated to meet the host country's specific market conditions, consumer tastes, or government regulations) or assets that are subject to the vagaries of a foreign government's policies (such as how its fiscal and monetary policies can affect the value of its outstanding debt). Accordingly, when business people sign a contract for a long-term trade deal or agree to make foreign investments that cannot be easily retrieved, they communicate their confidence in the stability of relations between those countries implicated in this transaction.

This remark about business people running political risks has three important implications. First and as already mentioned on several occasions, officials sometimes misrepresent—or lie. This possibility causes others to question their trustworthiness. In contrast, business people have only one interest which is to make money. They have no incentive to misrepresent, and can be expected to have every incentive to get the price right. In other words, there is no question that their business decisions reflect anything but their honest assessment about the profitability of their transactions.[27] Current market prices reflect their collective judgments and incorporate all available public information, including information on the current and likely future state of relationship between those countries involved in an economic exchange. If Sino-American relations were poised to worsen seriously, the share price of General Motors (which has a large share of China's automobile market) should instantaneously reflect concerns about this prospect and the interest rates offered by U.S. treasury bills (for which China has been a leading foreign buyer) should likewise be affected immediately. Thus, financial markets usually provide an accurate and timely barometer of interstate relations.

Second, economic interdependence tends to discourage posturing and bluffing by officials. Leaders cannot credibly threaten other countries without financial markets taking notice of these threats. They cannot engage in saber-rattling without roiling financial markets. The expected effects that such actions can have in destabilizing markets can thus discourage officials from making empty threats. By making such threats more costly, economic interdependence tends to make officials more honest in their diplomacy and less likely to misrepresent.

Third, financial markets provide telling signs when politicians are engaged in "empty talk," thus enabling observers to distinguish political noise from serious communication. Politicians often engage in rhetoric intended for domestic consumption, such as their statements made during an election campaign or congressional debate. For example, how much should Beijing be concerned when some Taiwanese politicians declare support for the island's *de jure* independence? These politicians' declared preference seems to be contradicted by Taiwan's increasingly heavy and highly asymmetric economic dependency on mainland China, to which it sends over 40% of its exports and 70% of its investments.[28] Today the economies on the two sides of the Taiwan Strait are practically integrated so that Taiwan will suffer devastating economic consequences should bilateral relations deteriorate seriously. My logic suggests that thriving cross-Strait economic relationship provides reassurance to Beijing that Taipei is not about to declare *de jure* independence.[29] Taiwan will have trouble replacing the Chinese market in the event of a political rupture, and its assets and operations on the mainland will be forfeited should this happen. By accepting increasingly intense economic ties with the mainland, Taipei has extended a surety to Beijing not to destabilize their relations. The enormous vulnerability that it has wittingly taken on in becoming heavily and asymmetrically dependent on the Chinese market presents a credible commitment in this regard. By exposing itself to this vulnerability, Taipei is in effect saying by its action that it trusts Beijing and it is also worthy of Beijing's trust. Realists tend to decry the lack of trust in interstate relations and especially between enduring rivals such as this pair, but they cannot explain their deep and dense economic relationship and the fact that Taipei's defense burden (military expenditures as a percent of its gross domestic product) has declined steadily in recent years. This latter trend would also seem to represent a form of costly reassurance.

None of these remarks should be taken to suggest that a serious deterioration of political relations across the Taiwan Strait or in other dyads (e.g., U.S.-Mexico relations) with similarly close commercial ties is impossible. It is possible since states with such ties have been known to go to war (e.g., World Wars I and II). These remarks do imply that when a state in such a deep and dense economic relationship knowingly takes actions that undermine bilateral trade and roil international financial markets, it is serious about escalating a political dispute and that it is highly resolved in advancing its agenda. When this state's actions demonstrate that it is willing to suffer serious economic costs, it is probably not bluffing.

As just mentioned, the stakes that the pertinent parties have in their ongoing economic ties represent a surety for their good behavior. Metaphorically, these stakes constitute "good faith" money deposited in an escrow account. The forfeiture of existing investments and future profits is the penalty to be paid for opportunistic behavior. There need not be an outside third party to impose these costs (such as intervention by the courts or a foreign power), as the dissolution of existing ties between the parties is itself the punishment for a breach of trust. As such, these ties represent "self-enforcing agreements."[30] If the ongoing ties are really valuable to both parties, it will not be in the interest of either to upset them.

Significantly, economic interdependence allows states to invest in their general rather than strictly bilateral reputation. To illustrate further, Beijing has thus far refrained from coercion against Taiwanese firms doing business on the mainland even when cross-Strait relations took a downturn during Chen Shui-bian's administration. The implicit threat directed at these firms as valuable hostages in the event of a political rupture presents an effective leverage so long as it is unexercised. Like the threat of nuclear deterrence, if one has to actually implement one's threat, this threat has failed. The value of hostages depends on their being kept alive. Moreover, any politically motivated retaliation against Taiwan's firms operating on the mainland will damage Beijing's general reputation for offering a hospitable home to foreign investors. Its self-restraint with respect to these firms serves to advertise its trustworthiness *not* to use trade or investment as a political instrument. Conversely, political intimidation directed against them would harm its general reputation for reliability as an economic partner. Thus, a state's action and inaction can both have ramifications beyond its immediate target. Finally, when a state actually undertakes actions that are tantamount to "killing" economic hostages, its behavior suggests that a conflict has reached a very serious stage and perhaps having already escalated to a point of military showdown.

Parenthetically, this discussion suggests that when a state undertakes economic sanction against another, this action has ramifications for third parties similar to those described in the preceding paragraph. When the U.S. freezes the bank accounts of Haitian generals and Iranian officials, imposes economic embargo on Iraq and North Korea, and orders the subsidiary of Dresser Industries based in France not to sell pipeline equipment to the USSR, other states take notice. Potential targets of future U.S. sanction are likely to take precaution and steer their businesses away from U.S. firms. As a result of such anticipatory reaction by prospective targets of economic coercion, future sanctions will encounter diminishing effectiveness.

Significantly and in contrast to China today, the USSR and its communist allies did not have extensive economic ties with the West during the Cold War. The absence of these ties deprived both sides those domestic voices that would have lobbied for moderation during stressful times. It also denied their respective officials the use of economic exchanges to communicate their trustworthiness and if need be, to deliberately disrupt these exchanges and upset the financial markets in order to demonstrate resolve when in crisis situations. Regarding the last point, Gartzke, Li, and Boehmer have argued that economic exchanges offer states an option to convey their resolve in confrontations without having to resort to the usual military displays (by knowingly acting in a manner that causes a market panic with serious injury to its own stakeholders, a state can signal to its counterpart that it is not engaging in "empty talk" and that its threats should be taken seriously).[31] Thus, economic exchanges have this side-benefit of enabling states to communicate resolve without, however, having to engage in military brinksmanship. The more a state can demonstrate its willingness to incur the economic costs caused by market turmoil of its own doing, the more credible is its announced intention. The extent of market turmoil and the ensuing economic costs enable observers to distinguish between political hot air and threats that need to be taken seriously. When interest rates jump and stock prices dive, we can infer that the political events driving these market reactions are probably not bluffs or empty talk.

The fact that China today is deeply embedded in global and regional trade and financial networks is vitally important as these ties serve as shock absorbers when interstate tensions rise. Furthermore, the USSR's economic isolation during the Cold War and even today made it much easier for Western countries to use sanctions and embargoes against it when they want to express serious political disapproval of Moscow's policies. Such attempts at economic denial are more difficult to undertake against China today because of its enmeshment in various interlocking manufacturing networks and entangling financial arrangements. It would be difficult for the U.S. to punish China economically without also hurting its formal or informal allies such as Taiwan, South Korea, and even Japan and Australia due to the ripple effects such action can cause. Thus by promoting interlocking financial interests and transnational production chains, globalization has this pacifying influence on interstate relations. A cannot hurt B, without also hurting C, D, and E and also A's own domestic stakeholders.

Indeed, U.S. economic interests will also be seriously hurt if Sino-American relations were to suffer a serious setback. The intense Sino-American trade, investment, and loan exchanges have been described as "superfusion" by Zachary Karabell.[32] Take the example of China's holding of a massive amount of U.S. debt.[33] As the creditor nation, it is vulnerable to the depreciation of the U.S. dollar compared to other currencies and commodities, and even to a possible debt repudiation in the worst-case scenario. By purchasing these debt instruments (Beijing has been Washington's largest foreign creditor until Japan overtook it recently; in February 2017, Japan owned $1.1 trillion of U.S. debt compared to China's $1.059 trillion),[34] China is in effect subsidizing the U.S. fiscal deficit—and enabling Washington to spend more on its military than it would otherwise have been able to do so without foreign borrowing (Beijing owns about 27.8% of U.S. foreign debt valued at $3.8 trillion, with the U.S. government and domestic investors owning the remaining $19.9 trillion of U.S. national debt).[35] Conversely, by relying on China to finance its public spending Washington is exposing itself to the danger of Beijing using its loans for political leverage and in the worst-case scenario, boycotting the U.S. credit market and even dumping on the market those loans that it already owns. Should financial markets have the slightest suspicion that such possibilities may come to pass, they will be thrown into catastrophic turmoil with U.S. interest rates skyrocketing and the value of its equity shares plummeting. There will also be market panic in China and elsewhere. If political relations were to really deteriorate to the point of armed confrontation, the value of the Swiss franc and commodities such as gold, oil, grain, and even the rates for freight insurance would climb and thus move in the opposite direction of stock and bond prices.

Parenthetically, the amount of U.S. debt owed to China dipped because Beijing sold treasury bills in order to use the proceeds to buy the *yuan* in order to prevent the Chinese currency from depreciating. This is ironic because Donald Trump had accused Beijing of manipulating its currency in order to make Chinese exports cheaper and therefore more competitive abroad. Between mid-2005 and early 2014 the *yuan* had in fact risen 30%. In recent years, Beijing has wanted to let market forces to play a greater role in determining its currency exchange rates and when it has intervened in the marketplace, it has in fact tried to stop the *yuan*'s value from falling.

Importantly, when the financial and commodity markets remain placid when public media and politicians in both countries engage in "America bashing" and "China bashing," this situation provides an impartial indication that things are not as bad as political rhetoric seems to indicate. That the markets have thus far reacted with equanimity to various incidents causing tension in Sino-American relations suggests that their participants think these events are very unlikely to cause a disastrous and irreparable breakdown in these countries' political relations. Indeed, the continuing trend of their rising economic exchanges points to credible mutual reassurance of benign intentions.

Deep and dense economic exchanges advance interstate trust in Russell Hardin's sense of "encapsulated interest."[36] As a creditor to the U.S., Beijing should wish to see the U.S. economy perform well so that Washington will be in a better position to repay its debts and to demand imports from China. Conversely, Washington should hope for the Chinese economy to do well so that it can continue to help funding its credit needs. By the same logic, as major suppliers of raw materials and agricultural commodities to the Chinese market, Australia and Brazil should want to see a vibrant Chinese economy elevating demand for their exports. In this sense, globalization and economic interdependence enable states to develop shared interests and thus to foster their mutual expectation of benign intentions. To paraphrase Hardin, in order for a state to trust another, it must believe that its counterpart is self-motivated to advance its interests.

Finally, the logic presented in this section suggests that financial markets are forward-looking. In late June 2015, two sets of interstate negotiations were facing looming deadlines. One of these pertained to the talks between Tehran and Washington about limiting Iran's nuclear program. Even though the price of oil is subject to many different influences, its direction of change should also offer a hint about what the traders of this commodity think about the probability of a deal being struck as in that event Iran would be able to bring additional supply to the market and therefore oil price would come under increased pressure. The other negotiation involved Greece and its European creditors. Would Greece default and even leave the Eurozone? Greek Prime Minister Alexis Tsipras had urged his countrymen to reject those conditions demanded by foreign creditors to provide Greece with further emergency funding. How would the referendum vote turn out? And should the Greeks reject their creditors' conditions, what would happen then? The movements of credit and security markets disclosed their participants' attempts to anticipate political developments. If these participants were pessimistic about Greece being able to borrow additional funds from abroad, the Euro should come under greater stress and demand for gold should rise. Moreover, Europe's already-depressed interest rates should become even lower and its stock markets (especially the share values of European banks) should fall. Again, these price movements can reflect many different influences, including adjustment to information about pending or anticipated political developments. Since Greece is a rather small economy, the markets' anticipations and reactions also pointed to their larger concerns about other possible developments. For example, would a possible Greek exit from the Eurozone be a harbinger of future contagion, such as those involving other distressed southern European economies? Thus, economic interdependence provides the conditions under which financial markets can present a barometer of current and likely future political relations.

I have argued in this section that when a state pursues economic openness and interdependence, it communicates to its counterparts that it trusts them and deserves to be trusted in return. Conversely, when it publicizes its reservations or objections to this interdependence or globalization (such as shown by President Trump's rhetoric about NAFTA and TPP), it sends the opposite message. This message is not just limited to a specific partner in each transaction, but is broadcast to the international community as a whole as a result of the economic posture that the pertinent state has announced or adopted. In assuming a general posture that favors economic openness and interdependence, it promotes diffuse reciprocity rather than specific reciprocity although the latter, such as in China's relations with Taiwan and the U.S., is clearly also very important. The key takeaway point is of course that China has made a hugely important economic reorientation from pursuing national autarchy and economic isolation to emphasizing international interdependence and openness. While much has been written about this reorientation and the growth it has brought to China's economy, not enough attention has been given to the implications that this transformation has had for building its reputation for trusting other countries and for being trustworthy itself.

Naturally, when multiple countries in a region undertake similar policies of economic openness and interdependence as they have in East Asia, they foster a general climate of mutual reassurance as discussed in the last chapter.[37] Moreover and importantly, states with liberal, open economies tend to converge in their behavior because of the forces of market competition. A state suffers reputational damage and thus loses its credibility in the eyes of market actors when it reneges on its commitment to a liberal, open economy.[38] Its economic competitors can consequently gain an edge on it. This competitive dynamic pushes states to converge in their policies, and sustains the momentum for greater economic interdependence. Additionally and as remarked earlier, economic interdependence creates its own domestic stakeholders and promotes transnational coalitions of liberal internationalists. It thus tends to have a lock-in effect that makes future attempts to reverse economic openness and interdependence more costly and difficult, a development which in turn helps to overcome the commitment problem emphasized by rationalist theorists as an obstacle in developing interstate trust. It is of course possible for voters and politicians to turn against economic openness and interdependence or to at least attach a higher priority to noneconomic issues such as immigration. Whatever may have been their motivation, those who supported Britain's exit from the European Union and those who supported Donald Trump's presidential candidacy communicated a lack of trust in other countries, a sentiment that is reciprocated by foreigners.

INTERNATIONAL ORGANIZATIONS

When a state joins an international organization, it communicates its intention to participate in multilateral diplomacy (just as increased foreign trade and foreign investment convey a favorable attitude toward economic multilateralism and interdependence). It can thus also invest in its reputation for trustworthiness and for trusting others by taking part in such institutions. Those states that favor international engagement and collective diplomacy are more inclined to participate in these institutions in the first place and, moreover, their participation is likely to further foster values conducive to such an outlook. Conversely, when a state declines to join these institutions and either implicitly or explicitly refuses to be bound by its rules and conventions, it shows its distrust of others. Many have criticized Washington's refusal to join Beijing's initiative to create the Asian Infrastructure Investment Bank (AIIB) and its attempts to persuade others (as it turned out unsuccessfully even with respect to its major allies except Japan) to do likewise.[39] The reasons given by the U.S. for its stance, whether sincere or contrived, indicate clearly its lack of trust in China's policies and intentions (with respect to, for example, Beijing's labor standards, human rights, legal transparency, and the manner in which the AIIB's funds will be disbursed in the future). It is seen by Beijing and other capitals as a transparent attempt to check Chinese influence abroad.

This stance has been ineffective in part because of partisan politics and a hamstrung president in Washington. For instance, the 2010 accord to reform the International Monetary Fund's voting formula was stalled in Congress for five years before it acted to ratify. Even though it is the world's second largest economy, China's vote percentage at this institution (3.66) was less than the Benelux countries (Belgium has 2.08% and the Netherlands has 2.34%).[40] Not surprisingly, such delay attenuates foreign confidence about the U.S. ability or willingness to implement even those deals that have already been negotiated with the executive branch. When President Barack Obama first asked the U.S. House of Representatives to approve the so-called fast-track authority to negotiate the Trans-Pacific Partnership (TPP) agreement with other Asia Pacific countries, an arrangement that Beijing again perceives to be designed to contain its rising influence, his request was rebuffed (on June 12, 2015). This vote was quickly reversed within two weeks by a narrow margin but it had already signaled a clear rebuke of the president, especially by many of his fellow Democrats who had voted against the bill. The TPP project also offers an example of how international agreements to expand trade can be very difficult to forge in a democracy, especially in the context of intense partisan contests. Both establishment and antiestablishment candidates in the 2016 U.S. presidential campaign, including Hillary Clinton, Bernie Sanders, and Donald Trump, had declared serious reservations and even outright opposition to this pact. President Trump withdrew the U.S. from it as one of his administration's first acts.

Public statements made by those opposing Obama's fast-track request indicated that they lacked trust in the executive branch's truthfulness and that they also did not trust other states to implement their obligations under a trade agreement. Even when the president did eventually get the authorization that he had sought (a provision that would not allow Congress to amend a proposed deal that he comes up with foreign partners, giving it only the option of approving or rejecting this deal), the contentious nature of the congressional debate communicates deep political division. This division suggests to foreign audiences that the president's negotiation room would be seriously constrained by domestic politics and that any trade deal would face stiff partisan opposition. In an opinion piece commenting on Washington's failed attempt to block the AIIB, former U.S. Secretary of Treasury Lawrence Summers points to a significant challenge posed by U.S. domestic politics, "As long as one of our major parties is opposed to essentially all trade agreements, and the other is resistant to funding international organisations, the US will not be in a position to shape the global economic system."[41]

What does it mean when a state complies with a treaty that it has ratified? Does the treaty cause the state to conform its behavior to its legal obligations, or is this state simply acting on its prior inclination before ratifying the treaty?[42] In other words, does international law (when states accede to international treaties and conventions) have an independent effect on states' behavior, or does it just reflect their preexisting intention? If the latter case, a state is simply doing what it was already disposed to do. When it signs and ratifies a treaty, this action only serves the purpose of advertising its preexisting intention, enabling it to distinguish itself from others that do not share a similar intention. This "screening" effect is consistent with the argument being pursued in this chapter, namely, a state can invest in its reputation for being trustworthy by joining international organizations. Naturally, to the extent that participation in international organizations also has a "constraining" effect on a state's behavior (i.e., to have an independent effect causing it to behave in a way that it would not otherwise have behaved), it makes another important contribution to its trustworthiness. Finally, when a state refuses to ratify international agreements or withdraws from them or when it declines to join international organizations, this decision also speaks to its reputation for being trustworthy and for its disposition to trust others.

Bruce Russett was most responsible for starting the systematic investigation of the relationship between intergovernmental organizations (IGOs) and military conflict.[43] In subsequent years, David Singer and Michael Wallace observe that the number of such organizations tends to increase after each bout of severe conflict,[44] and Harold Jacobsen concludes that "as the number of IGOs has grown, the amount of violence in the global political system has decreased."[45] Jacobson, Reisinger, and Mathers as well as William Domke, however, have found little statistical association between a state's number of IGO membership and its incidence of war involvement, although it seems that a state poised to start war is likely to leave IGOs (e.g., the withdrawal of Germany, Italy, and Japan from the League of Nations).[46] The strongest evidence that *joint* membership in IGOs tends to reduce (pairs of) states' propensity to get into militarized disputes has come from Bruce Russett and his co-authors.[47]

Bruce Russett and John Oneal propose six pathways whereby participation in intergovernmental organizations can promote peace by punishing norm violators, mediating disputes among member states, reducing information and transaction costs for international cooperation, encouraging states to adopt a broader and less myopic definition of their self-interests, socializing officials to embrace prevailing international norms, and fostering mutual responsiveness and new common identities among states.[48] Some of these causal mechanisms, such as those referring to socialization and common identification, are more relevant to promoting the strong form of trust (the next chapter's topic). Others are more relevant to the weak form of trust (such as the deterrent threat of punishing wrongdoers, and this punishment can take the softer form of shaming and shunning), or to those facilitative conditions that would hopefully make disputes easier to resolve and cooperation easier to undertake. As already indicated, my concern in this chapter is more with the signal a state sends to others when it joins and continues to stay in an international institution (or conversely, when it boycotts or withdraws from it).

More specifically, the key idea here is self-selection. When a state becomes a member of an international organization, this decision communicates at least a minimum amount of willingness to submit to this body's rules and procedures and thus to forfeit some amount of national autonomy and freedom of action.[49] Membership in an international organization therefore offers prima facie indication of a state's general disposition to engage in multilateral diplomacy and to coordinate its policies with others in undertaking collective action. It conveys a voluntary entanglement in world affairs and entails a certain loss of decision autonomy as opponents to U.S. membership in the League of Nations had argued. By even just implicitly rejecting a unilateral or isolationist approach of "going it alone," this membership decision signifies a state's investment in developing and participating in what Robert Keohane and Lisa Martin have described as the focal points of international cooperation.[50]

In his study of different U.S. leaders' attitudes toward joining the League of Nations, the United Nations, and NATO, Brian Rathbun shows the importance of social psychological motivations at work.[51] A disposition in favor of multilateralism, as indicated by support for such international security institutions, reflects a person's generalized trust, a belief in diffuse (as opposed to specific) reciprocity (that others can be expected to reciprocate one's cooperation and goodwill, even when they encounter prisoners' dilemma situations).[52] By definition, diffuse reciprocity does not depend on an expectation of a specific quid pro quo between two individuals or states.[53] Those who have a disposition to extend generalized trust are likely to be multilateralists inclined to pursue international cooperation even though this means taking on the risks of defection, entrapment, and free riding by others. In contrast, unilateralists and isolationists (who lack this generalized trust) are less willing to accept such risks. This point is germane to the semi-strong form of trust because multilateralists are optimists in the context of our earlier discussion of Axelrod's work.[54] When states pursue multilateralism such as joining international organizations, they knowingly take on binding legal commitments that limit their future policy discretion. Parenthetically, President Trump has voiced his skepticism of multilateral agreements and has indicated a preference to negotiate (or renegotiate) trade deals on a bilateral basis.

In Rathbun's analysis,[55] he recalls John Ruggie's definition of "qualitative multilateralism" as "an institutional form which coordinates relations among three or more states on the basis of 'generalized' principles of conduct—that is, principles which specify appropriate conduct for a class of actions, without regard to the particularistic interests of the parties or the strategic exigencies that may exist in any specific occurrence."[56] Generalized trust is required for the pursuit of this multilateralism because it is impossible to make strategic calculations due to the great uncertainties about various possible future contingencies and limited knowledge about the preferences and intentions of the large number of actors involved. For example, a commitment to the principle of collective defense entails such generalized trust since states do not know at the time of taking on this commitment which of them will be victimized by aggression (or for that matter, which one will be identified as an aggressor in the future) and the specific circumstances under which they will be called upon to act on their commitment.

Significantly and as explained previously, generalized trust reflects a judgment about other people's character (such as a belief in their willingness to honor commitments and to eschew opportunism). In contrast, strategic or instrumental trust is specific to a situation, and it is based on a calculation about a particular exchange of benefits. Generalized trust is moralistic and based on the logic of appropriateness. Rathbun, however, shows that U.S. leaders who shared a common identification with the Western Europeans had reached very different conclusions about the desirability of joining international security organizations when faced with the same structural circumstances but given their different disposition to extend generalized trust.[57] Thus according to him, common identification is not sufficient to encourage multilateralism but generalized trust is. Space limitation does not permit a more extensive discussion of the question of causal precedence: whether some minimal amount of trust is required to develop a common identity, or whether this development needs to occur before trust can be built.[58]

Generalized trust obviously fosters and sustains security communities and the strong form of trust, topics to be taken up in the next chapter. In the present context, it suffices to note that those disposed to trust generally are optimists who are willing to take a chance in believing in others' trustworthiness and they are also inclined to invest in their reputation for being nice (being optimistic and nice in the sense described earlier in the context of Axelrod's research).[59] Naturally, saying so does not deny that the particular form that multilateralism and generalized trust takes can be limited to only those "like us" and not all others.

A decision to join and participate in an international organization is in and of itself a marker of a state's willingness to trust others. It also shows that it can be trusted by others, indicating its willingness to work with other states rather than acting as a "lone ranger." Significantly, this remark does not mean that the strong and powerful will therefore eschew acting outside an international organization such as the United Nations, whether alone or multilaterally with a "coalition of the willing." A threat to exercise this outside option can be used strategically by a powerful state like the U.S. to open bargaining space and gain international endorsement of its preferred policy such as with respect to military intervention or peacekeeping in former Yugoslavia and the Middle East.[60] China's initiatives to launch the AIIB and the BRICS (Brazil, Russia, India, China, and South Africa) bank and currency pool also illustrate the pursuit of outside options (with respect to the International Monetary Fund and the World Bank).

Naturally, when states sign on to join those institutions entailing deeper and more enduring commitments having the effect of significantly infringing their sovereignty and limiting their future policy options, such as those regimes that have the quality of a constitutional pact,[61] their decision communicates a serious pledge to bind themselves to the pertinent norms and principles. These states can of course still break their promises, and realists are fond of reminding people about the fragility and unreliability of international organizations.[62] But such breach of trust is not without reputational costs as states take on legal obligations in order to enhance the credibility of their commitments to start with.[63] And as argued already, the severity of this possible penalty provides an *ex ante* indication of a state's intention to refrain from voluntary defection. Moreover and importantly, the penalty for noncompliance need not be imposed by just the pertinent international institutions or retaliation by other states. This penalty and therefore the mechanism to enforce compliance can come from market repercussions and domestic backlash.[64] For instance, many foreign lenders will boycott Greece if it defaults on its debts, and domestic conservation groups will protest against their own government's disregard of its treaty obligations to protect the environment.

Judith Kelley's study shows that some states that had ratified the treaty to join the International Criminal Court went on subsequently to sign a bilateral agreement with Washington, pledging not to turn over Americans accused of war crimes to this court.[65] This agreement is seen by many to be inconsistent with these states' earlier commitment to the ICC. However, many other states rebuffed the U.S. effort to get them to sign this bilateral agreement. The latter states therefore continued to honor their ICC treaty commitment even under heavy U.S. pressure. Kelley's research indicates that some states do take their treaty commitments seriously. International law constrains the behavior of those states that value highly the rule of law and their reputation for keeping their international commitments.[66] It appears that in this case as well as in the case of states pledging to the International Monetary Fund to refrain from placing restrictions on their current account transactions, democracies are not necessarily better at keeping their international commitments but those with a strong record for the rule of law are.[67] Significantly and as already remarked, the repercussions for violating preexisting commitments do not have to originate directly or primarily from the pertinent institutions or even from the other member states. Domestic groups, transnational coalitions, and financial markets also have an interest in monitoring states' compliance behavior and a capacity to discipline their conduct and punish their transgressions.

Kelley's article is instructive in two other ways.[68] First, support for the ICC provides a revealing test about whether a state is serious about its declared commitment to human rights and universal jurisdiction to punish war criminals. Do its deeds correspond to its words? The U.S. and China have both decided to remain outside of the Rome Statute creating this court. As just noted, Washington has furthermore lobbied strenuously all other states to agree not to turn over Americans to the court under any circumstance (even though such a low-probability event would not come to pass unless a government fails to prosecute its own citizens for alleged wrongdoing). The second significance of this episode is that many states resisted this U.S. pressure even when they can expect no material gains from supporting this treaty and indeed even when they can expect considerable material losses resulting from the U.S. threat to sanction them for noncooperation. Their behavior therefore suggests that contrary to realists' expectations, at least some states do sometimes prioritize norms and principles and value their treaty commitments more than their material interests. Those that have remained steadfast in honoring their treaty obligations even under external pressure and the threat of material deprivation are obviously more trustworthy than others that have not. As mentioned earlier, the choices states make in stressful situations are more informative about their true reliability or trustworthiness.

This discussion suggests that intergovernmental organizations can make a passive contribution to peace and in this sense, makes a stronger claim than Boehmer, Gartzke, and Nordstrom's view that "the presence of IGOs in and of themselves does relatively little to influence international conflict."[69] Being a member of such organizations will expose a state to greater reputational costs for its transgressions than otherwise (if it were otherwise, Washington and Beijing would have less reason to object to joining the ICC, for example). Intergovernmental organizations can also contribute passively to conflict avoidance in other ways such as by increasing interaction opportunity among their member states and extending the relevant officials' time horizon (the shadow of the future). In addition, these organizations can play an active role in encouraging their member states to conclude and comply with international agreements.[70] They can do so by mitigating information asymmetries among those states involved in a dispute and helping them to overcome concerns about the commitment problem, impediments that can otherwise prevent them from reaching an agreement. For example, by providing their good offices as an impartial observer and even as an enforcer of cease-fire agreements, international agencies can help civil-war combatants to end their fighting and settle for peace.[71] Finally, frequent contact among those states that interact in intergovernmental organizations can have a socialization or information effect, making it more possible for them to develop similar interests.[72]

Boehmer, Gartzke, and Nordstrom argue rightly that not all international institutions are the same. Some are more likely to have an impact on conflict avoidance and abatement than others.[73] Those that are structurally developed, consist of cohesive members, and have a strong mandate should have a greater impact. Of course, organizations with these characteristics are formed by those states that are likely to have substantial goodwill toward and trust in each other to begin with. They are also subsequently likely to attract additional members with similar traits, thus again indicating a selection process reflecting decisions by both the existing members and candidates for new membership. The evidence from David Bearce and Stacy Bondanella tends to support the view that only the more structurally developed institutions are likely to have an impact on shaping their member states' evolving interests as revealed by their voting record in the United Nations General Assembly.[74] Conversely, loose organizations with informal procedures are less likely to have an independent effect in promoting shared interests among their member states.

When a state becomes deeply embedded in an international organization with structurally more developed characteristics such as those described by Boehmer, Gartzke, and Nordstrom,[75] membership in it indicates this state's evident trustworthiness through self-binding. Germany's membership in NATO and the European Union provides such reassurance to its partners. The other European states are reassured that Berlin cannot easily make a quick "break out" to revive militarism without uprooting those institutional ties connecting them and thus setting off alarms long before such an attempt is likely to pay off. Therefore, Germany's being integrated and enmeshed in various European institutions is a mark of its trustworthiness. To some extent, Japan and South Korea's bilateral alliances with the U.S. have a similar effect. By integrating their armed forces with the Americans and submitting themselves to a joint military command under U.S. control, these countries signal to their neighbors that they will not "go it alone" (such as developing their own nuclear weapons). Significantly, in the current context of references to Germany, Japan, and South Korea, these countries' ability to pursue certain policies such as developing nuclear weapons and operating an independent military force is not in doubt. Their institutional affiliations and commitments gain importance for foreign audiences because these ties provide credible information about their future intentions (such as *not* to pursue their own nuclear weapons or independent armed forces even though they have an ability to do so). In this way, membership and participation in international organizations can transmit useful information to other states and their respective domestic publics.[76]

Parenthetically, in contrast to the multilateral nature of NATO, Washington has pursued a hub-and-spokes approach in conducting its alliance relationships in East Asia where these ties have been predominantly bilateral arrangements connecting each Asian country to the U.S.[77] Thus, Japan has been less embedded institutionally in East Asia than Germany has been in Western Europe. This fact and the more general phenomenon of thinner and shallower institutional networks in the former region reflect and also contribute to its greater trust deficit.

To continue on the theme that international organizations can provide reassurance and enhance trust in a passive fashion, consider the fact that military "intervention without some effort to gain [U.N. Security Council's] approval is now virtually obsolete, a remarkable feature of contemporary international relations that merits both theoretical and policy attention."[78] Why would powerful states, especially the U.S., bother with gaining U.N. authorization before undertaking coercive diplomacy when they clearly have the capabilities to carry out such policies without this organization's support and when the transaction and coordination costs involved in seeking U.N. authorization and, if successful, in organizing a multinational effort may be considerably larger than any additional material gains to be expected from this effort? It is plausible to suggest that the state considering this coercion, such as the U.S. vis-à-vis Iraq or Serbia, would gain legitimacy for its policy if it had obtained U.N. approval. The argument being pursued here, however, suggests another separate effect, one that is related to the information communicated to other states (and their informed publics) that are not the direct targets of the coercion being considered. This effect stems from the coercing state's instrumental or strategic calculation, and not its moral or ethical consideration.

When the U.N. Security Council is asked to authorize the use of military force by the U.S., Washington is making a choice to involve Russia and China (among others) which are likely to be skeptical about U.S. intentions. A choice to channel such a decision through the Security

Council reflects self-constraint by the U.S. since this approach will impose additional transaction and coordination costs on Washington and expose its plans and motivations to greater scrutiny. It would even run the risk of being rebuffed. By choosing to accept these costs and run this risk, the U.S. allays foreign concerns that it may have ulterior motives, and communicates that it instead has benign intentions. A choice to work under U.N. auspices also reassures Moscow and Beijing since they will now have some influence over the military operation if the resolution to authorize force is approved.[79] Whether or not this request to use force is approved, the U.S. makes a gain in its reputation for playing according to the rules and thus for being trustworthy in the eyes of other states. Moreover, if Russia and China go along with the resolution to authorize military intervention, their support conveys critical information to the leaders and citizens of other countries, including the American people,[80] indicating that the proposed action is legitimate and genuinely popular and that it is more likely to succeed (now with Russian and Chinese endorsement) than otherwise. Because Moscow and Beijing are presumably biased in not trusting Washington's motivations, support or endorsement coming from these usually more skeptical sources should be more reassuring to other countries and their citizens than typically friendly sources such as Washington's traditional allies, reassuring in the sense that Washington's declared motivations are probably sincere and not phony.[81] In this way international organizations can play another role, both active and passive, in building trust. Parenthetically, when a state gains U.N. authorization for one ostensible purpose but then applies it as a carte blanche for another purpose (e.g., turning back North Korean aggression versus unifying Korea under an anticommunist government, restoring Kuwaiti independence versus destroying Iraq's armed forces; imposing a no-fly zone in Libya to protect civilians versus engineering a regime change) in a bait-and-switch move, its reputation suffers and it will face greater difficulty in gaining similar authorization in the future.

There was a time when China had practically no presence in international organizations, as it belonged literally to less than a handful of them. It was not, for example, a member of the United Nations or any of its affiliated organizations before 1971.[82] Parenthetically and quite ironically considering its current policy on Taiwan, Washington had argued against China's membership in the United Nations on the grounds that the government in Taipei rather than Beijing was the legal representative of *all* of China. Since the 1970s, however, China has increasingly raised its foreign profile so that its presence in intergovernmental organizations has caught up with that of its peers.[83] Although it once advocated vigorous rejection of international arms control as a ploy by the powerful countries to dominate the weak ones, Beijing has changed its views since the 1960s and has ratified various international agreements aimed at arms limitation, including those intended to discourage the spread of nuclear weapons. If, as I have argued, a state's membership in international institutions and its formal commitment to international treaties can be taken as an investment in its reputation to play nice and according to the rules of collective diplomacy, China has certainly travelled a great distance in the last forty or so years. Whereas Beijing had ostracized and was in turn ostracized by various intergovernmental organizations (including the United Nations) in the earlier years of the People's Republic, it has more recently become an active participant in them. Just as with its switch from economic isolation and autarchy to economic openness and interdependence, there has been a huge transformation in China's presence in and its attitudes toward international organizations. In both respects, the amount of change has been very significant. The logic presented here would accordingly suggest that over time it has become more inclined to trust other states and has also deserved more trust from them.

Compared to its strong support of the United Nations in this organization's earlier years, the U.S. has become more disenchanted with international organizations over the years such as when it walked out of the International Labor Organization (ILO) and the United Nations Educational, Scientific and Cultural Organization (UNESCO). Voting in the U.N. General Assembly and Security Council usually involves symbolic expressions and strategic posturing. This said, Beijing is usually in the majority voting coalition in both bodies whereas Washington is by comparison more often in the minority.[84] Although in the first two and half decades of the United Nations the USSR was diplomatically isolated and had cast most of the vetoes in the Security Council in order to block resolutions repugnant to it, the U.S. has increasingly resorted to this means in more recent decades. A veto is by definition a decision by a minority of one to block or thwart a majority's wishes. Between October 1971 (when China joined the United Nations) and February 2017, the USSR/Russia had cast 25 vetoes, China 11, and the U.S. 78.[85] One finds the same voting pattern in the General Assembly where 511,292 votes were cast by individual states during 1974–2008, with 83.7% of them being yes votes, 4.6% no votes, and 11.7% abstentions. Thus, there was overwhelming support for those resolutions that came up for a formal vote. Compared to the aforementioned benchmark, China's record was 88.1% (yes), 2.8% (no) and 9.1% (abstentions) respectively and the corresponding figures for the U.S. were 20.2%, 56.2% and 23.6% respectively.[86] When Christopher Primiano and Jun Xiang compare China with France, Britain, and the U.S. on their voting record on U.N. resolutions pertaining to even *just* the issue of human rights, they find to their surprise that Beijing has supported these resolutions more frequently than the other three.[87] By definition, the extent to which a state finds itself usually aligned with the majority of states voting in support of U.N. resolutions is generally indicative of its being inside the international consensus. Conversely, those that find themselves often in the minority are more outside of this consensus. By this measure, Beijing has been more often within the international consensus on various issues voted on by U.N. members than Washington. Erik Voeten's analysis of roll-call votes on those issues that Washington has declared to be important to its foreign policy agenda suggests that the gap between U.S. preferences and those of the rest of the world had widened significantly even in the decade preceding George W. Bush's administration.[88]

Changing *levels* of participation in international organizations and support for them and for various international conventions described in this discussion are noteworthy. The *direction* of such overtime change is also noteworthy. When states persist in their customary behavior, this stasis is unremarkable as it points to a continuation of their existing policy orientation. But when they break from this pattern and even reverse it, this change is more informative and points to a new orientation or attitude. Beijing and Washington's involvements with the United Nations have seemingly evolved in two opposite directions, with the former becoming more supportive of and the latter less supportive of it over time. Washington's 2003 invasion of Iraq signals a particularly sharp departure from an emergent international consensus that states should seek U.N. approval before they undertake foreign military action. Moreover, another decision by the George W. Bush administration communicates an important reversal of the international norm to limit and control armament. This unilateral decision by the U.S. to withdraw from the ABM Treaty in 2002 and to concomitantly build missile defense systems launched a new era for weapons competition. It announced a U.S. intention to not just maintain nuclear equivalence but to pursue strategic superiority. The U.S. of course has the legal right to withdraw from the ABM treaty just as Japan, Germany, and Italy had the right to leave the League of Nations and North Korea to abandon the Nuclear Nonproliferation Treaty. The focus here, however, is not on the legality of such decisions but the respective governments' general policy intentions and postures communicated by these decisions. During recent decades, China has gradually altered its position from opposing international conventions intended to limit and control nuclear weapons to joining and supporting these efforts. Besides signing on to the relevant international treaties, it has participated as a member of the minilateral negotiations seeking to curtail Iran and North Korea's nuclear programs.

CONCLUDING REMARKS

People tend to think about interstate relations as football or chess matches which are contests producing a single winner. "But the world is rarely like that. In a vast range of situations mutual cooperation can be better for *both* sides than mutual defection. The key to doing well lies not in overcoming others, but in eliciting their cooperation."[89] China's recent ascent has been driven primarily by its rapid economic growth, and this growth has in turn been based on China's increasing economic integration with the rest of the world. That is, China's economic growth has been premised on its becoming more embedded in the global economy. The implication of this development should be clear in light of Axelrod's remark. As Nathan and Scobell observe, China "will not prosper like nineteenth-century colonial powers by exploiting and impoverishing other societies. ... Unlike Spain competing with Portugal in the sixteenth century, Holland competing with Spain in the sixteenth and seventeenth centuries, or Britain competing with France in the nineteenth century, China will not get ahead if its rivals do not. Their economic decline or destruction will not help China."[90] This view challenges the zero-sum perspective that motivates the typical discourse on Sino-American relations.

In this chapter, I have examined two important avenues to elicit interstate trust and promote interstate cooperation. They are economic interdependence and international organizations. Significantly, these two phenomena have a synergistic relationship. In their research on the so-called Kantian tripod (which claims that a republican form of government, a cosmopolitan disposition, and a confederation of like-minded governments contribute to peace among states), Russett and Oneal show that economic interdependence and participation in inter-governmental organizations are statistically associated with each other and with democracy.[91] All three variables make a separate and direct contribution to dampening the incidence of militarized disputes for politically relevant pairs of states. Each of these three variables also makes an indirect contribution to peace as a result of its positive effect on the other two. Thus, these variables appear to form a constellation of factors that reinforce each other and also interstate peace.

Other analyses have further shown that, for example, newly democratic regimes seek membership in regional organizations in order to demonstrate their commitment to continue political reform by locking in themselves and their successors to this project.[92] Supporters of liberal economic reform can likewise invoke international organizations to legitimize their policy position by contending that economic openness and interdependence signify China's new status as a responsible great power. International norms and institutions can be used strategically against domestic opponents to market reform, and China's international obligations are deployed to promote and lock in this reform.[93] Naturally, the causal arrow can also point in the other direction so that increasing economic openness and interdependence become a justification for more active participation in a larger number of international organizations. The combined effect of this synergism is to enhance the prospect for building interstate confidence and hence trust.

I began this chapter by asking a counterfactual question about Sino-American relations. If these two countries had held deep and abiding distrust of each other, would they have chosen to enter into those economic transactions that characterize their relationship today? I argue that by entering into a very close economic relationship that will entail severe costs in the event of a political rupture, these countries have been investing in their reputation for being both trusting and trustworthy. Naturally, countries with close economic relationships have been known to go to war as the belligerents of World War I did. At the same time, a close economic relationship should attenuate the observation made in Chapter 2, suggesting that there are strong, historically-based reasons for Beijing and Washington to distrust each other's intentions. Their "superfused" economies should temper this trust deficit. This condition also distinguishes current Sino-American relations from Soviet-American relations during the Cold War

Moreover, there are far more Chinese students who are studying (or have done so) in the U.S. than Russians now or in the past. There is thus another important linkage, especially because many Chinese residents in the U.S. are the children of high-ranking officials. They and other Chinese from affluent background own substantial assets in the U.S. This phenomenon in turn provides another example of hostage giving, indicating the level of trust that Beijing has in Washington. Presumably, China's leading officials would not send their offspring to study in the U.S. and affluent Chinese would not invest heavily in real estate in New York and California if they expected any potential severe turbulence in the two countries' relationship.

In the next chapter, I will discuss how Chinese officials' habits and beliefs and even perhaps their values might have been transformed as a result of their experience in participating in international organizations and interacting with their foreign counterparts. For now, it is important to note that the trend of rising Chinese membership and participation in international organizations is unmistakable. As already remarked, this increase over time shows an *ex ante* commitment to multilateral diplomacy. This observation does not imply that Beijing can therefore be trusted or that it will eschew the use of its power in seeking outcomes advantageous to it (which country does not?). It does, however, suggest an investment in Beijing's reputation to play nice and according to common rules. This investment is pertinent to a question raised earlier. Is a rising power more likely to defy and undermine international norms because it now has more capabilities to do so, or is it more likely to act responsibly because it now has a larger stake in the existing international order? Comparing Beijing's rhetoric and conduct during the Maoist years with its behavior today, the evidence points rather decisively in favor of the latter proposition. China's bellicosity was much more evident and its involvement in international organizations was much more limited in the first three decades of the People's Republic at a time when it was much weaker than now. It has moderated its rhetoric and engaged in more active multilateral diplomacy even while its power has grown significantly in recent decades. Therefore and at least in this respect, the direction of the pertinent trends belies the proposition that a rising China will destabilize the existing international order. Still, there are those who are cautious, skeptical, and even downright pessimistic about ongoing power shifts that in their view can or will lead to a Sino-American war.[94]

As Alastair Iain Johnston has concluded, "In sum, it is not a stretch to characterize Chinese diplomacy since the 1990s as being, in relative terms, more status quo-oriented than at any period since 1949. That is, China has joined most international institutions that regulate interstate behavior; inside the institutions, it generally has not tried to undermine the functioning or purposes of these institutions...."[95] Since these words were written, these tendencies have continued and become stronger. Moreover, recent developments appear to point in the opposite direction for the U.S. during the George W. Bush administration and prospectively more so in a Donald J. Trump administration. Current U.S. public opinion on foreign relations appears to be deeply divided and subject to sharp swings. Did the George W. Bush administration's foreign policies and would those of the Donald J. Trump administration represent an aberration of the traditional U.S. support for international conventions and organizations? In other words, should some of my earlier observations be taken to reflect a temporary departure from the historical orientation of successive U.S. governments? This is a large empirical question that cannot be taken up in this book but I will return to it briefly in the next chapter.

NOTES

1. Axelrod, *The Evolution.*
2. Michael Tomz, *Reputation and International Cooperation: Sovereign Debt across Three Centuries* (Princeton, NJ: Princeton University Press, 2007).
3. Axelrod, *The Evolution.*
4. Robert O. Keohane, "Reciprocity in International Relations," *International Organization* 40, no. 1 (1986): 1–27.
5. Axelrod, *The Evolution.*
6. Putnam, *Making Democracy Work,* and *Bowling Alone.*
7. Ikenberry, *After Victory.*
8. Robert O. Keohane and Joseph S. Nye, *Power and Interdependence: World Politics in Transition* (Boston: Little, Brown, 1977).
9. Albert O. Hirschman, *National Influence and the Structure of Foreign Trade* (Berkeley: University of California Press, 1945).
10. Joseph Grieco, "Anarchy and the Limits of Cooperation: A Realist Critique of the Newest Liberal Institutionalism," *International Organization* 42, no. 3 (1988): 485–507; and James D. Morrow, "When Do 'Relative Gains' Impede Trade?" *Journal of Conflict Resolution* 41, no. 1 (1997): 12–37.
11. Samir Amin, *Accumulation of a World Scale: A Critique of the Theory of Underdevelopment* (New York: Monthly Review Press, 1974); Paul A. Baran, *The Political Economy of Growth* (New York: Monthly Review Press, 1957); Fernando H. Cardoso, "Associated-Dependent Growth: Theoretical and Practical Implications," in *Authoritarian Brazil: Origins, Policies and Future,* ed. Alfred Stepan (New Haven, CT: Yale University Press, 1973), 142–178; and Andre G. Frank, *Capitalism and Underdevelopment in Latin America* (New York: Monthly Review Press, 1967).
12. Putnam, "Diplomacy and Domestic Politics."
13. Lobell, "The Second Face."
14. Norman Angell, *The Great Illusion: A Study of The Relation of Military Power to National Advantage* (London: Putnam's Sons, 1913).
15. Katherine Barbieri, *The Liberal Illusion: Does Trade Promote Peace?* (Ann Arbor: University of Michigan Press, 2002); Erik Gartzke, Quan Li, and Charles Boehmer, "Investing in the Peace: Economic Interdependence and International Conflict," *International Organization* 55, no. 2 (2001): 391–438; Edward D. Mansfield and Brian Pollins, eds., *Economic Inter-*

dependence and International Conflict (Ann Arbor: University of Michigan Press, 2003); and Bruce M. Russett and John R. Oneal, *Triangulating Peace: Democracy, Interdependence, and International Organizations* (New York: Norton, 2001).

16. "Top U.S. Trade Partners," U.S. Department of Commerce (2016), accessed June 2, 2017, http://www.trade.gov/mas/ian/build/groups/public/@tg_ian/documents/webcontent/tg_ian_003364.pdf.

17. Nan Zhong, "China Becomes Top U.S. Trade Partner" *China Daily* (January 10, 2015), accessed June 2, 2017, usa.chinadaily.com.cn/business/2015-11/06/content_22385828.htm.

18. Michael Mastanduno, *Economic Containment: CoCom and the Politics of East-West Trade* (Ithaca, NY: Cornell University Press, 1992).

19. Levi and Stoker, "Political Trust," 476.

20. Fearon, "Signaling Foreign Policy Interests."

21. Fearon, "Rationalist Explanations."

22. Legro, *Rethinking the World,* and "What China Will Want;" and Solingen, *Regional Orders,* and "Pax Asiatica."

23. Stephen D. Krasner, *Defending the National Interest: Raw Materials Investments and U.S. Foreign Policy* (Princeton, NJ: Princeton University Press, 1978).

24. Kupchan, *How Enemies Become Friends.*

25. Katherine Barbieri and Jack S. Levy, "Sleeping with the Enemy: The Impact of War on Trade," *Journal of Peace Research* 36, no. 4 (1999): 463–479; and Paul A. Papayoanou and Scott L. Kastner, "Sleeping with the (Potential) Enemy: Assessing the U.S. Policy of Engagement with China," *Security Studies* 9, no.1/2 (2000): 157–187.

26. Steve Chan, "Commerce between Rivals: Realism, Liberalism, and Credible Communication across the Taiwan Strait," *International Relations of the Asia-Pacific* 9, no. 3 (2009): 435–467; Scott L. Kastner, "When Do Conflicting Political Relations Affect International Trade?" *Journal of Conflict Resolution* 51, no. 4 (2007): 664–688, and *Political Conflict and Economic Interdependence across the Taiwan Strait and Beyond* (Stanford, CA: Stanford University Press, 2009); and Tse-kang Leng, *The Taiwan-China Connection: Democracy and Development across the Taiwan Straits* (Boulder, CO: Westview, 1996).

27. Gartzke, Li, and Boehmer, "Investing in the Peace."

28. Chan, "Commerce between Rivals."

29. Ibid.

30. Beth Yarbrough and Robert Yarbrough, "Reciprocity, Bilateralism, and Economic 'Hostages': Self-Enforcing Agreements in International Trade," *International Studies Quarterly* 30, no. 1 (1986): 7–21.

31. Gartzke, Li, and Boehmer, "Investing in the Peace."

32. Karabell, *Superfusion.*

33. Chan, "Money Talks;" and Drezner, "Bad Debts."

34. Kimberly Amadeo, "U.S. Debt to China: How Much Does It Own?" accessed May 31, 2017, https://www.thebalance.com/u-s-debt-to-china-how-much-does-it-own-3306355.

35. Ibid.

36. Hardin, *Trust and Trustworthiness.*

37. Solingen, "Pax Asiatica."

38. Beth A. Simmons, "International Law and State Behavior: Commitment and Compliance in International Monetary Affairs," *American Political Science Review* 94, no. 4 (2000): 819–835.

39. Robert Keatley, "China's AIIB Challenge: How Should America Respond?" *The National Interest* (April 18, 2015), accessed June 2, 2017, nationalinterest.org/feature/americas-big-strategic-blunder-not-joining-chinas-aiib-12666; Stephen S. Roach, Zha Daojiong, Scott Kennedy, and Patrick Chovanec, "Washington's Big China Screw-up," *Foreign Policy* (March 26, 2015), accessed June 2, 2017, http://foreignpolicy.com/2015/03/26/washingtons-big-china-screw-up-aiib-asia-infrastructure-investment-bank-china-containment-chinafile/; Lawrence Summers, "Time US Leadership Woke Up to New Economic Era," *Financial Time* (April 5, 2015), accessed June 2, 2017, http://www.ft.com/cms/s/2/a0a0 1306-d887-11e4-ba53-00144feab7de.html#axzz3XJUVoUHN; and Hugh White, "AIIB: China outsmarts US diplomacy on Asia bank," *The Age* (March 31, 2015), accessed June 2, 2017, http://www.theage.com.au/comment/aiib-china-outsmarts-us-diplomacy-on-asia-bank-20150330-1 maoq7.html.

40. "IMF Voting: Who has the Power?" *The Guardian* (May 19, 2011), accessed June 2, 2017, www.theguardian.com/business/2011/may/19/imf-voting-who-has-the-power-dominique-strauss-kahn.

41. Summers, "Time U.S. Leadership."

42. Judith Kelley, "Who Keeps International Commitments and Why? The International Criminal Court and Bilateral Nonsurrender Agreements," *American Political Science Review* 101, no. 3 (2007): 573–589; Michaela Mattes and Greg Vonnahme, "Contracting for Peace: Do Nonaggression Pacts Reduce Conflict?" *Journal of Politics* 73, no. 4 (2010): 925–938; Sim-

mons, "International Law;" Beth A. Simmons and Daniel J. Hopkins, "The Constraining Power of International Treaties: Theory and Method," *American Political Science Review* 99, no. 4 (2005): 623–631; and Jana von Stein, "Do Treaties Constrain or Screen? Selection Bias and Treaty Compliance," *American Political Science Review* 99, no. 4 (2005): 611–622.

43. Bruce M. Russett, *International Regions and the International System: A Study in Political Ecology* (Chicago: Rand McNally, 1967).

44. J. David Singer and Michael D. Wallace, "Intergovernmental Organizations and the Preservation of Peace, 1816–1964: Some Bivariate Relationships," *International Organization* 24, no. 3 (1970): 520–547.

45. Harold K. Jacobson, *Networks of Interdependence: International Organizations and the Global Political System* (New York: Knopf, 1984), 199.

46. Harold K. Jacobson, William Reisinger, and Todd Mathers, "National Entanglements in International Governmental Organizations," *American Political Science Review* 80, no. 1 (1986), 156; and William K. Domke, *War and the Changing Global System* (New Haven, CT: Yale University Press, 1988), 148.

47. Russett and Oneal, *Triangulating Peace*; and Bruce M. Russett, John R. Oneal, and David R. Davis, "The Third Leg of the Kantian Tripod for Peace: International Organizations and Militarized Disputes: 1950–1985," *International Organization* 52, no. 3 (1998): 441–467.

48. Russett and Oneal, *Triangulating Peace*, 444–449.

49. Steve Chan, "Can't Get No Satisfaction? The Recognition of Revisionist States," *International Relations of the Asia Pacific* 4, no. 2 (2004): 207–238.

50. Robert O. Keohane and Lisa L. Martin, "The Promise of Institutionalist Theory," *International Security* 20, no. 1 (1995): 39–51.

51. Rathbun, *Trust in International Cooperation*.

52. Ibid., 5.

53. Keohane, "Reciprocity in International Relations."

54. Axelrod, *The Evolution*.

55. Rathbun, *Trust in International Cooperation*, 19.

56. John G. Ruggie, "Multilateralism: The Anatomy of an Institution," *International Organization* 46, no. 3 (1992), 571.

57. Rathbun, *Trust in International Cooperation*.

58. Adler and Barnett, *Securities Communities*; Vincent C. Keating and Nicholas J. Wheeler, "Concepts and Practices of Cooperative Security: Building Trust in the International System," in *The Legacy of the Cold War: Perspectives on Security, Cooperation and Conflict*, eds. Vojtech

Mastny and Zhu Liqun (Lanham, MD: Lexington Books, 1998), 57–78; and Wendt, *Social Theory*.

59. Axelrod, *The Evolution*.
60. Erik Voeten, "The Political Origins of the UN Security Council's Ability to Legitimize the Use of Force," *International Organization* 59, no. 3 (2005): 527–557.
61. Ikenberry, *After Victory*.
62. John J. Mearsheimer, "The False Promise of International Institutions," *International Security* 19, no. 3 (1994/95): 5–49.
63. Sartori, *Deterrence by Diplomacy*.
64. Xinyuan Dai, "Why Comply? The Domestic Constituency Mechanism," *International Organization* 59, no. 2 (2005): 369–398; and Simmons, "International Law."
65. Kelley, "Who Keeps."
66. Ibid.
67. Simmons, "International Law."
68. Kelley, "Who Keeps."
69. Charles Boehmer, Erik Gartzke, and Timothy Nordstrom, "Do Intergovernmental Organizations Promote Peace?" *World Politics* 57, no. 1 (2004), 29.
70. Sara M. McLaughlin and Paul R. Hensel, "International Institutions and Compliance with Agreements," *American Journal of Political Science* 51, no. 4 (2007): 721–737.
71. David E. Cunningham, *Barriers to Peace in Civil War* (Cambridge: Cambridge University Press, 2011); Virginia P. Fortna, *Peace Time: Cease-Fire Agreements and the Durability of Peace* (Princeton, NJ: Princeton University Press, 2004); Barbara F. Walter, *Committing to Peace: The Successful Settlement of Civil Wars* (Princeton, NJ: Princeton University Press, 2002); and Suzanne Werner and Amy Yuen, "Making and Keeping Peace," *International Organization* 59, no. 2 (2005): 261–292.
72. David H. Bearce and Stacy Bondanella, "Intergovernmental Organizations, Socialization, and Member-State Interest Convergence," *International Organization* 61, no. 4 (2007): 703–733.
73. Boehmer, Gartzke, and Nordstrom, "Do Intergovernmental Organizations."
74. Bearce and Bondanella, "Intergovernmental Organizations."
75. Boehmer, Gartzke, and Nordstrom, "Do Intergovernmental Organizations."

76. Terrence L. Chapman, "International Security Institutions, Domestic Politics, and Institutional Legitimacy," *Journal of Politics* 51, no. 1 (2007): 134–166; and Alexander Thompson, "Coercion through IOs: The Security Council and the Logic of Information Transmission," *International Organization* 61, no. 1 (2006): 1–34.

77. Victor Cha, *Alignment despite Antagonism: The United States-Korea-Japan Security Triangle* (Stanford, CA: Stanford University Press, 1999); and Hemmer and Katzenstein, "Why Is There."

78. Thompson, "Coercion through IOs," 2.

79. Thompson, "Coercion through IOs."

80. Terrence L. Chapman and Dan Reiter, "The United Nations Security Council and the Rally 'Round the Flag Effect," *Journal of Conflict Resolution* 48, no. 6 (2004): 886–909; and Voeten, "The Political Origins."

81. Chapman, "International Security Institutions."

82. Samuel S. Kim, *China, the United Nations and World Order* (Princeton, NJ: Princeton University Press, 1979).

83. Johnston, "Is China a Status Quo Power?"

84. Steve Chan, "On States' Status-quo and Revisionist Dispositions: Discerning Power, Popularity and Satisfaction from Security Council Vetoes," *Issues & Studies* 51, no. 3 (2016): 1–28; Xun Pang, "Dissimilarity of Trade Network Positions and Foreign Policy Divergence: Structure or Strategy?" presented at the conference on "China's Threat," Tsinghua University, Beijing (2014); and Erik Voeten, "Clashed in the Assembly," *International Organization* 54, no. 2 (2000): 185–215, and "Resisting the Lonely Superpower: Responses of States in the United Nations to U.S. Dominance," *Journal of Politics* 66, no. 3 (2004): 729–754.

85. "Security Council: Veto List," United Nations (February 2017), accessed February 28, 2017, http://research.un.org/en/docs/sc/quick/veto.

86. Peter Ferdinand, "Foreign Policy Convergence in Pacific Asia: The Evidence from Voting in the UN General Assembly," *British Journal of Politics and International Relations* 16, no. 4 (2014), 665.

87. Christopher Primiano and Jun Xiang, "Voting in the UN: A Second Image of China's Human Rights," *Journal of Chinese Political Science* 21, no. 3 (2016): 301-319.

88. Voeten, "Resisting the Lonely Superpower."

89. Axelrod, *The Evolution*, 189–190 (emphasis in original).

90. Nathan and Scobell, *China's Search*, 276.

91. Russett and Oneal, *Triangulating Peace*.

92. Jon C. Pevehouse, "With a Little Help from Friends? Regional Organizations and the Consolidation of Democracy," *American Journal of Political Science* 46, no. 3 (2002): 611–636, and "Democracy from Outside-in? International Organizations and Democratization," *International Organization* 56, no. 3 (2002): 515–549.

93. Johnston, *Social States*, 209.

94. Mearsheimer, "China's Unpeaceful Rise," and Tammen et al., *Power Transitions*.

95. Johnston, *Social States*, 207.

CHAPTER 5

A STRONG FORM OF TRUST GROUNDED IN APPROPRIATENESS AND UNTHINKABILITY

Trust in its strong form is based on shared identity rather than interests. When this happens, the logic of appropriateness and unthinkability prevails over the logic of consequences. The former logic takes over when a person decides his or her action on the basis of what is considered right, proper and moral, whereas the latter logic is based on a person's calculations of what he or she stands to gain or lose in a situation. The former logic applies to members of a security community who take for granted their counterparts' goodwill. They practice generalized rather than particularistic trust. They may continue to disagree but they literally cannot imagine themselves using force to settle their disagreements. Naturally, Sino-American relations are far from reaching this strong form of trust. The next section discussing these countries' support for international norms and institutions supports strongly this observation. But beliefs, attitudes, and values can change, and these processes have converted some countries that were former enemies into current friends.

This chapter reviews the relevant histories from some of these formerly contentious dyads. It also presents some evident changes in Beijing's support for international norms and institutions, and some notable incidents of undermining these norms and institutions committed by both it and Washington that have the effect of elevating others' distrust of them.

SUPPORT FOR INTERNATIONAL NORMS AND INSTITUTIONS

It was mentioned in the last chapter that states sometimes commit themselves to international norms and principles even when they can expect little material gains from doing so and even when they may suffer material losses as a consequence. It was also mentioned that during the years of China's rapid rise, Beijing has increased its participation in international institutions. This increased participation was accompanied by evident changes in Beijing's attitudes toward various international issues. Alastair Iain Johnston's careful study shows evidence of three microprocesses of socialization—mimicking, social influence, and persuasion—affecting Chinese diplomats who had participated in the Conference on Disarmament, the Comprehensive Nuclear Test Ban Treaty, the Convention on Certain Conventional Weapons, and the ASEAN (Association of Southeast Asian Nations) Regional Forum.[1] Both in their statements and actions, Chinese diplomats have moved closer to prevailing international norms, such as abandoning their earlier opposition to arms limitation agreements and switching to a position of favoring them. Beijing has participated, for example, in minilateral talks to encourage Tehran and Pyongyang to discontinue their efforts to develop nuclear weapons. It has also voted in support of U.N. resolutions to sanction these countries in order to encourage them to dismantle their weapons programs. Its changing attitudes about international norms and principles reflect at least in part the effects of exposing its diplomats to the pertinent forums and institutions. This development lends support, albeit still quite tentative and limited, to those sociological and social psychological perspectives claiming that social interactions can transform people's outlooks and even their identities. Although their cross-national evidence cannot identify the specific causal processes involved, Bearce and Bondanella show a general pattern whereby joint membership in the more "structured" type of intergovernmental organizations tends to promote interest convergence by pairs of states (with the latter variable indicated by the concordance of their votes in the United Nations General Assembly).[2] This pattern tends to support the proposition that participation in intergovernmental organizations socializes states to develop common interests. Such convergence can in turn promote common identification over time such as in the process leading to the formation of security communities.[3]

As Johnston remarks, the critical transformative period of Chinese diplomacy happens to coincide with the collapse of the USSR and the ascent of the U.S. to a position of undisputed global supremacy. The transformation of Chinese official disposition as just noted would not be congruent with realists' expectation. Realists would have expected more strenuous Chinese resistance to U.S. primacy and a decision by China and other major states to join in a collective effort to balance against overwhelming U.S. power. Contrary to this expectation, such reaction did not materialize from either China or the other major powers.[4] Rather, China has without doubt become more integrated into the international community both economically and diplomatically during this period of U.S. preponderance and its own relative rise.

The direction of China's evolving support for international norms and conventions is unmistakable even though one may rightly question its speed and evenness. Rosemary Foot and Andrew Walter have undertaken a thorough and balanced assessment that helpfully compares Chinese and American conformity to incipient international norms rather than focusing just on Beijing's conduct in isolation.[5] As such, their analysis provides an empirical foundation for reasonable discourse beyond rhetorical assertions about a particular country's ostensible revisionist impulse or the behavior to be expected from a supposed responsible stakeholder.

This analysis of Chinese and American policies in five important issue areas (the use of force, macroeconomic surveillance, the nonproliferation of nuclear weapons, climate change, and financial regulation) provides a far more nuanced picture than conveyed by such rhetoric.

The pertinent global normative standards continue to be contested and are therefore in flux. Support for these norms is also a matter of continuing domestic debate both in Beijing and Washington. These countries' adherence to and support for international norms have been uneven across different issues. They have also evolved over time. Beijing has changed its views on nuclear nonproliferation and has adapted its policy position and practices to conform to expectations codified in various international arms control and limitation treaties. It has also aligned itself more closely to accepted international banking conventions according to the standards established and propagated by leading financial institutions in the U.S. and Western Europe. Furthermore, it has reversed its previous skeptical views on U.N. peacekeeping operations, and has begun to make contributions to these missions. In other issue areas, Beijing has resisted international pressure to change its policy. It has, for example, declined to let market forces to fully determine its currency value.

This resistance, however, is not unique to China. The U.S. has also failed to respond fully to international demands that it take more decisive actions to address its chronic budget deficit and monetary expansion. Although U.S. officials have regularly lectured other countries about financial prudence, lax regulations and the speculative excesses of its financial institutions were behind the devastating setback to its own economy and to the rest of the world in the Great Recession starting in 2008. As many observers have also pointed out, although Washington has pressed other countries (most notably Iran and North Korea) hard to refrain from horizontal proliferation of nuclear weapons, it has not restrained itself from vertical proliferation with the aim of improving its own nuclear weapons on a continuing basis. It has moreover withdrawn from the Anti-Ballistic Missiles Treaty, and has proceeded to develop a missile defense system in Europe and Asia. Even though it says it favors limitations on the sale of conventional armament, the U.S. is the world's largest weapons exporter by far. In addition to the International Criminal Court, the U.S. has obstructed or has at least not helped the prospects for reaching a global consensus on collective efforts to limit the emission of greenhouse gases, to ban the use of antipersonnel mines, and to codify responsibility for humanitarian intervention. As Bruce Russett and John Oneal remarked some time ago:

> The United States has undermined its moral authority in recent years by refusing to sign or ratify a long list of multilateral treaties, covering just about the full spectrum of international issues. These include the Comprehensive Test Ban Treaty, the Land Mines Convention, the Law of the Sea Convention, the International Convention on the Rights of the Child, the treaty to establish a permanent International Criminal Court, and the Kyoto Protocol on global warming. None of these agreements is flawless, and they should be improved, but most other countries have ratified them or will do so…. Watching all this, even some of America's friends perceive the United States as a state that invokes international law to bind others but ignores it when it seems in its immediate self-interest to do so.[6]

George W. Bush came to the White House in January 2001. Thus his administration's policy orientation could not be held responsible for the general phenomenon just referred to because most of these accords predated it. In other words, this phenomenon cannot be described as an aberration from traditional U.S. support for international organizations and treaties, reflecting *just* this administration's policy orientation. The League of Nations and the International Trade Organization (the Havana . Charter, 1948) come to mind as earlier examples of Congress refusing to approve U.S. membership in international organizations. Erik Voeten's analysis of roll-call votes in the United Nations shows also a widening preference gap between the U.S. and most other states *before* 2001, a development that was happening at a constant rate in the preceding decade.[7] More recently, Donald Trump has withdrawn the U.S. from the Trans-Pacific Partnership and the Paris accord on climate change, two agreements that his predecessor (Barack Obama) had negotiated.

These remarks are not intended to deny that the U.S. has played a leading and indeed, indispensable role in promoting many important international organizations and norms in the post–1945 world—but rather that the U.S. has also often recoiled from binding itself to various international institutions and conventions and that this tendency is not just limited to the George W. Bush administration. Thus, Washington's behavior can sometimes appear to be highly inconsistent with its rhetoric on the appropriate conduct to be expected from a responsible stakeholder. Because of its preeminent international status and its habit of lecturing other states, this behavior is especially damaging to efforts to organize international collective action and to galvanize mutual respect for the rule of law. On some issues such as creating international regimes for the prosecution of alleged war criminals and the protection of earth's environment, Beijing and Washington have often found themselves in the same minority opposing an emergent international norm. On these occasions, they have been part of the problem rather than part of the solution. This said, these two countries have also sometimes collaborated to promote some international agreements. For example, in 2013 China was instrumental in brokering an interim deal in the Doha Round of trade negotiations, and in 2014 it joined the U.S. in pledging to limit the emission of carbon gases, a joint effort that contributed to the successful conclusion of the international agreement to reduce global warming at the Paris conference in November 2015. This Paris accord and others (such as the deal to restrain Iran's nuclear program, multilateral trade agreements like NAFTA and TPP, U.S.-Australia arrangement to resettle refugees, and even U.S. defense commitments to NATO, Japan, and South Korea) have been severely criticized by President Trump. Parenthetically, Beijing has announced that it will abide by the Paris accord regardless of Washington's participation.

In addition to the aforementioned issues, there are controversies about cyber espionage, drone attacks, and the torture of suspected terrorists. U.S. intelligence agencies have charged Russian hacking to harm the candidacy of Hillary Clinton, a charge about which Trump has expressed doubts publicly. Private U.S. companies have routinely come under cyber espionage whose source can be traced back to China. This practice surely undermines foreigners' perception of this country's trustworthiness. Similarly, its frequent failure to protect foreigners' intellectual property and its widespread practice of commercial counterfeiting are also a common source of legitimate complaints from abroad. In June 2015, China was widely reported to have made a successful hacking attempt to gain access to sensitive personnel files of a large number of current and former U.S. government employees, although the Obama administration declined to officially make this charge.

At about the same time, Wikileaks.org revealed that the U.S. government has itself been spying on three current and recent French presidents. Earlier disclosures by Edward Snowden have reported that the U.S. National Security Agency has also eavesdropped German Chancellor Angela Merkel's telephone conversations. When a country spies on other countries, it obviously distrusts them. If Washington has acted in this fashion toward its allies in Paris and Berlin, Beijing can hardly expect to be treated any better. According to Snowden, the U.S. National Security Agency had also hacked China's cell phone and telecommunications companies and its university computers.[8] The U.S., in collaboration with Israel, had reportedly also deployed Stuxnet, a computer virus, successfully to ruin a large portion of Iran's nuclear centrifuges. Again, it would not be unreasonable for Beijing to suspect that it could be the target of a similar virus attack or surreptitious attempts to gain its classified information like those that have been alleged against it.

To what extent do these actions constitute transgressions or violations of existing international norms? Stewart Patrick shows that most international rules are subject to contestation and they are routinely violated by states, including China and the U.S.[9] For example, China has often been guilty of violating international norms protecting intellectual property. In other areas such as spying, it seems all governments engage in this activity. If one is to rely on public opinion around the world to indicate global normative standards, a large majority of people in most countries oppose government surveillance programs that violate their citizens' privacy, the use of drones to kill suspected terrorists, and the application of so-called enhanced interrogation techniques against prisoners suspected of being terrorists.[10]

Public opinion around the world tends to be highly critical of U.S. conduct in these areas. At the same time, despite these criticisms people in most countries have generally more favorable views of the U.S. than China. Those from liberal democracies and traditional U.S. allies, such as in Western Europe and Japan, hold the U.S. in much higher esteem than China. The general popularity enjoyed by the U.S. points to a sense of strong affinity among those countries sharing a common identity as part of the North Atlantic security community that Deutsch and his coauthors had written about sixty years ago.[11] Judging by the views held by the Japanese and South Koreans, this community has since then expanded to include these East Asian countries. Public attitudes around the world point to a general convergence indicating greater U.S. popularity than China. With the exception of the Muslim world, more people think that the U.S. can be trusted than China (such as in these countries' respect for their citizens' privacy rights). Collective judgments such as these tend to be more right than wrong. They suggest that China will have to provide more convincing evidence in order to persuade public opinion around the world that it is trustworthy. At the same time, although the U.S. has a larger reservoir of goodwill around the world, recent polls show that this good standing can be jeopardized by unpopular actions such as its invasion of Iraq and its use of drones to kill suspected terrorists.

In some of China's neighboring countries such as Japan and the Philippines, the mass public tends to have rather unfavorable views of it although in other countries (e.g., Pakistan, Malaysia) the reverse tends to be the case. Moreover, public opinion can change over time as suggested by South Koreans' attitudes toward China. This opinion is subject to change depending on how a country's mass public perceives and reacts to Beijing's policies such as with respect to its sovereignty claims over islets in the East and South China Seas. These observations are equally applicable to the U.S. so that, for example, Washington's regional neighbors have often held heterogeneous views about its policies and intentions (e.g., Nicaragua versus Guatemala, Venezuela versus Canada, and Cuba versus the Dominican Republic).

In contrast to the regulation of proper conduct in cyberspace, international law on the legitimate use of force is clearer. Article 51 of the United Nations Charter recognizes a state's inherent right to undertake self or collective defense in the event of an armed attack against a member of the United Nations. It seems a stretch, however, to argue that this provision would entitle a state to use force against another state in the absence of such an attack and without the United Nations approval. Having failed to gain the Security Council's authorization for the second Gulf War (Operation Iraqi Freedom), the U.S. led a "coalition of the willing" to invade Iraq and overthrow Saddam Hussein's government. The claim that a state has the right to unilaterally decide when to wage a preventive war (sometimes mistakenly confused with a preemptive war, referring to a state initiating a military strike when it faces the imminent danger of being attacked) in order to deter some vague future threat is especially dubious on legal grounds and sets a dangerous precedent for other states to resort to the same behavior. Military interventions without U.N. authorization have a corrosive effect on international norms and trust. For instance, if it is permissible for outside powers to use military force to aid the cause of secessionists in Kosovo, should it also be condoned in Bangladesh, Cyprus, or Ukraine? Washington was critical of the actions taken by India, Turkey, and Russia, respectively, in these latter episodes.

China had also used military force to teach Vietnam "a lesson" in its border war with the latter country in 1979. Since its seizure of the Crescent group of Paracel islands from the South Vietnamese in 1974, Beijing has refrained from using force in its ongoing maritime disputes in the East and South China Seas. It has, however, declined international adjudication and has thus far argued for bilateral negotiations with the other claimant states. Although China has signed the United Nations Convention on the Law of the Sea (UNCLOS), it has specifically opted out of the provision for compulsory dispute settlement by invoking Article 298. It has therefore protested against the involvement of the Permanent Court of Arbitration when the Philippines submitted its dispute with China to this body for adjudication.

On July 12, 2016, when this tribunal rejected Beijing's claim of historical rights in the South China Sea, China reiterated its refusal to recognize this court's jurisdiction. Parenthetically, this court's ruling pertains to the application and interpretation of the UNCLOS (which the U.S. has yet to ratify) but it specifically lacks jurisdiction in settling sovereignty disputes. Its ruling therefore does not settle the question of which of the contesting states has a better sovereignty claim, only that China's claim of "historical rights" does not entitle it to the resources in the disputed area.[12] In this court's opinion, none of the Spratly features in dispute constitute "islands," and that they are all "rocks" because they cannot sustain independent human existence and economic activity—including the largest land feature, Taiping or Itu Aba, under Taiwan's control (Taipei has also rejected the court's jurisdiction and its ruling). Because the disputed land features do not qualify as islands in the court's opinion, they are not entitled to their own exclusive economic zones extending 200 nautical miles, and they can only claim a territorial sea limited to twelve nautical miles. This ruling relates not only to China, Taiwan, and the Philippines; it also pertains to other countries such as Japan and the U.S. which have also made extensive territorial claims based on land features that cannot be considered islands according to this ruling.

Washington has acted similar to Beijing when it challenged the jurisdiction of the International Court of Justice in a case involving Nicaragua's
complaints about U.S. support of the *contras* seeking to overthrow its
government and U.S. mining of its harbors. This court is the highest
arbitration organ of the United Nations, and in its ruling of June 1986
it rejected Washington's justification for its intervention in the name
of humanitarian assistance and on the grounds that the Nicaraguan
government was trying to establish "a totalitarian communist dictator-
ship." This ruling is also pertinent to other subsequent U.S. interventions,
when it stated that "With regard more specifically to alleged violations
of human rights relied on by the United States, the Court considers that
the use of force by the United States could not be the appropriate method
to monitor or ensure respect for such rights."[13] When the U.S. challenge
to the Court's jurisdiction failed and the Court ruled against the U.S.
for violating international law, Washington blocked the enforcement of
this judgment by vetoing the U.N. Security Council resolution calling
for its full and immediate compliance. As Graham Allison has remarked,
"None of the five permanent members of the UN Security Council have
ever accepted any international court's ruling when (in their view) it
infringed their sovereignty or national security interests."[14]

THE LONG PROCESS OF BUILDING AMITY AND TRUST

Some adversarial states have been able to reach political reconciliation,
setting aside their previous animosity and establishing strong trust as a
basis for durable peace and friendship. The evolution of relations between
Britain and the U.S., Argentina and Brazil, Norway and Sweden, and
France and Germany comes to mind. These were former enemies or
rivals who had somehow managed to reach political accommodation
and went from there to create a strong bond of mutual confidence and
respect. They had reversed their once acrimonious and even hostile
relations to become members of a security or moralistic community to
the extent that the idea of going to war against each other has literally

become unthinkable and unimaginable. Their leaders and citizens take for granted the goodwill and trustworthiness of their counterparts. With the expansion of their security or moralistic community such as those binding the North Atlantic, the Scandinavian, and the MERCOSUR (*Mercado Comun del Sul*, a trade bloc consisting of Argentina, Brazil, and their neighbors) countries, particularistic trust has turned increasingly albeit unevenly to generalized trust.

Charles Kupchan has undertaken a wide range of case studies to investigate why peace has broken out between some former enemies, converting them eventually to trusted friends.[15] His conclusions are germane to the question of whether trust is possible in Sino-American relations and if so, which factors tend to help its promotion. Some of these factors may facilitate trust building but are not critical or even necessary for this process. Some appear beneficial but are not within the direct control of policy makers, as they pertain to entrenched social conditions or long-standing cultural orientations that are not easily transformed by official action. Any change in these conditions or orientations will entail a protracted process. Still, Kupchan's analysis shows some surprising cases where deft statecraft has managed to foster friendly relations between odd couples, such as Britain and Japan in the early 1900s and China and the USSR in the 1950s.[16] But because these countries lacked a strong foundation in social and cultural affinity, their friendly relations also turned out to be fragile and vulnerable to reversal.

One of the most important conclusions from Kupchan's analysis pertains to the claim that democracy is necessary to build trust in international relations. "This book directly challenges such conventional wisdom. It refutes the claim that democracy is necessary for peace, demonstrating that non-democracies can be reliable contributors to international stability."[17] When some of the formerly contentious dyads decided to settle for political accommodation (e.g., Britain and the U.S., Argentina and Brazil, and Norway and Sweden), they were hardly polities with effective legislative oversight, judicial independence, or universal suffrage, critical traits that we associate with democracy today. Landed oligarchs, military generals, and monarchists were influential actors at the moment of *abertura*, or political opening, for launching the reconciliation process. In some cases, the relevant countries also did not have deep and dense economic connections. Amitav Archaya observes that ASEAN "evolved toward a security community without sharing liberal-democratic values or a substantial degree of intra-regional economic interdependence."[18]

Moreover, autocracies have also been able to effectively reassure each other and work either together among themselves or with more liberal polities to pursue stable peace, cooperation, and even political amalgamation. The Concert of Europe, the experiences of German and Italian unification, and the formation of the Sino-Soviet alliance and the Gulf Cooperation Council offer some relevant examples. As Kupchan explains, the effective management of European peace and stability by the Concert of Europe came to its demise not because the autocrats had wanted to dismantle this institution but rather because its two more liberal member states (Britain and France) had knowingly undermined it for reasons related to appeasing their domestic constituents in the context of democratic opening. Similarly, although it may be difficult to recall today, in the 1950s relations between Moscow and Beijing were based on a genuine and mutual fondness and ideological solidarity between their leaders and citizens. Kupchan remarks that "[the] Sino-Soviet treaty of 1950 was much more than a mutual commitment to collective defense against common enemies. From the outset, both parties demonstrated a remarkable degree of confidence in the other's intentions, readily engaging in acts of reciprocal restraint and accepting mutual vulnerability."[19]

Kupchan's historical analysis suggests that democracy or even regime similarity is *not* a necessary condition to build interstate trust or undertake cooperation. This is good news because if it were otherwise, establishing trust and stability in current Sino-American relations would be impossible.

Moreover, because democratization is necessarily a long and challenging process with the danger of occasional reversals, one is encouraged about the prospect of stabilizing Sino-American relations and addressing these countries' trust deficit without having to wait for this process to come to a conclusion. Kupchan's analysis of the Concert of Europe also introduces an important cautionary note. It was the rise of populism in democratizing Britain and France that motivated their leaders to undertake policies that undermined the existing concert arrangement. These democratizing countries were the ones that had defected from the concert norms whereas their autocratic counterparts were ready and disposed to uphold the political status quo and lend support to monarchical solidarity. Commenting on the demise of the concert arrangement that had guaranteed European peace and stability for three decades, Kupchan concludes that "Britain had in effect become a revisionist power, seeking to extend its geopolitical influence and export its liberal ideology."[20] This observation comports with the view that with a greater role for public opinion in its foreign policy process and also greater elite fragmentation, a democratizing China may not necessarily be a more conciliatory China. Scholars continue to debate about whether democracy holds the key to international peace and whether factors other than democracy—such as capitalism, territorial settlement, or a receptive civic culture—are more important and relevant.[21]

A second conclusion emerges from Kupchan's analysis. Strategic restraint as shown by the policies undertaken by the pertinent states rather than institutionalized restraint reflecting the domestic politics of these countries is the leading factor for building interstate trust. Autocrats face less institutionalized restraint at home but if they reach out to seek political accommodation and reconciliation with their counterparts (whether democratic or autocratic), they have encountered success. Strategic restraint involves costly signals to reassure another state of one's benign or at least nonhostile intentions. Such reassurance can be reflected by a state's deliberate action or inaction, such as to limit or even demobilize its military forces, to undertake policy coordination and consultation with another state, and to refrain from challenging another state's domestic order or infringing its traditional sphere of influence. A state can also communicate its trustworthiness by pursuing open trade, entering into legal commitments, and generally facilitating its citizens' social interactions with foreigners. Significantly, Kupchan's analysis makes a compelling case that rising economic and social exchanges tend to follow rather than precede official reconciliation and political rapprochement. Trade, social integration, and joint membership in cooperative arrangements (whether the Zollverein as a precursor to German unification, the European Coal and Steel Community as a precursor to the Common Market, and the MERCUSOR for the South American countries) tend to be motivated by geostrategic calculations and as such, these cases support the "political primacy" argument claiming that politics and diplomacy drive such developments. Similarly and as argued previously, the "superfusion" characterizing current Chinese and U.S. economic and financial relations reflects and is concomitantly a product of earlier political rapprochement based on geostrategic calculations.

These remarks do not deny that changing economic relations may have a reciprocal impact on government decisions. For instance, Taiwan's business firms have in the past often sought to bypass official restrictions against trading with and investing in mainland China. Over time, the burgeoning economic ties across the Taiwan Strait have constrained Taipei from taking actions that would be inimical to those interests repre-sented by these ties (mainly large, internationally oriented conglomerates and financial institutions).[22] Thus in this sense, economics has led politics and it can have a reciprocal significant impact on politics. Moreover, Taipei's very reluctance to limit or reverse cross-Strait economic ties is indicative of its political disposition and preference—namely, it gives a higher priority to promoting the island's economic well-being than pursuing its *de jure* independence. The DPP administration headed by Tsai Ing-wen will provide a test to this proposition.

Significantly, economic interdependence is not a fortuitous occurrence, and it does not just stem from the actions of entrepreneurs or existing economic complementarities between the two sides of a transaction. Thus, despite their economic complementarities, physical proximity, and even cultural affinity, trade has languished between North and South Korea, India and Pakistan, and Israel and its Arab neighbors. Cordial and stable political relationship—and expectations that such relationship will endure—make economic interdependence possible. Conversely, the absence of this factor tends to hamper such interdependence and indeed, even regular commercial intercourse. By implication, a deterioration of political relationship can upset and even reverse economic ties. This perspective of "politics in command" comports with the argument that economic interdependence both indicates the current state of two countries' political relationship and also predicts its likely future.

The initiation of a process leading to mutual trust and stable peace usually starts with a major, unilateral concession by one side of a relationship to the other side. This attempt at reconciliation has been typically dictated by this initiating country's difficult, even dire, internal and/or external circumstances. It wants accommodation not out of some sense of altruism but as an attempt to relieve the pressures confronting it. Mikhail Gorbachev's policies to seek détente and retrenchment abroad and perestroika and glasnost at home are an obvious example. In 1972 Mao Tse-tung also agreed to proceed with Sino-American strategic cooperation in order to face the threat coming from Moscow without first settling Taiwan's status with Washington. Anwar Sadat's domestic problems had also influenced his decision to visit and conciliate with Israel.

This line of argument suggests that it will probably take a major disruptive event or disconcerting trend, perhaps even a new leader who is not committed to an old and discredited policy,[23] in order to engineer a breakthrough in bilateral relations and to establish a new level of trust and cooperation. It has often taken a systemic disturbance to shock officials from their entrenched policies, and enduring rivalries have tended to end as a result of events such as defeat in foreign wars or domestic revolutions.[24] Moreover, when leadership transitions bring to power officials who do not have a vested stake in defending the old policies and who are receptive to "new thinking," these occasions present promising opportunities to turn a new page on a country's foreign relations. The converse can also be pertinent. In the absence of evidence pointing to a series of dramatic and indisputable policy failures and a powerful and decisive new leader, officials and bureaucrats can continue to follow decrepit policies for a long time even though these policies' shortcomings should have become obvious to them. Thus, Soviet leaders before Gorbachev continued with business as usual even though there were clear signs that their country was in serious and steady decline for many years.

This said, when a state seeks accommodation during a time a stress, its gestures are more apt to be seen as a measure of expediency or one that has been forced upon it by its dire circumstances. These gestures may therefore be interpreted as a transient compromise pending this state's future recovery. They may at best engender a weak form of trust, and at worst incline the other side to increase its pressure in order to extract additional concessions from it. Thus ironically, states are not disposed to befriend a competitor with a costly, unilateral policy of accommodation unless they are faced with urgent geostrategic challenges abroad or acute political or economic difficulties at home. Yet conciliatory or reassurance signals sent under these circumstances also happen to be the least persuasive and the most susceptible to misinterpretation and even exploitation. As a corollary to these observations, the stronger side of a relationship should be in a better position to undertake an initial, even unilateral, concession to jump start a process of reconciliation because it can more afford to take this risk should its overture not be reciprocated. Yet ironically, precisely because it enjoys an upper hand, this state is less likely to undertake this step for the simple reason that it expects to prevail in any possible economic or military showdown.

Any leader who initiates a policy of accommodation will face serious domestic backlash (e.g., Anwar Sadat, Yitzhak Rabin, and Mikhail Gorbachev). As already mentioned, politically secure leaders are in a better position to make concessions in order to reach foreign agreements. Yet, difficult domestic and international circumstances are often required to shock officials into initiating a new line of policy. This seemingly contradictory combination implies that leaders of authoritarian systems (e.g., Castro, Gorbachev, Mao, and Sadat) may be better able to undertake conciliatory overtures when confronted with difficult domestic and/or foreign circumstances. Politically insecure, democratic leaders may be more constrained and/or disinclined to do so. They run greater political risks should their overtures to accommodate and conciliate with a foreign rival fail to be reciprocated.[25] In order to establish mutual trust and stable peace, it is important for one of the contending parties to first make a large and hence credible unilateral gesture to accommodate the other. But as Kupchan's analysis makes clear,[26] the other party must be receptive to this overture. In order to sustain the process of reconciliation and rapprochement, the elites of both countries must exercise reciprocal restraint. Timing becomes critical as the windows of opportunity to initiate and reciprocate accommodation must be simultaneously open in both countries.[27] The political clocks in both countries (such as election cycles, leadership transitions, and periods of significant popular discontent with existing policies and pressure to undertake reform coming from dissident elements) must be operating in synchrony so that they are aligned to set off a virtuous cycle of trust and cooperation begetting further trust and cooperation.

The process of turning enemies into friends described by Kupchan starts, as already mentioned, with a policy of unilateral accommodation by one side of a relationship.[28] In the second stage, it entails reciprocal restraint by both sides. Both of these stages involve more the elites than the masses. A convergence of elite values and expectations takes hold slowly, and only after the consolidation of this convergence does this process enter the third and fourth stages involving respectively "social integration" and "narrative generation" inclining the people of the two countries involved to embrace common identification. These latter stages see an increase in social and economic exchanges, accompanied by the mass media of each country presenting and propagating a benign image of the other country. Mass attitudinal transformation follows from these developments, and reflects largely successful elite entrepreneurship. Critically, the process just described is an elite-led phenomenon. This top-down nature of socioeconomic integration and even political union was demonstrated some time ago in the case of the European Common Market.[29] Mass attitudes expressing a friendly disposition and close affinity followed rather than preceded elite cooperation and the creation of intergovernmental organizations to coordinate common policies.

Naturally, to the extent that the two countries involved in the latter stages of rapprochement have compatible social orders and shared cultural heritage, this process will make progress more easily and it will less likely run into trouble. For example, incompatible social orders are likely to engender protests and obstruction from those domestic groups (such as import-substituting industries, military establishments, and conservative oligarchs) that stand to lose in distributional struggles if the new relationship takes hold. Therefore, the process of building trust and ensuring stable peace is more likely to be consolidated and more resistant to reversal when facilitated by compatible social orders and a common cultural heritage. However, the latter conditions are not essential to foster and sustain such process. The Sino-Soviet alliance and the Anglo-Japanese alliance thrived for at least a while without either compatible social orders or a common cultural heritage. It is true that these alliances did not last very long. It may also be recalled that compatible social orders did not prevent Anglo-French rivalry or the breakup of the Dreikaiserbund (among Russia, Austria-Hungary, and Prussia). Nor did a common cultural heritage prevent war between Prussia and Austria or for that matter, the American Civil War. Thus, these conditions are hardly sufficient for establishing mutual trust and durable friendship—or for disqualifying such relationship as attested by contemporary Japanese-American relations, two countries that cannot be said to share a common cultural heritage or ethnic identity.

In fact and in seeming contradiction to the expectation that countries sharing a common cultural heritage should show greater affinity for each other, recent Pew surveys of mass attitudes in Asia point in the opposite direction.[30] Unfavorable views of China were most pervasive in the three countries that are culturally most similar to China: Japan (89%), Vietnam (74%), and South Korea (37%). At the same time, more citizens of these three countries held favorable views of the U.S. than in other Asian countries (68%, 78%, and 84% respectively).[31] Probably more as a reflection of U.S. unpopularity than Chinese popularity, favorable ratings of China were highest in Asia's three Muslim countries: Pakistan (82%), Malaysia (78%), and Indonesia (63%).[32] Cultural affinity cannot explain this phenomenon, whereas anti-Americanism might be at work as unfavorable views of the U.S. ran as high as 62%, 41%, and 26% respectively in these countries.[33]

The good news for Sino-American relations is that compatible social orders and a shared cultural heritage are not necessary for building a relationship based on mutual trust. One would despair if they were, because clearly China and the U.S. have neither compatible social orders nor a common cultural heritage and since it will surely take a long time, if ever, for these conditions to converge for these countries. Equally important, even if this convergence occurs in the long run, there is relatively little that officials can do to directly influence them at the present. In other words, these macro social or cultural phenomena are not amenable to policy intervention—they are not subject to the officials' direct control. But strategic restraint is something that is within their power to practice.

CONCLUDING REMARKS

Henry Kissinger, former U.S. Secretary of State, has remarked that the U.S.-British relationship:

> involved a pattern of consultation so matter-of-factly intimate that it became psychologically impossible to ignore British views. [These countries] evolved a habit of meetings so regular that autonomous American action somehow came to seem to violate club rules... The relationship existed on no legal claim: it was formalized by no document; it was carried forward by succeeding British governments as if no alternative was conceivable. British influence was great simply because it never insisted upon it.[34]

Kissinger's description applies to a special bilateral relationship and not generalized trust among member states of a security community. Although constant diplomatic contact does not in itself constitute evidence of trust, it enables officials to have the opportunity to exchange information, seek consultation, and offer reassurances to each other.

Sino-American relations have not nearly approached Kissinger's description of British-American relations. But diplomatic contact between the former pair has been on the rise. In recent years top U.S. and Chinese leaders have exchanged state visits almost on an annual basis. They have met regularly in their respective countries and during APEC's (Asia Pacific Economic Cooperation) summit conferences. In April 2009, Barack Obama and Hu Jintao also initiated the U.S.-China Strategic and Economic Dialogue, institutionalizing annual meetings by high-level officials of both sides alternating between their two capitals. Consisting of a strategic track and an economic track, this new format replaced the Senior Dialogue and Strategic Economic Dialogue started by the George W. Bush administration.

Officials of both countries also meet regularly in other multilateral settings such as in those intergovernmental organizations that China has taken a seat in recent years. Even though there are optimistic signs that Beijing has become more integrated into the international community, there continue to be incidents suggesting that both it and Washington prefer sometimes to stand outside of and even in opposition to emergent global norms. On various security and nonsecurity matters, both countries have often chosen to hold out against these norms. Such behavior undermines their trustworthiness in each other's eyes as well in other states' perceptions.

A strong form of trust indicates that people act on the basis of diffuse rather than specific reciprocity. They take for granted that others in their community are trustworthy and do not intend to do them harm (at least not deliberately if they can help it). Elites and masses in the relevant security community share a "we feeling." Common identity more than shared interests motivates their behavior. Naturally and as already stated, China and the U.S. are far from reaching this stage in their relationship. But an examination of the historical experiences of other countries that have made great advances in establishing mutual trust and durable friendship suggests that structural conditions (such as similar social order, cultural heritage, and political institutions) are facilitative but not determinative of whether states can succeed in this endeavor. As Kupchan argues, strategic restraint—the policies that states undertake to reassure each other of their benign intentions—is a more decisive factor.[35] This conclusion in turn suggests that Beijing and Washington's diplomacy can have a more immediate and direct impact on overcoming their trust deficit. Strategic restraint is something that officials in both countries, whether democratic or authoritarian, can undertake to build trust and improve relations—a topic that I will take up in the next chapter.

Notes

1. Johnston, *Social States*.
2. Bearce and Bondanella, "Intergovernmental Organizations."
3. Deutsch et al., *Political Community*.
4. Stephen G. Brooks and William C. Wohlforth, "Hard Time for Soft Balancing," *International Security* 30, no. 1 (2005): 72–108, and *World out of Balance: International Relations and the Challenge of American Primacy* (Princeton, NJ: Princeton University Press, 2008).
5. Rosemary Foot and Andrew Walter, *China, the United States, and Global Order* (Cambridge: Cambridge University Press, 2011).
6. Russett and Oneal, *Triangulating Peace*, 304.
7. Voeten, "Resisting the Lonely Superpower."
8. Evan Osnos, "Why China Let Snowden Go," *The New Yorker* (June 24, 2013), accessed June 2, 2017, http://www.newyorker.com/news/evan-osnos/why-china-let-snowden-go.
9. Stewart Patrick, "What, Exactly, Are the Rules?" *The Washington Quarterly* 39, no. 1 (2016): 7–27.
10. "Global Balance of Power," Pew Research Center (December 15, 2016), accessed June 2, 2017, http://www.pewglobal.org/topics/global-balance-of-power/; and "Global Publics Back U.S. on Fighting ISIS, but Are Critical of Post-9/11 Torture," Pew Research Center (June 23, 20150), accessed June 2, 2017, http://www.pewglobal.org/2015/06/23/global-publics-back-u-s-on-fighting-isis-but-are-critical-of-post-911-torture/.
11. Deutsch et al., *Political Community*.
12. Robert Beckman, "The South China Ruling: Game Changer in the Maritime Disputes," RSIS Commentary No. 180/2016 (July 18, 2016).
13. "International Court of Justice Ruling in USA v. Nicaragua," Center for the Study of Interventionism (June 27, 1986), accessed June 2, 2017, www.interventionism.info/en/International-Court-of-Justice-ruling-in-USA-v.-Nicaragua.
14. Graham Allison, "Of Course China, Like All Great Powers, Will Ignore an International Legal Verdict," *The Diplomat* (July 11, 2016), accessed June 2, 2017, http:thediplomat.com/2016/07/of-course-china-like-all-great-powers-will-ignore-an-international-legal-verdict/ quoted in Amitai Etzioni, "The China Options," (February 8, 2017), accessed June 2, 2017, https://paper.ssrn.com/so13/paper2.cfm?abstract._id=2913748, 8.

15. Kupchan, *How Enemies Become Friends.*
16. Ibid.
17. Ibid., 3.
18. Quoted in ibid., 216.
19. Ibid., 160.
20. Ibid., 248.
21. Erik Gartzke, "The Capitalist Peace," *American Journal of Political Science* 51, no. 1 (2007): 166–191; Douglas M. Gibler, "Bordering on Peace: Democracy, Territorial Issues, and Conflict," *International Studies Quarterly* 51, no. 3 (2007): 509–532; Douglas M. Gibler and Jaroslav Tir, "Settled Borders and Regime Type: Democratic Transitions as Consequences of Peaceful Territorial Transfers," *American Journal of Political Science* 54, no. 4 (2010): 951–958; and Edward D. Mansfield and Jack Snyder, "Democratization and the Danger of War," *International Security* 20, no. 1 (1995): 5–38, and *Electing to Fight.*
22. Kastner, *Political Conflict.*
23. Legro, *Rethinking the World,* and "What China Will Want;" and Miroslav Nincic, *The Logic of Positive Engagement* (Ithaca, NY: Cornell University Press, 2011).
24. Paul F. Diehl, ed., *The Dynamics of Enduring Rivalries* (Urbana: University of Illinois Press, 1998); Paul F. Diehl and Gary Goertz, *War and Peace in International Rivalry* (Ann Arbor: University of Michigan Press, 2000); and Gary Goertz and Paul F. Diehl, "Enduring Rivalries: Theoretical Constructs and Empirical Patterns," *International Studies Quarterly* 37, no. 2 (1993): 147–171, and "The Initiation and Termination of Enduring Rivalries: The Impact of Political Shocks," *American Journal of Political Science* 39, no. 1 (1995): 30–52.
25. Michael P. Colaresi, "When Doves Cry: Unreciprocated Cooperation and Leadership Tenure," *American Journal of Political Science* 48, no. 3 (2004): 555–570, and *Scare Politics: The Politics of International Rivalry* (Syracuse, NY: Syracuse University Press, 2005).
26. Kupchan, *How Enemies Become Friends.*
27. Nincic, *The Logic.*
28. Kupchan, *How Enemies Become Friends.*
29. Barry B. Hughes and John E. Schwarz, "Dimensions of Political Integration and the Experience of the European Community," *International Studies Quarterly* 16, no. 3 (1972): 263–294.

30. "Views of China and the Global Balance of Power," Pew Research Center (June 23, 2015), accessed June 2, 2017, http://www.pewglobal.org/2015/06/23/2-views-of-china-and-the-global-balance-of-power/.

31. "America's Global Image," Pew Research Center (June 23, 2015), accessed June 2, 2017, http://www.pewglobal.org/2015/06/23/1-americas-global-image/.

32. Pew, "Views of China."

33. Ibid.

34. Quoted in Hopf, *Social Construction*, 293.

35. Kupchan, *How Enemies Become Friends.*

Chapter 6

Conclusion

The Practice of Strategic Restraint

Experts who are teachers and researchers of international relations saw "the rising power of China" as the most important issue facing the U.S. They put this development at the very top of a list of the most urgent and critical international relations items in a 2011 survey.[1] This issue was in their view even more important than "global climate change." These responses from U.S. experts are not significantly different from the survey results coming from the non-U.S. experts. When combined, the collective judgment from these two groups shows that "the rising power of China" was edged out by "global climate change" by just a small margin as the most important issue facing the world. Among various competing issues that were thought to influence the future of international relations, China's rise took the top place or nearly the top place in the minds of these scholars.

The same 2011 survey reports a worrisome concern. The respondents saw a relatively small but hardly insignificant probability that China and the U.S. would go to war in the next decade. On a scale of 1 to 10 (with 10 indicating the greatest likelihood), the U.S. participants gave an estimate of 1.33. When combined with the responses from the non-U.S.

participants, their collective judgment remains practically the same at 1.34. More ominously, when asked to extend their forecast to the next thirty years, the probability of a Sino-American war estimated by these two groups rose to 2.27 and 2.28 respectively.[2] Although we do not know the reasons behind these experts' seeming pessimism, the trust deficit between the two countries might be one of them.

Much of recent discourse on Sino-American relations has been framed in terms of the power-transition theory,[3] which claims that the danger of war increases when a late rising power catches up to an incumbent hegemon. This proposition was further popularized by Graham Allison's recent project on "Thucydides's Trap,"[4] referring to this ancient historian's claim that the Peloponnesian war was "inevitable" and that its "truest cause, but the least spoken of, was the growth of Athenian power, which presented an object of fear to the Spartans and forced them to go to war."[5]

As I have written elsewhere,[6] the power-transition theory seeks to explain the outbreak of systemic wars—large and intense armed conflicts led by the world's two most powerful states. These are struggles at the very pinnacle of the interstate system, and they can shake the very structure of this system and revise the world order. This theory, however, also offers a political construction with a particular interpretation of interstate dynamics from the dominant power's perspective. It suffers from several weaknesses.[7]

One of these weaknesses is that it directs attention to the capabilities and motivations of the rising power without at the same time considering the declining power's decision situation. Yet an acute sense of vulnerability and even a feeling of desperation on the part of declining states were clearly an important part of the historical context leading to war. I have mentioned Germany's disposition to wage a preventive war in 1914 before a window of opportunity closed on it.[8] Austria-Hungary's worries about its disintegrating empire were also not irrelevant to its decision to issue its harsh ultimatum to Serbia. Thus, in order to explain the dynamics of conflict escalation, one must study not just the situation facing the rising power(s) but also that which confronting the declining power(s).

Another problematic aspect of the power-transition theory pertains to its focus on the dyadic relationship between the two (supposedly) most powerful countries. Yet at any one time, there are more than just one rising power. On the eve of World War I and again World War II, there were several rising powers, including the U.S., Germany, Japan, and Russia. London chose to accommodate some of them while opposing others. Thus, agency matters as much as structure. That Britain ended up fighting Germany and that the U.S. and Russia/the USSR subsequently joined the British coalition were not unrelated to London's statecraft. Multilateral interactions determined the outcomes of these global conflicts rather than just a bilateral contest for power. Had the U.S. not fought on the British side, the outcome of both world wars would have been very different.

Yet a third common error on the part of those who invoke the power-transition theory to comment on contemporary Sino-American relations is that China is today still only a regional power that lacks any global reach to enable it to challenge the U.S. position as the incumbent global hegemon. It is a fundamental mischaracterization to conflate Beijing's policy differences with Washington pertaining to its immediate neighborhood with its ostensible desire to upend the world order dominated by Washington. As Jack Levy and William Thompson have remarked,[9] analysts should determine how the regional distribution of power interacts with the global distribution of power. One can reasonably argue that World Wars I and II happened at a time when the European regional subsystem dominated the global system, so that the conflict dynamics among Europe's major states escalated and spread to cause a worldwide conflagration. Conversely, during the Cold War the Soviet-American rivalry at the global level permeated and intensified conflicts at the regional level such as those between Israel and its Arab neighbors, India and Pakistan, North and South Korea, and Ethiopia and Somalia. Although

East Asia's importance has risen relative to that of other regions, it is farfetched to argue that Beijing has acquired a capability to contest Washington's global supremacy. China remains a regional power that lags far behind the U.S. dominance of the global commons. Significantly also, Berlin was far more concerned about its security situation in Europe before the two world wars in comparison to its desire to displace Britain's global influence. Thus the power-transition theory's characterization of the two world wars as an epic contest for world domination is also inaccurate in this case.

Those who apply the power-transition theory and even some scholars outside of this research tradition often imply or assert that China is a dissatisfied or revisionist power, and conversely, the U.S. is a satisfied or status-quo power or was such a country during the period when it was a rising power.[10] Some even contend that a hegemon is by definition a satisfied or status-quo power.[11] Such a claim naturally raises the question of what additional analytic leverage one gains by calling attention to a country's satisfaction or dissatisfaction (or its revisionist or status-quo orientation) since having power is tantamount to being satisfied—a move that not only strips any separate substantive content from the latter concept but one that also automatically classifies any country disagreeing with the incumbent hegemon as an anti–status quo challenger. By default, anyone who disagrees with the hegemon is dissatisfied not only with the latter, but also with the international order.

One thus conflates a sense of dissatisfaction with a country's current status or situation with a revisionist motivation to challenge and replace the existing international order. Naturally, a country can be dissatisfied without necessarily wanting to alter the basic rules of international order (which country does not want to improve its international status or influence, and thus be described as dissatisfied?). Those who attribute a revisionist or status-quo motivation to countries also do not usually engage in a detailed and systematic discussion about what exactly are these rules. As I have mentioned earlier and will return to discuss later in this chapter, these rules should be about the recognition of the ruling elites' legitimacy and the Westphalian principle of state sovereignty, the sanctity of borders, the acceptance of limits on one's discretion to use military force, the observance of international agreements and treaty commitments, and the recognition of other major states' spheres of influence. Recent Washington policies promoting regime change abroad, extending the extraterritorial jurisdiction of U.S. laws, attacking Serbia, Iraq, and Afghanistan, and enlarging the NATO alliance to include former Soviet-bloc countries show a more revisionist tendency to rewrite the rules of international order than Beijing.

China's territorial claims in the East and especially South China Seas have been seen by some as a sign of its dissatisfaction and even its revisionist disposition. Japan and Germany in the mid- and late 1800s and early 1900s have been similarly depicted as dissatisfied and revisionist as a result of their drive to expand their empire. Ken Organski and Jacek Kugler include the Franco-Prussian War and the Russo-Japanese War (in addition to the two world wars) as appropriate instances to test their power-transition theory.[12] Although these wars elevated Prussia/Germany and Japan's international status, it is not clear how else had the basic nature of international order been transformed by them. What these authors omit from their analysis is equally important. They exclude the Spanish-American War and dismiss the U.S. overtaking of Britain as an instance of power transition. In contrast to Germany and Japan, the U.S. had made far greater territorial gains. John Mearsheimer quotes Henry Cabot Lodge's observation that the U.S. had "a record of conquest, colonization, and territorial expansion unequaled by any people in the nineteenth century."[13] Compared to China's maritime claims today, the U.S. had made even more far reaching acquisitions. It had annexed the Hawaii archipelago, carved out a U.S. zone in Panama, and seized Puerto Rico, Cuba, Guam, and the Philippines after the Spanish-American War.

Thus, the power-transition theory's conclusions are based on a very selective reading of history. Their advocates do not take up the one

214 TRUST AND DISTRUST IN SINO-AMERICAN RELATIONS

instance when an incumbent leader (Britain) was actually overtaken by a latecomer (the U.S.), and on this occasion and between this dyad the power transition was actually peaceful. But they insist on warning about the danger of war following a possible overtaking of the U.S. by China, a development that may or may not come to pass. They claim that a power transition between Germany and Britain had occurred before 1914 and again 1939, even though Germany's economy and its per capita income did not surpass Britain's on the eve of both world wars. Only its army was bigger. The occurrence of the two world wars is attributed to this supposed overtaking—even though the U.S. and not Britain had become the world's most powerful country and even though Germany never came close to matching, not to mention overtaking, U.S. power. In contrast, China's economy did overtake Japan's recently but war has not happened between them. Therefore, one may reasonably question the selective use of history to support the power-transition theory's claims and ask for the pertinent criteria for determining when a valid falsification of this theory has occurred.

Trust enters into this discussion of power-transition theory because from the perspective of the leading but declining hegemon, it is critical for it to discern the rising power's future intentions. Can this latecomer be counted on to have benign intentions after a power transition? If it cannot be trusted, then launching a preventive war when the declining power still has an advantage becomes relevant. Realizing such thinking may occur to its counterpart, the latecomer would want to reassure the currently dominant state in order to avoid being attacked. It would also want to reassure its neighbors that it does not have insatiable ambition, so that they will not mobilize a countervailing coalition to contain it. Organski and Kugler are right in pointing out that Britain won both world wars because it had stronger allies.[14] Japan, Germany, and Napoleonic France lost because they did not know when to stop their campaign to expand; they turned the other major powers into their enemies by attacking them repeatedly and sealed their own fate by fighting them simultaneously.

The allies opposing these aggressors cooperated even though they did not necessarily trust each other. As already indicated, cooperation is possible without trust (in its strong form). All that is required for cooperation to happen is for the parties to believe that they have a shared interest and that their counterpart will return their cooperation with cooperation (i.e., that they can expect reciprocity). The U.S. and the USSR cooperated in reaching various arms control and arms limitation agreements, but these agreements did not necessarily indicate that they have a deep trust in each other's intentions. Instead, each side expected that the other side will not attack because it has retained a capability to launch a devastating counter-attack. It also relies on stringent verification to ensure that the other side does not cheat. Such verification would not have been undertaken if they had relied on blind faith. Moscow and Washington concluded these agreements because these deals serve a common interest. But as I have argued earlier, these deals can be fragile because they will expire or collapse when states redefine their interests. The definition of these interests reflects and is derived from their identity. Therefore, the strong form of trust based on common identification provides a more robust and enduring basis for cooperation.

RECAPITULATING THE MAIN CAVEATS AND CONCLUSIONS

It is worth reiterating that the analysis of trust and distrust in Sino-American relations refers to their leaders' reciprocal perceptions. As such, what matters is how one side sees the other and not how one wishes to be seen by the other side or what one thinks is the objective truth. After all, it is the other side's image of oneself—whether fair or unfair, accurate or inaccurate—and not one's self-image that will determine its actions. Moreover, it is only natural that given their different experiences and circumstances, people are likely to have different recollections and perceptions. In reflecting on the various past incidents and historical memories I have mentioned, the appropriate question to ask is whether it is probable and even reasonable for the other side to hold those views and beliefs attributed to it. One may of course complain that the other side has a distorted view or inaccurate understanding of oneself, and claim that this view or understanding is biased. Such argument, however, is in itself ineffective in altering this counterpart's behavior. It will take credible and tangible action to persuade it that its view and understanding are incorrect. One has to invest in one's reputation for being trustworthy by undertaking actions with severe self-imposed negative consequences if one breaches trust. In other words, trust is not something to be taken for granted and must instead be established and maintained by deliberate and assiduous effort.

It is also worth remembering that people are prone to selective recall— what Amos Tversky and Daniel Kahneman call the retrievability bias.[15] They are more likely to recall recent events happening to themselves or to those close to them, and events that are either very traumatic to them or cast them in a highly favorable light. Conversely, they are less likely to recall distant, unfamiliar events that occurred to strangers (thus distance not only in time, but also in a cultural, psychological, and physical sense). Moreover, people are likely to be more attentive to evidence that supports their existing views than that which contradicts these views. Because most officials tend to be socialized to see international relations as a Hobbesian world, they are likely to be less receptive to information suggesting that others deserve their trust. Therefore, they will demand more massive and compelling evidence to accept others' trustworthiness, and conversely, their trust in others is more easily shaken by slender and even ambiguous evidence implying that the latter may be unreliable or unfriendly.

It is also only natural that people dislike being told that others may perceive them in an unfavorable light or are likely to question their trustworthiness. Only rarely do they pause to reflect whether their words and deeds may have given others a plausible reason to have negative views about them. Mutual distrust can deepen and become entrenched due to the effects of mirror images on both sides of a relationship, effects that stem from their mental or analytic habits showing the following tendencies.[16] When they see their counterpart undertaking an undesirable or unpopular action, they are inclined to explain this action by pointing to this counterpart's natural disposition—that is, its innate character or purposeful intention. But when they themselves undertake a similar action, they tend to resort to circumstantial explanation—such as by pointing to situational factors beyond their control. Thus, when a person fails to show up on time for an appointment, he or she is likely to find excuses such as his/her alarm clock did not work or traffic congestion was responsible for his/her tardiness. But when the role is reversed, he or she is likely to see his/her counterpart's tardiness as an indication of the latter's inherent character flaw (such as his/her basic irresponsibility or lack of consideration for others) or even as a sign of intentional attempt to do harm (such as a deliberate snub).

Attribution theory also presents corollary propositions about how people interpret favorable events or positive experiences. They are more likely to explain these events and experiences as a matter of their own volition or disposition when explaining or presenting their own actions. Thus, when discussing their own steps to retrench their military or to limit their armament, they are likely to say that this action demonstrates their peaceful intentions. Conversely, when another country engages in similar behavior (especially when this country is not trusted), they are likely to point to its dire circumstances (e.g., its stressful economic conditions, its budgetary difficulties) and thus to dismiss this behavior as a sign of its benign intentions. For readers who may question this or that episode in my previous discussion of the historical reasons for mutual distrust in Sino-American relations, it is important for them to keep in mind such common psychological tendencies. To address the problem of mutual distrust, one will need to understand why the other side holds the views it has about oneself, and not just tell this counterpart to accept one's self-image.

The preceding chapters offer the following conclusions. First, China and the U.S. have a tumultuous and even mostly antagonistic history since 1949. While there were periods of détente and rapprochement, this relationship also experienced periods of deep suspicion and outright hostility. The vicissitudes undergone by this relationship show that cooperation is possible, although it will take a long road to build mutual trust in its strong form. The higher the level of historical distrust, the more challenging and arduous will be the efforts needed to reverse it. Not only do these efforts need to persuade the leaders and people of the other country, but they must also overcome skepticisms and oppositions within one's own country. Because each country currently has a strong distrust of the other, more persuasive evidence would be necessary to convince it to trust its counterpart. Thus, both sides have a steep hill to climb in order to gain the other side's trust (in contrast, countries that have had a long history of cooperation would have an easier time to augment and consolidate their mutual trust).

A corollary of this observation is that even a minor incident in Sino-American relations can cause major damage to each side's perceived trustworthiness. Their mutual trust is more vulnerable to setback and officials on both sides are more inclined to interpret even ambiguous events as evidence of a breach of trust. In contrast, Franco-American and German-American relations are much better able to withstand adverse publicity such as that which disclosing the U.S. government spying on French and German officials. Similarly, although Israeli-American relations have been tumultuous recently over many issues (e.g., Jewish settlements in occupied Arab land, Washington's nuclear deal with Tehran, and mutual accusations of spying and meddling in the other country's domestic politics), their traditional friendship will endure despite their occasional frictions.

Second, the weak form of trust only offers a transient source for confidence in stable future relations. It is built on a flimsy foundation as changing circumstances can easily alter a state's future intentions. At the same time, the strong form of trust sets a very high bar so that it can even be in short supply in domestic situations such as those described by Robert Putnam's analysis of the civic culture prevailing in southern Italy.[17] Recent surveys have also indicated a general decline in Americans' trust in their fellow citizens. In interstate relations, interactions among the Scandinavian countries come closest to approximate this sense of belonging to a common moralistic community and to exemplify the practice of generalized trust. Even among member states of the North Atlantic security community, we have heard recent reports that the U.S. government has spied on French and German leaders. This being the case, the strong form of trust is clearly beyond the reach of Sino-American relations for a long time to come. Even though these countries have cooperated on some issues such as in their joint efforts to combat terrorism or to curb nuclear proliferation, this cooperation reflects much more strategic calculation and instrumental convenience than common identification or moral convergence. This same observation, however, also says interstate cooperation is possible even without strong bonds of trust.

Third, one cannot hold out much hope for diplomatic exchanges, military consultations, and summit meetings between the leaders of the two countries to make much of an immediate and substantial tangible impact on reversing the current trust deficit in Sino-American relations. Moreover, even when progress is being made through these contacts and through these countries' diplomats participating and even collaborating in various multilateral venues, this result is likely to be fragile and subject to reversal. One need just to recall that in the 1950s there were much more intense, even intimate, interactions between the Chinese and Soviets who shared an ideological affinity as well. Sino-Soviet cooperation, however, was not immune to subsequent acrimony that became so serious that both Beijing and Moscow had thought of the other country as its greatest security threat at the height of their dispute. There is therefore the danger of backsliding even in those cases showing seemingly strong political solidarity and mutual trust. In contrast to Sino-Soviet relations in the 1950s and early 1960s, there are more robust and symmetric economic bonds between China and the U.S. today. The effects of these growing and cumulative economic ties on domestic interest groups should tend to stabilize foreign relations, acting as a shock absorber in times of stress. But as attested by the outbreak of World War I, close commercial and financial relations cannot be counted on to override leaders' geostrategic decisions.

Fourth, interstate trust is, at least initially, built on the basis of political calculations. The process of building trust has typically started by a weaker or needier state's unilateral and costly concession. It is an attempt to seek accommodation based on this state's difficult domestic and/or foreign circumstances. Leaders are less likely to undertake such overtures unless they are motivated by strong pressures to do so. Thus ironically, when things are going well for the leaders of both countries, neither side is likely to take bold initiatives and both are more disposed to make only incremental changes to their existing relations. Yet, as observed earlier, when a country's leaders try to build trust and conciliate with their counterparts, their circumstances are such that this communication is more likely to be dismissed as insincere and to be construed as a temporizing attempt reflecting their current weakness rather than future benignity. The tendency for the trust-building process to typically start with concessions made by the weaker side in a relationship is furthermore ironic because it is the stronger side that should feel more secure in its position and that should therefore be more able to afford to take a chance in undertaking a conciliatory initiative without making itself more vulnerable. Naturally, the window of opportunity must be open on both sides for an overture to be reciprocated and for a process of building trust to become cumulatively effective. Thus, conditions in both countries must be aligned so that leaders on both sides are receptive to conciliatory steps to revamp their relations such as those shown in Franco-German ties after World War II and, more recently, in 2015, in U.S.-Cuban relations.

Fifth, the dominance of political calculations in the trust-building process suggests that economic and cultural conditions tend to play a secondary role. As Charles Kupchan shows,[18] politics tends to trump economics. Trade and investment usually follow the flag as the proponents of the "political primacy" perspective argue (there are exceptions such as when Taiwan's business people managed to change Taipei's earlier policy of refusing any contact with mainland China). Conversely, political deterioration in official relations can threaten to end economic exchanges. Dense economic ties and close cultural affinity have not in the past prevented European states from going to war or for today's China and Japan to be deeply suspicious of each other's intentions. These remarks do not deny that economic interests can sometimes prevail over politicians' natural inclinations or alter their initial preferences, such as when even pro-independence politicians in Taiwan are leery of openly advocating policies that would limit or disrupt the island's commerce with mainland China. As for mass attitudes, they tend to follow changes in states' official relations (just recall the panda craze immediately after the thawing of Sino-American relations). Favorable public opinions about another country rise when official relations between the two sides improve, and they fall when these relations deteriorate. Most citizens do not have strong opinions about foreign relations, and their views do not usually constrain their leaders' foreign policy discretion. This said, latent public attitudes can be mobilized by the political opposition to challenge the incumbent leaders' policies and to criticize these leaders' performance in office. The bitter partisan debate about "who lost China" in Washington and the scare politics of McCarthyism during the early 1950s left a lasting legacy on U.S. foreign policy.[19] Thus, whether public opinion is subject to elite influence or whether it can constrain leaders' policy discretion depends in part on whether the leadership is cohesive and united. When there is elite rivalry and leadership division, competing factions are likely to engage in partisan mobilization often to the detriment of international cooperation.

Sixth, some of the factors that have been mentioned to contribute to trust building are not within the power of officials to influence, at least not in a direct and immediate sense. Thus, a country's cultural tradition is beyond a leader's ability to manipulate even though he or she can orchestrate publicity to influence public opinion. Similarly, the character of a country's regime and its basic social order are not usually something that can be altered easily or quickly (although the massive changes set off by Mikhail Gorbachev's reforms come to mind as a possible counter example). Moreover, how the people of a country change their identity in such a way that it gradually incorporates foreigners beyond their borders is still a poorly understood process. What is clear, however, is that this evolution involves a protracted process of many years and even decades, and that a shared identity based on a sense of belonging to the same moralistic community represents the culmination of a long journey to build trust. These remarks suggest that when analyzing or recommending how states can enhance mutual trust, attention should be directed to those things that officials have more direct control over—such as the topics of communicating reassurance through economic interdependence and subscribing to emergent international norms addressed by the semi-strong form of trust. Although many scholars and officials have focused their attention on regime character (especially whether a counterpart state is a democracy) and power shifts (such as China's recent power gains), these factors do not appear to be the most important or relevant ones for building trust.

As Kupchan has shown,[20] autocratic or authoritarian states have also been quite capable of strategic restraint and these states have also been able to elicit cooperation and trust. As for power shifts, it is appropriate to counsel leaders of those countries gaining power and those that are already powerful to resist the inclination to put less trust in others and to work harder to reassure others that they themselves can be trusted. It is of course difficult to imagine leaders of any country who would not wish to see an improvement in their country's power and international position. But they would do well as a general proposition to "bark less and wag more." In his study of the peaceful power transition between Britain and the U.S., Yongping Feng includes strategic restraint as a critical factor.[21] It enabled both states to alter their identities and redefine their interests. Britain's cooperation also helped the U.S. to ascend rapidly as Washington was able to focus its resources on internal development rather than external competition.

Finally, countries that have built strong trust have started their process with a convergence of the values and beliefs held by their elites rather than mass publics. This process is usually a top-down phenomenon, one that is led by elite opinions that only subsequently and after a long period spreads to feelings of amity and common identification at the mass level. Economic and cultural exchanges can have a greater impact on enhancing interstate trust to the extent that they affect the elites' perceptions of their self-interests and even their self-identities. Whether the relevant countries share compatible social orders and cultural traditions can facilitate or complicate this convergence but this sociocultural congruence is neither a sufficient nor a necessary condition for ensuring trust. There is a low level of trust in Sino-Japanese relations even though these countries share a similar cultural heritage and have close economic ties. The U.S. Civil War also shows that these conditions are not nearly as important as a convergence of elite values and beliefs in keeping trust and securing peace. Similarly, the reversal of Sino-Soviet friendship in the 1960s and 1970s shows that ideological similarity, regime affinity, and compatible social orders were unable to withstand the effects of a loss of confidence and trust by the elites on both sides.

THE PRACTICE OF STRATEGIC RESTRAINT

Strategic restraint trumps the other hypothesized variables in building mutual trust.[22] It is something that officials can directly control, and it can have a more immediate impact in ameliorating a trust deficit than macro factors pertaining to a country's regime type, cultural heritage, and its people's political outlook. What would strategic restraint entail?

My previous discussion has already touched on several critical norms that contribute to the practice of this restraint which can be manifested by a state's appropriate action as well as inaction under given circumstances. These norms pertain mainly to limitations on the pertinent states' freedom to use military force, their adherence to treaty obligations, and their recognition of the geostrategic boundaries of their competition.[23] When great powers tended to agree on these normative rules in the past, they were better able to maintain peace, stability, and trust in their relations. Conversely, when they refused to be bound by these rules, conflict among them was more pervasive and intense. When states collectively and consistently follow a code of conduct in the three areas just mentioned, they promote a restrictive and rule-based normative order. When they routinely and flagrantly violate these rules, their behavior indicates a permissive environment akin to that of structural anarchy. This behavior, when repeated by many states, also fosters such an environment. Thus, as Alexander Wendt has observed, "anarchy is what states make of it."[24]

The practice of strategic restraint follows from an adherence to a restrictive normative order, one that is based on the great powers' self-binding and co-binding to a common code of conduct. At the very core of this code are the standards to be applied to judging a state's legitimate use of military force. For reasons already explained, this use of military force against another country (or entity) is suspect when it is undertaken without authorization from the United Nations. Washington's extra-legal use of drones to kill suspected terrorists and its claim that it has the right to launch a preventive war in order to avert a possible future threat are controversial and set dangerous precedents. The U.S. invasion of Iraq in 2003 was especially damaging to its perceived trustworthiness. This was a war of choice rather than necessity,[25] and its justification was based on false claims.[26] Washington's air campaigns against Serbia, Libya, and Syria would also tend to augment rather than attenuate Beijing and Moscow's suspicions about its ulterior motives (Russia has also undertaken a bombing campaign in Syria albeit at the behest of the incumbent government in Damascus). These episodes do not pertain to

China directly but would nevertheless raise Beijing's concerns about Washington's general intentions.

Of course, China and Russia have also used military force such as when they fought Vietnam in 1979 and Georgia in 2008, respectively. Russia has also intervened against Ukraine although in this case it appears to have relied more on Ukrainian separatists rather than committing its own forces directly and overtly. Just as with the numerous U.S. military interventions against various small Caribbean and Central American countries, it is implausible that these neighbors posed a threat to China and Russia's national security. These episodes would therefore incline other states to distrust all three—although unlike many episodes involving the U.S. use of force (e.g., Grenada, Panama, the Dominican Republic, Iraq, Afghanistan), those recent conflicts fought by China and Russia were limited wars that did not result in changing an opponent's regime or taking over its country. Border conflicts should in principle be more amenable to settlement because they involve tangible resources or objects that are divisible,[27] whereas conflicts over a regime's character or a country's political orientation involve transformative struggles over intangible (and hence, indivisible) values and as such they are likely to be more intense and intractable. Ceteris paribus, the farther away from its homeland a country uses its military force, the less likely that its action is motivated by defensive rather than offensive interests. When a state fights at or near its border, this phenomenon does not necessarily mean that it has defensive motivations. But when it fights in distant lands, its defensive rationale is more suspect. This said, it is also true that most countries are incapable of intervening militarily abroad and only one country, the U.S., is capable of waging a large-scale, protracted war far away from its homeland. In other words, that most countries—including China—have not fought long-distance wars may just reflect their lack of capability rather than their lack of motivation. As a general heuristic, geographic distance provides a more objective measure of a state's stake and motivation in a conflict than relying on officials' words.

Border conflicts are less ambitious and easier to settle than wars seeking regime transformation or overseas conquest.

It is also pertinent to note that China has since 1974 refrained from using direct military force in its maritime disputes in the East and South China Seas.[28] Western analyses and reports have given much attention to Beijing's increased military capabilities and its expansive territorial claims in the Paracel and especially the Spratly archipelagoes. China, however, has thus far generally pursued a policy course that can be best described as "reactive assertiveness."[29] Trevor Moss describes this posture as "China doesn't pick fights, but ... if someone picks a fight with China it will offer a forceful response."[30] Michael Swaine and Taylor Fravel have similarly remarked, "As in its approach to the South China Sea, Beijing has not altered its existing strategy in the East China Sea arena [in its sovereignty dispute with Japan over the Senkaku/Diaoyu Islands], choosing instead to defer settlement and engage in political and diplomatic negotiation while defending its existing claims to disputed territory."[31] This depiction is at variance with the characterization one encounters more often in the Western media, one that attributes to Beijing a bellicose posture and an ambitious agenda.

With respect to China's ongoing sovereignty disputes in the East and South China Seas, Beijing has signed the U.N. Convention of the Law of the Sea although as mentioned already, it has explicitly opted out of the provision that would have required China to submit to compulsory dispute settlement through international arbitration. The U.S. has yet to join UNCLOS. As remarked in the last chapter, Beijing has refused to acknowledge that the Permanent Court of Arbitration has jurisdiction over its sovereignty disputes and it has declined to participate in its proceedings or to accept its ruling against China's claim of "historical rights." The U.S. has similarly rejected that the International Court of Justice had any jurisdiction to adjudicate Nicaragua's complaints about Washington's support of the *contras* and its mining of that country's harbors.

Washington's withdrawal from the Anti-Ballistic Missiles Treaty, announced by President George W. Bush in December 2001, was a significant departure from its traditional advocacy of international regimes to limit armament. Although it had tried to convince Moscow and Beijing that its effort to build missile defense systems was not aimed at them, neither was convinced. In response to Washington's claim that its national missile defense (NMD) will only target rogue states like North Korea and Iran, a Russian general retorted that this is "an argument for the naïve or the stupid.... This system will be directed against Russia and against China."[32] Washington's abrogation of the ABM Treaty and its pursuit of NMD signified a decision to abandon the *status quo ante* of mutual assured destruction, and communicated an intention to seek nuclear superiority.

Kegley and Raymond have used the opinions of international jurists and legal scholars to code historical periods when the norm of *pacta sunt servanda* (treaties are binding) prevailed and to distinguish these periods from others when the opposite norm of *rebus sic stantibus* (by reason of changed circumstances) was frequently invoked by states to repudiate their alliance commitments.[33] They found that when there is a strong international norm demanding that treaty obligations be binding on states, militarized disputes and wars are less frequent and intense. Conversely, more lax observance of international accords and greater insistence on each state's decision autonomy and policy freedom tend to be accompanied by more pervasive strife. Thus, respect for the sanctity of states' international commitments appears to have the general effect of building trust and dampening conflict.

By giving prior notice that it was going to withdraw from the ABM Treaty and that it also intended to abrogate its defense treaty with Taiwan, Washington was exercising an option provided by these accords. Thus it did not violate the terms of these treaties. The message conveyed by these decisions, however, seems clear. It could not be said to have enhanced other states' confidence in Washington's benign intentions, especially in Moscow and Taipei. As mentioned previously, given the vast military advantage that the U.S. already enjoys over other countries—including Russia and China[34]—it is not unnatural for them to ask why it continues to develop its armament while insisting that other countries limit theirs. The gap between U.S. strategic forces and those possessed by Russia and China has widened so much that two scholars were led to conclude that Washington can now effectively launch a disarming first strike, thus dismantling the basis of mutual assured destruction that has provided stable nuclear deterrence between the superpowers.[35] This view is echoed by another analyst who concludes "... major powers have a basis to fear that U.S. NMD could evolve into a serious effort to acquire meaningful nuclear superiority, an effort that would make sense only if the United States had expansionist rather than status quo aims."[36] The U.S. announced in 2012 an official policy to ensure that "our forces will be strong enough to dissuade potential adversaries from pursuing a military build-up in hopes of surpassing, or equaling, the power of the United States."[37]

The core issue of contention in Sino-American relations pertains to the status of Taiwan. The official joint communiqué establishing these countries' diplomatic relations in 1979 states: "The United States of America recognizes the Government of the People's Republic of China as the sole legal Government of China. Within this context, the people of the United States will maintain cultural, commercial, and other unofficial relations with the people of Taiwan." [38] It moreover declares that "[the] Government of the United States of America acknowledges the Chinese position that there is but one China and Taiwan is part of China." A joint communiqué of course lacks the legal binding force of a treaty, but it nevertheless declares the intentions and commitments of the states involved. The word "acknowledges" used in this context was deliberately ambiguous. One meaning of this word given by the Merriam-Webster dictionary is "to recognize the rights, authority, or status of." Another meaning is "to take notice of" or "to make known the receipt of." Naturally, the Chinese side prefers the former interpretation whereas the U.S. side prefers the latter. Although this ambiguity might have served a purpose when the two countries were negotiating over establishing formal diplomatic relations, it points to a constant irritant that undermines trust and has the potential to escalate tension. Former U.S. Secretary of State Henry Kissinger has stated bluntly that "[for] us to go to war with a recognized country where we have an ambassador over a part of what we would recognize as their country would be preposterous."[39] Although some U.S. politicians invoke Taiwan people's right to self-determination, it is also clear that Washington does not support this island's political independence should a majority of its voters decide to pursue this course. Nor has the U.S. prioritized the right to self-determination on the part of those who live in Kashmir, Palestine, or Crimea, and it did not initially favor attempts by Bangladesh and Croatia to secede from Pakistan and Yugoslavia respectively—nor did it recognize the Confederacy's right to do so.

Taiwan should provide the litmus test for Sino-American trust. Its status is highly salient to Beijing, and dispute over this status is the most likely cause for a military confrontation between Beijing and Washington. Thus far the U.S. has pursued a deliberate policy of strategic ambiguity.[40] Washington declines to commit itself publicly and explicitly to how it will act should there be a cross-Strait crisis. Its public statements favor a peaceful settlement, a preference that has been widely interpreted to suggest that it will resist Beijing's use of military force to seize Taiwan but it will also oppose Taipei's attempt to declare *de jure* independence. From Beijing's perspective, by nullifying Beijing's military threat to Taiwan this U.S. policy has the effect and even the intent of perpetuating Taiwan's continued *de facto* separation from China. As Beijing improves its military capabilities, it will naturally be more inclined to ask why it should go along with a deal whereby it accepts Washington's help to prevent Taiwan's *de jure* independence in exchange for this island's *de facto* independence in seeming perpetuity. The U.S. has pursued extended deterrence to protect Taiwan's *de facto* independence, and this policy requires it to demonstrate its resolve by "tying hands" and/or "sinking costs."[41] Washington's willingness to defend Taiwan against a possible Chinese attack, however, has become more questionable over time.[42] Various scholars have proposed different approaches to resolve or at least to alleviate the current stalemate in order to avert a possible future crisis fraught with risks.[43]

Whereas the advantages and disadvantages of these proposals may be debated, two things appear to be relatively clear. First, regardless of the actual nature of Washington's decision, its action or inaction on the Taiwan issue will most likely get Beijing's attention. In other words, given its importance to Beijing this issue will carry more weight in its perception of Washington's intentions than almost all others. Beijing's perception in this case is also influenced by its belief that rather than an intrinsic interest in Taiwan's fate, Washington cares about this island's status more out of a derivative concern about its relations with China and its support for Taipei has been motivated primarily by a desire to thwart and frustrate Beijing's political agenda. Second, whatever Washington may decide, its policy will have an effect not only in Beijing but also in Taipei. The U.S. cannot accommodate China and gain its trust without simultaneously undermining its relations with Taiwan and arouse concerns about its steadfastness in other allied capitals. An attempt to reassure Beijing may very well be perceived as a breach of trust and a betrayal of Washington's self-avowed principles not only by Taipei but also some parts of Washington itself.

Mutual respect for each great power's sphere of influence is the third element in those restrictive normative orders that have historically accompanied or promoted international peace and stability. Self-restraint from interfering in areas where another great power has traditionally had important geostrategic interests helps to demarcate the boundaries of interstate contest and provides a basis for reciprocal accommodation. This is another important contentious issue in Sino-American relations, and the USSR/Russia's recent experience should be instructive for China. Despite Moscow's asymmetric and even unilateral concessions in ending the Cold War, it has not been fully accepted by the West and recent events show that the West has actually increasingly encroached on Russia's traditional sphere of influence (e.g., Iraq, Yugoslavia, Afghanistan, and even Ukraine). Thus, it is not unreasonable for Moscow and others like Beijing to conclude that the USSR/Russia's accommodative policies have not been reciprocated. Seen from their perspective, NATO's expansion to include the Eastern and Central European states can easily be interpreted as an aggressive advance to exploit Russia's moment of weakness. Attempts to seek Ukraine's political and economic reorientation away from Russia and toward Western Europe represent another example of failed self-restraint and an infringement on Moscow's traditional sphere of influence.

Moreover, it will not escape Beijing's attention that whereas the U.S. had during the Cold War at least tacitly recognized the USSR's sphere of influence in Eastern and Central Europe, it has thus far not been willing to acknowledge China's strategic interests in its near abroad. The U.S. had fought three long bloody wars in countries bordering China (Korea, Vietnam, and Afghanistan), and in Beijing's eyes its support has been the key reason sustaining Taiwan's separation from China. Washington is also supporting those countries contesting China's maritime claims in the East and South China Seas. It has undertaken forward deployment of its military forces that routinely operate right up to China's eastern, southern, and western borders. It has military bases and formal or tacit allies along these borders. Amitai Etzioni argues that the delineation of spheres of influence is a critical part of the trust-building process to stabilize relations among great powers.[44] Currently, the lines demarcating the intersection of U.S. and Chinese influence in East Asia are ambiguous and needless to say, highly contentious.

In addition to limiting the use of military force, complying with international accords, and respecting states' traditional spheres of influence, strategic restraint is manifested by voluntary decisions to eschew opportunism. Abstention from opportunism can be indicated by a decision not to depreciate a country's currency when others are doing so in the midst of an economic crisis with the aim of promoting their exports abroad. It can also manifest itself in not demanding other countries to change their domestic rules and regulations that are widely seen to have the aim of helping one's own firms gaining access to their markets. The U.S. was perceived to have exploited the Asian financial crisis in insisting on such changes as a condition for South Korea and other countries to obtain foreign credit. Conversely, China had resisted the temptation to devalue its currency during this period. Moreover, Beijing had injected liquidity into international financial markets during the last Great Recession rather than withdrawing funds from abroad.[45]

To the extent that a country has a free and independent press, a vibrant and critical political opposition, a long tradition of pacifism or neutrality, and a large segment of its public opposed to foreign war and intervention, these features reassure its foreign counterparts. They provide built-in domestic resistance to a leader who may otherwise entertain foreign aggression. These groups can also serve the role of domestic watchdog to assuage foreign concerns, and they can be trusted to sound off alarms long before an aggressive leader will be able to implement his or her plan. Germany and Japan's constitutional provisions and strong popular sentiments opposing foreign military involvement enhance foreigners' confidence that these countries are not likely to harbor expansionist ambitions (although in July 2015 the Japanese Diet approved policy changes that would enable this country's armed forces to participate in foreign military missions). This said, sometimes democracies' domestic institutions fail to brake the rush to war as shown by the absence of a thorough debate by the media, the political opposition, and the mass public in the period leading up to the U.S. invasion of Iraq in 2003.[46] Institutional restraints and public opinion did not in this case stop a war of choice as the proponents of democratic peace theory would have expected.

Germany's enmeshment in various European and North Atlantic institutions provide an additional insurance against its possible defection through the effects that these institutions have on constraining or binding the behavior of their member states.[47] Japan's alliance with the U.S. also serves partly this purpose by curbing Tokyo's military autonomy and tethering it to Washington. In this sense, the U.S.-Japan defense treaty serves as a *pactum de contrahendo*, or a pact of restraint.[48] The U.S. role in this relationship has been described as a "cork in the bottle." As such, it contributes to trust in Tokyo's nonbelligerent intentions on the part of Japan's neighbors. Naturally, this restraining effect is offset by the opposite impression created by an alliance, which is to bolster opposition to an intended target. Thus, alliances can have these dual effects. Allies want to undertake joint effort against a third party but they also want to use the alliance to influence a partner's foreign policy (so that, for example, they are better able to avoid entrapment by this partner to get them engulfed in an unwanted conflict).[49]

Whether Beijing perceives the U.S.-Japan treaty is more useful to it as a restraint on a militarily tethered Japan or whether it becomes more concerned that this alliance is part of the U.S. grand design to contain China and block its ascent will depend on Washington's words and deeds. To the extent that Washington has in recent years urged Tokyo to actually increase its defense spending and raise its overseas military profile, and to the extent that it has abandoned a previously ambiguous posture pertaining to how it will act in a potential confrontation between China and Japan in their dispute over the Senkaku/Diaoyu Islands, these developments are more likely to alarm than reassure Beijing. The uproar created by Beijing's announcement of an air-defense self-identification zone (an announcement requiring foreign aircraft flying in an area in the East China Sea that overlaps with other countries' jurisdictional claims to identify themselves to Chinese authorities) in November 2013 was revealing. Washington, Tokyo, and Seoul all criticized this announcement even though they have all previously made similar unilateral declarations (the U.S. policy, however, did not require foreign aircraft flying to non-U.S. destinations to identify themselves to U.S. authorities).

Naturally, China does not have those domestic and foreign features just mentioned with respect to Germany and Japan. Beijing will therefore have to communicate its trustworthiness in other ways such as through its involvement in multilateral forums and international organizations. By entangling and embedding itself in these institutions and cross-national networks of international commerce and finance, it can convey its intention to exercise strategic restraint. These decisions represent self-limiting safeguards, ones that make a decision to defect in the future more costly although not impossible. Thus China's increasing enmeshment in the web of international relations points to its greater trustworthiness. Compared to the U.S., China is about twice as much involved in foreign trade given its economic size.

It should be recalled that this enmeshment also serves an important defensive purpose—it makes much more difficult for a foreign power like the U.S. to single out China for punitive sanction without also hurting other countries. These other countries therefore, as a result of China's enmeshment in international commerce and finance, become Beijing's tacit partners in reducing China's vulnerability to a possible U.S. attempt to coerce it economically.

Strategic restraint also requires sensitivity to how one's actions and statements in the domestic realm can have undesirable repercussions abroad, creating issues and causing problems for counterpart leaders in their domestic politics. "America bashing" and "China bashing" may be popular with certain segments of the domestic audience and help a politician to display his or her nationalist credentials. Yet rhetoric intended primarily for domestic consumption can provide political ammunition to hardliners in other capitals, creating an echo chamber of escalating recriminations. In this way the dynamics of domestic politics can abet and entrench mutual distrust. The hardliners on both sides of a relationship can turn out to be each other's best allies as they seek to battle their respective domestic liberal opponents. Scapegoating a foreign country by hardliners in one country can be an open invitation to their soul mates in the other country to return the favor, and the resulting dynamic produces a political atmosphere that will hardly be conducive to fostering mutual trust.

Moreover, when rival elite factions engage in competitive bidding to demonstrate that they can take a tougher position against a foreign competitor, they climb on to an escalator that may be difficult for them to get off. This situation makes it politically more challenging for leaders to initiate a conciliatory process by making concessions to their foreign counterparts in the first place or to reciprocate such gestures in order to sustain this process. Leaders who are personally inclined to undertake friendly policies will be hamstrung by domestic political forces that are deeply suspicious of and strongly antagonistic toward the other country. Especially in a close election, democratic leaders want to avoid being charged by their opponents for being "soft" on or "cuddling" a foreign adversary. As Chinese domestic politics becomes more pluralistic with rival political factions competing for power, this dynamic of scapegoating foreigners and rival elite factions trying to outbid each other on their nationalist credentials may also become more intense. There is relatively little that incumbent officials on both sides can do to moderate or silence outspoken politicians favoring a more confrontational approach to Sino-American relations.

Strategic restraint in the domestic arena may be especially difficult when a country's elite is divided and when politicians on each side may be tempted to mobilize and exploit the mass public's nationalist impulses. We can sometimes catch a glimpse of this phenomenon such as when supporters of the Trans-Pacific Partnership, including President Obama himself, invoked a threat or challenge from China as an extrinsic reason for this cooperative project which should be intrinsically beneficial for all the states involved.[50] These supporters of TPP argued that somehow if the U.S. president was denied fast-track authority to negotiate this trade agreement, China rather than the U.S. would be making economic rules in the future. Thus even nonrealists sometimes resort to realist arguments to advance their favorite policy. Such issue framing, even if only intended to sway domestic political opinion, is unnecessarily provocative and will inevitably have repercussions abroad, including those that tend to incite similar rhetoric from the other side. As another example, Washington's announced policy of pivot to Asia will surely be noticed by Chinese officials and provide political fodder to hardliners who question Washington's motivations and demand Beijing to take counter-actions to respond to this U.S. initiative. Whether intended or not, this announcement has the effect of undermining bilateral trust and when it is followed by only a small amount of resource commitment and effort mobilization, it also erodes confidence on the part of Washington's regional allies.

From Beijing's perspective, the current alignment of U.S. domestic politics can be worrisome. Republicans tend to emphasize the security threat posed by rising Chinese military power, whereas Democrats tend to focus on the Chinese economic menace to American jobs and Beijing's denial of human rights to its own citizens. Although many differences separate those located at the two opposite ends of the U.S. political spectrum, China may represent a focal point where these partisans can actually find common ground. Parenthetically, one can also discern a strong bipartisan apprehension about and even distrust of Saudi Arabia when an overwhelming majority of Democrats and Republicans in the U.S. Congress overrode President Barack Obama's veto and passed the bill to allow U.S. citizens to sue Saudi Arabia over the latter's alleged complicity in the 9/11 terrorist attack. To the extent that American politics has shifted away from the proverbial "median voter" to a more bimodal distribution of political opinions, this evolution points to more vigorous partisan struggles and a greater difficulty to secure a governing coalition, including one that can politically sustain bold initiatives that will be required to advance reciprocal adjustment and build mutual trust in Sino-American relations.

If a politically secure leader is in a stronger position to make concessions and seek accommodation with a foreign country, current and future Chinese officials will not likely have the same stature or authority as Mao Tse-tung or Deng Xiaoping to initiate bold domestic or foreign policies that make a sharp break from the status quo. Domestic power in China is no longer embodied in strong or popular figures in a cult of personality. It is more decentralized and institutionalized today, devolving to more autonomous agencies and to provincial and regional units. At the same time, civil society has become more vibrant and pluralistic, and the mass public is less quiescent and more politically informed. Popular opinion has also become more critical and even cynical, often questioning and challenging the legitimacy of communist rule and the sincerity and corruptibility of leading cadres. Thus Chinese leaders will become more rather less constrained by changing domestic political conditions, and they are likely to become more fearful of a domestic backlash should they face a humiliating setback in their foreign policy. They are almost certainly more reticent and less inclined to take those political risks that would be entailed in launching a new bold foreign initiative, especially when it may entail mass perceptions of making concessions on national sovereignty. Already public opinion is critical of government policies for being too weak and compromising rather than too assertive. All of this implies that ongoing political trends do not necessarily favor a more accommodating China as proponents of the democratic peace theory would expect. Naturally, it is useful to distinguish democracy from populism, with the former defined to feature the formal institutions of regular elections, universal suffrage, and political contest among competing parties. It is, however, also important to ask whether a country has a civic culture that respects individual rights and personal liberties. A regime can be popular but undemocratic (such as in Maoist China), and a country can be democratic but illiberal (such as today's Iran) or liberal but undemocratic (such as Britain and the U.S. before the advent of universal suffrage).

Naturally, because it will take both parties to build mutual trust, the political situations in both countries must be aligned to enable their leaders to initiate and sustain this process. The political windows of opportunity should be open on both sides at the same time in order for them to jump through. Ongoing political changes in China and the U.S. imply that these windows may be closing, and the critical precipitating event inclining leaders to seriously ponder new bold policy departures is not yet visible. It is, however, easier to imagine how these windows may become shut. A global recession can increase mass disaffection in both countries by exacerbating income inequality, economic dislocation, and popular resentment against incumbent officials. Already we can see signs of popular anger and this anger can turn against economic openness and interdependence, as shown by Britain's vote to exit the European Union and the popularity of Donald Trump's campaign message. Economic hardship also makes citizens more receptive to nationalist demagogues and antiforeign and anti-immigrant rhetoric.

The effects of ongoing domestic political changes in China are accompanied by this country's continued economic openness and its rising interdependence with the rest of world. This important development represents a costly investment in maintaining the international status quo, and it also has had the effect of entrenching and legitimating those domestic groups that have a large and expanding stake in doing so. China is the largest or second largest foreign creditor to the U.S. (it has alternated this position with Japan in the recent past), and it is a leading trade partner for the U.S. It is poised to become the world's largest foreign investor by 2020 and to overtake the U.S. economy in absolute size in the next couple of decades. Thus, it will become more entangled and embedded in the global political economy. This prospective development does not imply that adverse political changes cannot alter a country's economic policy and outlook—indeed, the U.S. under a Trump administration can very well reverse its traditional liberal economic orientation. Such reversal, however, can be quite costly in tangible and intangible ways.

Soviet-American relations during the Cold War lacked a significant economic dimension. Moreover, unlike Soviet-American relations during that time, China is not currently engaged in a worldwide ideological competition with Washington. Nor is it seeking to build a countervailing alliance. It has not made any attempt to challenge U.S. primacy in those regions that Washington considers to be critical to its national security or that are within its traditional sphere of influence (Western Europe, the Middle East, and Latin America). Inaction or self-abstention in these respects is important although its significance is sometimes overlooked. The one region with unclear and changing boundaries of Sino-American geostrategic competition is of course those areas in Northeast and Southeast Asia located in physical proximity to China. As discussed earlier, power shifts may raise the threshold for both China and the U.S. to trust the other side, thereby increasing the risks related to those tectonic frictions engendered by these uncertain boundaries.

In this regional context, trust in Sino-American relations impinges on third parties and is in turn impinged by them. Thus, for example, a rapprochement between Beijing and Seoul would incline Pyongyang to become more skeptical of the reliability of its Chinese ally. Similarly, Washington's reassurances to Taipei and Tokyo can undermine its credibility in Beijing's eyes. When relations between Beijing and Washington improve, this development can similarly cause concerns in the other capitals just mentioned. Thus, the process of building and sustaining trust is not a strictly bilateral matter. Changes in bilateral relations can have positive or negative multilateral reverberations. We can see this dynamic most clearly in recent Middle Eastern politics. Washington's nuclear deal with Tehran encountered serious resistance from both Tel Aviv and Riyadh. These traditional U.S. allies saw this event to portend a U.S.-Iranian rapprochement under the Obama administration. It augured in their view an impending realignment of Washington's Middle Eastern policies to their detriment. They were not reticent to say that their trust in the U.S. has been shaken. This example illustrates the complexities involved in the practice of strategic restraint because this restraint or reassurance directed at one party may have repercussions in managing one's relations with others. Calibrating and balancing a country's ties with multiple significant others, especially in the case of a global hegemon like the U.S., is no easy task. This illustration also points to the changeability of some situations or relations, as President Obama's policy toward Tehran can be reversed by President Trump. In the new Trump administration, China and the U.S. may seek a grand bargain whereby Washington gets Beijing's cooperation in dealing with North Korea in return for its accommodation of Beijing's interests pertaining to Taiwan. Such transactional politics, however, reflects convergent interests rather than abiding trust.

CONCLUDING REMARKS

I have drawn from the international relations literature to illuminate Sino-American relations. In doing so, I have placed this particular case in the general context of cross-national patterns. I have also tried to suggest a multivariate perspective, showing that trust is a joint product of multiple factors. Some of these factors are critical while others are less relevant or necessary. The confluence of factors and events tends to be more important than any single variable.

Prognostication is a dangerous business but it is possible to offer some hopefully informed conjectures based on how those variables and propositions introduced in the preceding analysis can interact. Although there continues to be significant distrust in Sino-American relations, these relations are also more robust and healthier today than in the past. Trust in this relationship, however, can come under serious strain and be severely tested. This challenge does not have to stem from a direct bilateral dispute. After all, China and the U.S. do not have any territorial dispute and Beijing is not threatening America's traditional spheres of influence. The source is more likely to be Taiwan, North Korea, or Japan which is engaged in a maritime dispute with China. Thus, the pathway to a possible destabilization of Sino-American relations is likely to originate from a third party which abets Beijing or Washington's felt need to bolster, reassure, or shelter it. Efforts by Beijing and Washington to foster or reinforce a protégé's trust in it can produce the so-called chain-ganging dynamic.[51] This ally's actions are in turn likely to be motivated by its domestic politics implicating its ruling elite's legitimacy, effectiveness, and even physical survival.

Partisan rivalry and popular discontent are two domestic conditions that can incline incumbent leaders to take risks in starting foreign confrontations as suggested by the diversionary theory of war. A severe economic downturn can also introduce an exogenous shock to the existing equilibrium. It can be the catalyst setting off a cascade of events that saps the incumbent officials' credibility and legitimacy, sharpens partisan divisions, and exacerbates mass disenchantment. The consequent economic distress and rising inequality engender an acute sense of relative deprivation, and mobilize angry voters to reject establishment politicians and their policies to foster economic openness and interdependence. In a nondemocracy like China, mass alienation can similarly produce leadership insecurity and dissention within its ranks. Nationalist and even xenophobic politicians can ride on the coattail of intense popular discontent, and those with more moderate views are hamstrung by partisan divisions to initiate or sustain attempts to promote trust abroad.

Domestic conditions interact with foreign developments such that if several countries experience the same challenging circumstances at the same time, their policy responses can feed on each other, thus creating a spiral that increases tension and decreases trust. Sharp and rapid power shifts among some countries can compound uncertainty and anxiety about existing interstate commitments and alignments. These concerns gain special salience for those states whose security, economic health, and domestic political power and legitimacy are tied to foreign support. Rising powers will set a higher threshold for trusting others, whereas declining powers will demand more reassurance from others. These concurrent dynamics and cross-cutting currents can be confounding but a restrictive normative order can provide an important safety net to guard against unwelcome perturbations.

Mutual understanding or mutual accommodation, rather than mutual trust, is perhaps a more appropriate and realistic way to talk and think about Sino-American relations at this time. As already explained, this relationship is characterized by only a weak form or a semi-strong form of trust. It lacks the genuine sense of shared purpose and common identity that comes from the strong form of trust. There was, however, even within the recent past a glimpse of the latter possibility.

A window of opportunity appeared to have opened after the end of the Cold War (1989), the USSR's collapse (1991), and the September 11 (2001) terrorist attack on the U.S. In 1990–1991 almost the entire international community, including Russia and China, was in support of the U.S.-led effort to evict Saddam Hussein from Kuwait (Operation Desert Storm). The United Nations was actually for once decisive, expeditious, and effective in its rebuke of Iraq's aggression, and the major states were unanimous in their condemnation of and opposition to this aggression (China had voted in support of all U.N. resolutions against Iraq except when it abstained on Resolution 678 that authorized the use of military force against that country). Similarly, international opinion was overwhelmingly sympathetic to and supportive of the U.S. campaign to combat terrorism after the tragedy of 9/11. Francis Fukuyama has famously heralded the arrival of a new era with people all over the world rallying around the ideals of democracy and capitalism.[52] Communism had collapsed in Europe and many authoritarian regimes had also fallen in other parts of the world. While not officially renouncing communism, China had embraced capitalism and opened its economy to foreign trade and investment. It had also ceased its earlier support of armed insurrections abroad.

When one thinks back to other historic occasions "after victory,"[53] such as in the wake of the Napoleonic Wars and World Wars I and II, they provided an opportunity to develop and consolidate institutions and rules for international cooperation. The victors, sometimes joined by the vanquished, would craft constitutional pacts that would offer a chance for them to bind themselves as well as others to a new or reinvigorated set of principles and conventions to regulate their future conduct and provide a basis for common expectations of proper behavior. What happened this time when circumstances appeared equally propitious to start a new consensual global order?

The U.S.-led invasion of Iraq in 2003 (Operation Iraqi Freedom) was a critical turning point, signaling Washington's determination to start a preventive war even in the face of significant international opposition and without the necessary U.N. authorization. Other instances of U.S. and/or NATO use of force against Serbia, Libya, and Syria, and Washington's resort to drone attacks in Afghanistan, Pakistan, and Yemen exacerbated foreign concerns about the limits that the U.S. was willing to accept on the exercise of its overwhelming power. Official rhetoric aimed at promoting regime change abroad, especially that which directed against Iran and North Korea (after Iraq's Saddam Hussein was overthrown by the U.S. invasion), indicated that Washington had a revisionist rather than status-quo agenda. Other significant episodes, such as the decision to withdraw from the ABM Treaty and the enlargement of NATO, would lend support to the same interpretation. They suggest that the U.S. is interested in further increasing its power and expanding its reach even though it is already far ahead of any plausible competitor, including China.

In July 2015, another issue with potentially significant implications for fostering or diminishing interstate trust was taking shape. This issue pertained to Iran's nuclear program. After years of negotiation with multiple partners but led by the U.S., a deal was finally reached that would curb Tehran's nuclear program in return for the international community to lift its sanctions against that country. This deal was supported by the other parties to the negotiation process, including China, Russia, Britain, France, Germany, and the European Union. The United Nations Security Council voted unanimously in support of it, as did the European Union's foreign ministers. It was, however, opposed vigorously by Israel and met considerable skepticism from domestic critics of the Obama administration. The politics of domestic approval in this case was reminiscent of some other international agreements negotiated by the U.S. in the past, such as the acrimonious debates involving the Panama Canal Treaty and the Strategic Arms Reduction Treaty. Although the latter treaties were eventually ratified, the process that led to this outcome showed how domestic politics can undermine foreign confidence in the ability of a democracy's chief executive to deliver on a negotiated deal and that even if ratified, future progress on similar negotiations might be stymied as a result of the strong domestic opposition disclosed by this experience. Unlike on these two occasions, in 1999 the U.S. Senate refused to ratify the Comprehensive Nuclear Test Ban Treaty despite President William J. Clinton's support for it. Russia has ratified this treaty but China has also thus far failed to ratify it.

The 2015 nuclear deal with Tehran has involved other negotiation partners and international organizations and as such, it engaged the latter more directly in developing and enforcing the terms of this multilateral agreement. President Obama was able to muster 42 Democratic Senators to support the Iran deal. Even though those opposed to this accord (consisting mostly of Republican senators) commanded a majority, they did not have enough votes to stop a Democratic filibuster (which would have required 60 votes) or to override a presidential veto (which would have required 67 votes). Because Congress did not disapprove this accord within sixty days, President Obama was able to secure this deal even though most U.S. legislators were opposed to it. This outcome was a close call, and the process leading to it revealed sharp partisan divisions and deep reservations inside the U.S. Had this process delivered a different outcome, it would have signaled even more strongly a U.S. inclination to "go it alone." The nuclear deal negotiated by President Obama with Iran was not considered a treaty which would have required a two-thirds majority of the Senate to ratify but only as an agreement that would go into effect barring a resolution of disapproval by the Senate. Because it is an agreement reached by a chief executive, this deal can be reversed by a future president—something that several candidates competing to be the Republican Party's nominee for the 2016 U.S. presidential election had announced to be their intention if elected.

Although President Donald Trump said he would cancel the nuclear deal with Iran, he has not yet done so at this writing. He has, however, fulfilled his campaign promises to pull the U.S. out the Trans-Pacific Partnership and the Paris climate accord, thus signaling a strong rejection of U.S. leadership of multilateral diplomacy. These episodes point to actual or prospective defection from cooperation. They reinforce the proposition that a really powerful country is less inclined to trust others, and that democratic politics can be messy and present a doubled-edged sword in matters of trust.

This discussion calls attention to how leaders define their country's interests and how others perceive their intention to pursue these interests. Different leaders of the same country may define these interests differently. There are of course areas where Beijing and Washington's interests (as their leaders have currently defined them) converge, such as in preventing nuclear proliferation and combating international terrorism. In these areas cooperation is possible and even likely (such as in their joint efforts to discourage Iran and North Korea's nuclear programs). A convergence of national interests naturally provides a basis for strategic (or instrumental) trust—the belief that the other side can be relied on to do the right thing because it is in its interest to protect or advance one's own interest. Thus cooperation is possible when leaders perceive shared interests and expect reciprocity, and it does not necessarily require the strong form of trust.

There are also areas where Beijing and Washington are likely to define their national interests differently and indeed, in a fundamentally incompatible way. When this is the case, their mutual distrust is understandable and even natural. Thus, for example, if Chinese leaders believe that the U.S. military presence and alliances in the Western Pacific pose a basic threat to their country's security and if the U.S. leaders believe that this presence and the alliances are in their country's basic national interest, then it is difficult to imagine how various attempts aimed at enhancing mutual trust can help avoid or dampen their conflict stemming from this incompatibility.[54] Only a change in how they define their interests can do that. And as suggested earlier, the definition of national interests often derives from how leaders see—that is, identify—themselves. Thus, shared identity usually provides the strong basis for developing and sustaining moralistic or generalized trust.

Distrust does not necessarily imply misperception. But when misperception exists, its correction helps to develop trust—such as if Beijing misunderstands Washington's policy toward Taiwan, attributing to the U.S. an interest and intention to keep this island from becoming reunited with China when Washington does not in fact have this agenda. Among other things, continued U.S. arms sales to Taiwan have contributed to this Chinese perception and given Washington's pledge made in the 1982 joint communiqué, serve as an indication of its untrustworthiness in Beijing's eyes.[55] As another example, if Beijing believes that Washington intends to overthrow unfriendly regimes but Washington actually does not have this intention to promote regime change abroad, then it would make sense for Washington to reassure Beijing that it does not have such intention (or did not have this intention in Nicaragua, Grenada, Panama, Iraq, Afghanistan, Libya, Syria, and so on), and thus to allay Beijing's concerns and remove its distrust caused by this misperception. But if a counterpart state actually has the incompatible interests and uncongenial intentions attributed to it, then the resulting tension is not a result of misperception or a problem produced by distrust. Until the two countries' leaders show credible signs that they are willing to voluntarily accommodate the other side's key interests, mutual trust will be elusive. Naturally, the strong form of trust requires such mutual accommodation and reciprocal adjustment to come from empathy, moral impulses, and social bonds engendered by joint membership in a security community rather than material or strategic calculations. In this case, trust is no longer driven by interests but rather by a sense of what is proper, legitimate and just.

Many of those events that have contributed to mutual distrust in Beijing and Washington occurred at a time of unrivaled and undisputed U.S. preponderance in international relations, and also during a period of China's rapid rise. They have aroused reciprocal concerns in both capitals that the other side's increased capabilities have made it more assertive and ambitious in its foreign relations, encouraging it to push its advantages and expand its interests. Although, as already suggested, contact between American and Chinese officials and analysts has increased enormously compared to the days when their countries did not have diplomatic ties, mutual suspicions have largely persisted with relatively few signs of dissipation. Moreover, with regard to the key elements of a restrictive normative order—accepted limits to the use of military force, consistent observance of a country's international obligations and commitments, and reciprocal respect for each country's traditional sphere of influence—there are still few indications of a common understanding. Mutual trust will be fragile and fleeting until there is a stronger common understanding and indeed, a common identity among the elites of both countries. This said, it is also undeniable that there has been significant progress when one compares the current state of affairs with the situation prevailing during the 1950s and 1960s. This progress gives hope to the belief that further improvement in bilateral relations is possible in the future. Cooperation initially undertaken on the basis of mutual interests can transform over time people's identities and shift their reasoning from the logic of consequences to the logic of appropriateness.

NOTES

1. Daniel Maliniak, Susan Peterson, and Michael J. Tierney, "TRIP around the World: Teaching, Research, and Policy Views of International Relations Faculty in 20 Countries," (May 2012), accessed June 2, 2017, www.wm.edu/offices/itpir/_documents/trip/trip_around_the_world_2011.pdf, 82.
2. Ibid., 84–85.
3. Organski and Kugler, *The War Ledger*; and Tammen et al., *Power Transitions*.
4. Allison, "The Thucydides Trap."
5. Donald Kagan, *The Outbreak of the Peloponnesian War* (Ithaca, NY: Cornell University Press, 1969), 2–3.
6. Chan, *China, the U.S.*, and "The Power Transition Discourse."
7. For reviews of the power-transition theory, see Chan, "The Power-Transition Discourse;" Jonathan M. Dicicco and Jack S. Levy, "Power Shifts and Problem Shifts: The Evolution of the Power Transition Research Program," *Journal of Conflict Resolution* 43, no. 6 (1999): 675–704; Richard N. Lebow and Benjamin Valentino, "Lost in Transition: A Critical Analysis of Power Transition Theory," *International Relations* 23, no. 3 (2009): 389–410; Levy, "Power Transition Theory;" David P. Rapkin and William R. Thompson, "Power Transition, Challenge and the (Re)emergence of China," *International Interactions* 29, no. 4 (2003): 315–342; and John A. Vasquez, "When Are Power Transitions Dangerous? An Appraisal and Reformulation of Power Transition Theory," in *Parity and War: Evaluations and Extensions of the War Ledger*, eds. Jacek Kugler and Douglas Lemke (Ann Arbor: University of Michigan Press, 1996), 35–56.
8. Copeland, *The Origins*; Lebow, "Windows of Opportunity;" and Levy, "Preventive War," and "Declining Power and the Preventive Motivation for War," *World Politics* 60, no. 1 (1987): 82–107.
9. Jack S. Levy and William R. Thompson, "Hegemonic Threats and Great-Power Balancing in Europe, 1495–1999," *Security Studies* 14, no. 1 (2005): 1–33, and "Balancing on Land and at Sea: Do States Ally Against the Leading Global Power?" *International Security* 35, no. 1 (2010): 7–43.
10. See, for example, Mearsheimer, "China's Unpeaceful Rise."
11. See, for example, Tammen et al., *Power Transitions*, 9.
12. Organski and Kugler, *The War Ledger*.

13. Quoted in John J. Mearsheimer, *The Tragedy of Great Power Politics* (New York: Norton, 2001), 238.
14. Organski and Kugler, *The War Ledger*.
15. Amos Tversky and Daniel Kahneman, "Judgment under Uncertainty: Heuristics and Biases," *Science* 185, no. 4157 (1974): 1124–1131.
16. Mercer, *Reputation and International Politics*.
17. Putnam, *Making Democracy Work*.
18. Kupchan, *How Enemies Become Friends*.
19. Daniel Ellsberg, "The Quagmire Myth and the Stalemate Machine," *Public Policy* 19 (1971): 217–274; and James C. Thomson, "How Could Vietnam Happen: An Autopsy," *The Atlantic Monthly* (April 1968), accessed June 2, 2017, http://www.theatlantic.com/magazine/archive/1968/04/how-could-vietnam-happen-an-autopsy/306462/.
20. Kupchan, *How Enemies Become Friends*.
21. Yongping Feng, "The Peaceful Transition of Power from the UK to the US," *Chinese Journal of International Politics* 1, no. 1 (2006): 83–108.
22. Kupchan, *How Enemies Become Friends*.
23. Kegley and Raymond, *A Multipolar Peace*, 194.
24. Alexander Wendt, "Anarchy is What States Make of It: The Social Construction of Power Politics," *International Organization* 46, no. 2 (1992): 391–425.
25. Mearsheimer and Walt, "An Unnecessary War."
26. Kaufman, "Threat Inflation;" and Mearsheimer, *Why Leaders Lie*.
27. Fearon, "Rationalist Explanations."
28. M. Taylor Fravel, "All Quiet in the South China Sea: Why China Is Playing Nice (For Now)," *Foreign Affairs* (March 22, 2012), accessed June 2, 2017, https://www.foreignaffairs.com/articles/china/2012-03-22/all-quiet-south-china-sea.
29. "Dangerous Waters: China-Japan Relations on Rocks," International Crisis Group (2013), accessed June 2, 2017, https://www.crisisgroup.org/asia/north-east-asia/china/dangerous-waters-china-japan-relations-rocks. The description "non-confrontational assertiveness" has also been used; see Mingjiang Li, "China's New Security Posture: Non-Confrontational Assertiveness," *East Asia Forum* (June 4, 2011), accessed June 2, 2017, www.eastasiaforum.org/2011/06/04/china-s-new-security-posture-non-confrontational-assertiveness, and "China's Non-Confrontational Assertiveness in the South China Sea," *East Asia Forum* (Jun 14, 2012), accessed June 2, 2017, http://www.eastasiaforum.org/2012/06/14/china-s-non-confrontational-assertiveness-in-the-south-china-sea/.

30. Trevor Moss, "China's Not-So-Hard-Power Strategy," *The Diplomat* (June 28, 2012), accessed June 2, 2017, http://thediplomat.com/2012/06/28/chinas-not-so-hard-power-strategy.
31. Michael D. Swaine and M. Taylor Fravel, "China's Assertive Behavior, Part Two: The Maritime Periphery," *China Leadership Monitor*, 35 (2011), accessed June 2, 2017 https://www.google.com/url?sa=t&rct=j&q=&esrc=s&source=web&cd=3&ved=0ahUKEwjqm_CM9Z_UAhXhh1QKHe3pDWQQFgg4MAI&url=https%3A%2F%2Fdspace.mit.edu%2Fopenaccess-disseminate%2F1721.1%2F71259&usg=AFQjCNHMkA2OZNc0NnlVY3iPGGuG3BbMhQ, 11.
32. Quoted in Robert A. Pape, "Soft Balancing against the United States," *International Security* 30, no. 1 (2005), 43.
33. Kegley and Raymond, *A Multipolar Peace.*
34. Posen, "Command of the Commons."
35. Lieber and Press, "The End of MAD."
36. Pape, "Soft Balancing," 34.
37. The White House, "The National Security Strategy of the United States of America," (September 2002), accessed June 2, 2017, http://nssarchive.us/NSSR/2002.pdf, 30.
38. "Joint Communiqué of the United States of America and the People's Republic of China)," Taiwan Documents Project, accessed June 2, 2017, http://www.taiwandocuments.org/communique02.htm.
39. Quoted in Patrick Tyler, *A Great Wall, Six Presidents and China: An Investigative History* (New York: Perseus, 1999), 225.
40. Richard C. Bush, *Untying the Knot: Making Peace in the Taiwan Strait* (Washington, DC: Brookings Institution Press, 2005), and *Uncharted Strait: The Future of China-Taiwan Relations* (Washington, DC: Brookings Institution Press, 2013); and Nancy B. Tucker, *Dangerous Strait: The U.S.-Taiwan-China Crisis* (New York: Columbia University Press, 2015).
41. Fearon, "Signaling Foreign Policy Interests."
42. Chan, *China's Troubled Waters.*
43. Richard K. Betts, *American Force: Dangers, Delusions, and Dilemmas in National Security* (New York: Columbia University Press, 2012); Bruce Gilley, "Not So Dire Straits: How the Finlandization of Taiwan Benefits U.S. Security," *Foreign Affairs* 89, no. 1 (2010): 44–56, 58–60; Charles Glaser, "Will China's Rise Lead to War? Why Realism Does Not Mean Pessimism," *Foreign Affairs* 90, no. 2 (2011): 80–91; Kenneth Lieberthal, "Preventing a War over Taiwan," *Foreign Affairs* 84, no. 2 (2005): 53–63; Rigger, "Why Giving Up;" Phillip C. Saunders and Scott L. Kast-

ner, "Bridge over Troubled Waters: Envisioning a China-Taiwan Peace Agreement," *International Security* 33, no. 4 (2009): 87–114; and Tucker and Glaser, "Should the United States."

44. Etzioni, "Spheres of Influence."
45. Norrlof and Reich, "American and Chinese Leadership."
46. Kaufman, "Threat Inflation," and "Selling the Market Short."
47. Ikenberry, *After Victory.*
48. Schroeder, "Alliances, 1815–1945."
49. Snyder, *Alliance Politics.*
50. Etzioni, "Integrating China."
51. Christensen and Snyder, "Chain Gangs."
52. Francis Fukuyama, *The End of History and the Last Man* (New York: Free Press, 1992).
53. Ikenberry, *After Victory.*
54. James Steinberg and Michael E. O'Hanlon, *Strategic Reassurance and Resolve: U.S.-China Relations in the Twenty-First Century* (Princeton, NJ: Princeton University Press, 2015), 13.
55. Steinberg and O'Hanlon, *Strategic Reassurance,* 130.

POSTSCRIPT

Donald Trump won the election on November 8, 2016, and became the U.S. president on January 20, 2017. His inaugural speech signaled a change from past U.S. policies, declaring that "From this day forward, it's going to be only America first—America first."[1] In his administration's early days, he issued executive orders to pull the U.S. out of the Trans-Pacific Partnership agreement, to temporarily ban visitors from seven predominantly Muslim countries and foreign refugees from entering the U.S, and to build a wall on the U.S.-Mexico border (declaring that Mexico will pay for it).

Trump had promised that he would also renegotiate the terms of NAFTA with Mexico and Canada and that he would rescind the deal that Obama had reached with Iran to curtail the latter's nuclear program. He had also said "the concept of global warming was created by and for the Chinese in order to make U.S. manufacturing non-competitive,"[2] and indicated that he would pull the U.S. out of the Paris accord to combat global warming (which he did on June 1, 2017, repudiating U.S. support for this global agreement signed by 195 states). He had, moreover, questioned U.S. commitments to its NATO allies, causing concerns especially among the newer members of this alliance in Eastern and Central Europe. In Asia, he had demanded that Japan and South Korea pay more for the U.S. military presence there. He implied that a decision by these countries to develop nuclear weapons would not be a particular concern for him. He promised to label China a "currency manipulator" (but later reversed himself)[3]—even while Beijing was trying to *prevent* the *yuan* from weakening rather than to depress its value. He averred that "we can't continue to allow China to rape our country,"[4] and threatened to impose a 45% tariff on Chinese exports to the U.S.

He had also made many disparaging remarks about women, Muslims, immigrants, and racial/ethnic minorities.

While he was the president-elect, Trump spoke to Tsai Ing-wen, Taiwan's president, in an unprecedented phone conversation that was evidently prearranged. This conversation rattled Beijing because there had never been any such high-level contact since Washington broke diplomatic relationship with Taipei in 1979, and it represented a breach of the official U.S. policy that there is only one China and Taiwan belongs to China. Beijing lodged a diplomatic protest with the Obama administration, and Trump responded to the controversy by questioning publicly "why we have to be bound by a 'one China' policy'?"[5] He reportedly reversed himself on this position after a phone conversation with China's leader Xi Jinping in February 2017.

He tweeted that "the United States must greatly strengthen and expand its nuclear capability"[6] and when asked to expand on his comment, he was quoted saying "let it be an arms race"[7] and the U.S. would win it. He planned to propose a 10% increase in U.S. military spending while trimming the budgets of other agencies, including the State Department and the Environmental Protection Agency.

Trump's actions and statements indicate a turn to a more unilateral, protectionist, and even isolationist and nationalist approach to U.S. foreign policy. They also imply a disposition to seek rapprochement with Russia and confrontation with China. He expressed a certain admiration for Vladimir Putin and was dismissive of U.S. intelligence reports of Russian hacking intended to hurt the electoral prospects of his Democratic opponent, Hillary Clinton. He even claimed that electoral fraud was responsible for Clinton having won the popular contest by nearly three million votes.

At the time of this writing, information on Trump's foreign policy is still limited although its general orientation seems clear. For example, he is skeptical of multilateral institutions and prefers to engage in bilateral negotiations instead. His views signal strongly a break from past U.S. policies, thus creating uncertainties and shaking confidence abroad. They suggest a rejection of economic interdependence and international organizations, and a disinvestment in U.S. reputation for trustworthiness. To the extent that his statements communicate a willingness to renege on commitments made by his predecessors or a disposition to pursue unilateral assertiveness, they further undermine foreigners' trust in the U.S. As explained before, a person's attitudes toward vulnerable, unpopular, or needy groups provide an indication of his/her trustworthiness, or at least this person's capacity for empathy. Even if Trump's statements turn out to be only political hot air, they can still cause concern because they point to a discrepancy between words and deeds. Given the overwhelming power of the United States, foreign countries are in a weak position to oppose it. Restraint will have to come more from its domestic sources such as its political institutions, its people's ideological inclinations, and its leaders' natural impulses and self-control.

The 2016 U.S. election also shows that the American people are deeply divided in their opinions on various domestic and foreign issues. This division and the sharp disagreements among the elite indicate a heightened prospect of political gridlock and the possibility of policy vacillation and even reversal. For all the aforementioned reasons, foreign countries are more likely to hedge their relations with the U.S. with the advent of Trump presidency. The transparency of democratic politics presents a doubled-edged sword that can sometimes reassure foreigners but also occasionally alarm and distress them.

NOTES

1. Donald J. Trump, "From this Day forward," accessed June 2, 2017, https://www.youtube.com/watch?v=u2IhFUwp2O0.
2. Donald J. Trump on climate change, accessed June 2, 2017, https://twitter.com/realdonaldtrump/status/265895292191248385?lang=en.
3. Donald J. Trump on Chinese currency manipulation, accessed June 2, 2017, http://www.politifact.com/truth-o-meter/promises/trumpometer/promise/1412/declare-china-currency-manipulator/ and https://twitter.com/realdonaldtrump/status/853583417916755968?lang=en.
4. Donald J. Trump, "China Rape," accessed June 2, 2017, http://www.cnn.com/2016/05/01/politics/donald-trump-china-rape/.
5. Donald J. Trump, "U.S. Not Necessarily Bound by 'One China' Policy," accessed June 2, 2017, http://www.reuters.com/article/us-usa-trump-china-idUSKBN1400TY.
6. Donald J. Trump, "U.S. Must Greatly Expand and Strengthen Its Nuclear Capability," accessed June 2, 2017, https://twitter.com/realdonaldtrump/status/811977223326625792?lang=en.
7. Donald J. Trump, "Let It Be an Arms Race," accessed June 2, 2017, http://www.nbcnews.com/politics/politics-news/trump-nukes-let-it-be-arms-race-n699526.

Index

Abu Ghraib, 82
Acheson, Dean, 64
air-defense self-identification zone, 130, 233
Al Qaeda, 53, 65, 82, 84
al-Assad, Bashar, 84
Allende, Salvador, 48, 59
Anti-Ballistic Missile (ABM) Treaty, 31–32, 119, 171, 227, 243
Arbenz, Jacobo, 48
Asia Pacific Economic Cooperation, 203
Asian financial crisis, 62, 232
Asian Infrastructure Investment Bank, 156–158, 162, 178
Association of Southeast Asian Nations, 184, 195
attribution theory, 217
audience costs, 88, 117–118, 132
axis of evil, 53, 78
balance-of-power theory, 18
bandwagon, 18
Bay of Pigs, 71, 81, 94
binding, 139, 161, 188, 194, 227–228, 233
  co-binding, 25, 33, 224
  self-binding, 28, 33, 166, 224
bluff, 28, 77, 109–111
BRIC, 108, 162
Bush, George H., 53, 65, 80, 82, 84, 104, 119, 170–171, 175, 187–188, 203, 227, 250
Bush, George W., 53, 65, 80, 82, 84, 104, 119, 170–171, 175, 187–188, 203, 227, 250

Carter, Jimmy, 24, 79, 81, 115, 119
Castro, Raúl, 115, 200
Chamberlain, Neville, 2
chain-ganging, 21, 241
Chen Shui-bian, 36, 150
Chiang Kai-shek, 36
China's rise, 18, 65, 90, 99–100, 209, 250
Chinese embassy in Belgrade, the bombing of, 11
Clinton, Hillary, 157, 189, 254
Clinton, William J., 81, 244
Cold War, 10, 18, 22, 40, 53–54, 65–67, 74, 91, 94, 109, 129–130, 143, 151, 173, 179, 211, 231, 239, 242
collective action, 63, 122, 133, 160, 188
commitment problem, 5, 109, 144, 156, 165
Common Market, 197, 201
Comprehensive Nuclear Test Ban Treaty, 184, 244
Concert of Europe, 195–196
Conference on Disarmament, 184
Convention on Certain Conventional Weapons, 184
constitutional pact, 163
Churchill, Winston, 2
Cuban Missile Crisis, 30, 44, 86
Cultural Revolution, 74
defense burden, 68, 149
de Gaulle, Charles, 60
democratic peace, 27, 44, 73, 93, 132, 232, 237

Democratic Progressive Party, 121, 197
Deng Xiaoping, 52, 237
distributional coalitions, 124
diversionary incentive (or theory), 115
domestic ratification, 24, 34, 121
Dreikaiserbund, 201
Dulles, John Foster, 10
economic interdependence, 21, 29, 125, 137–156, 172, 176–177, 195, 198, 222, 255
encapsulated interest, 13, 153
Eisenhower, Dwight, 81
entrapment, 21, 36, 160, 233
European Coal and Steel Community, 197
European Union, 17, 145, 156, 166, 238, 243–244
Eurozone, 154
Ford, Gerald, 123
Franco-Prussian War, 49, 213
free riding, 14, 59, 160
Gaddafi, Muammar, 9, 78, 137
German-Soviet Non-Aggression Pact, 4
Glaspie, April, 64
Gorbachev, Mikhail, 6, 37, 50, 128, 198–200, 222
Great Leap Forward, 74
Great Recession, 62, 186, 232
Gulf Cooperation Council, 195
Gulf of Tonkin Resolution, 81, 84
hedging, 14
hegemonic stability theory, 68
Helms-Burton Act, 54
Hitler, Adolf, 2, 4, 6, 123
Hu Jintao, 203
hub-and-spokes approach, 167
Hussein, Saddam, 9, 53, 61, 64–65, 77, 82, 84, 104, 137, 191, 242–243

intergovernmental organizations, 159, 165, 169, 172, 179–180, 185, 201, 203, 205
Intermediate-Range Nuclear Force Treaty, 128
International Convention on the Rights of the Child, 187
International Court of Justice, 193, 205, 226
International Criminal Court, 104, 119, 163, 178, 187
International Institute for Strategic Studies, 67, 92
International Labor Organization, 169
International Monetary Fund, 62, 157, 162–163
international organizations, 121, 137–139, 156–174, 177, 179, 182, 187–188, 234, 244, 255
International Trade Organization, 187
involuntary defection, 19, 115–116, 118–119, 128
Iran-contra scandal, 82
Jiang Zemin, 80
Johnson, Lyndon B., 81, 84
Kantian tripod, 172, 179
Kennan, George, 52
Kennedy, John F., 84
Kennedy, Robert, 30
Khrushchev, Nikita, 50
Kissinger, Henry, 203, 229
Korean War, 9, 52, 63–64, 71, 79, 91, 113
Kuomintang, 26, 52–53, 64, 76, 121
Kyoto Protocol, 187
Land Mines Convention, 187
League of Nations, 16–17, 116, 139, 159–160, 171, 187
learning theory, 19

Lee Teng-hui, 79, 115
logic of appropriateness, 17, 29–31, 44, 161, 183, 247
logic of consequences, 17, 29, 183, 247
logic of unthinkability, 31
Ma Ying-jeou, 77
MacArthur, Douglas, 63
Mao, Tse-tung, 114, 198, 200, 237
masking effect, 48–50
Mercado Comun del Sul, 194, 197
Merkel, Angela, 189
Milosevic, Slobodan, 77
Monroe Doctrine, 22
moral hazard, 36
Morsi, Mohammed, 48
Mossadegh, Mohammad, 48, 59
multilateral institutions, 28–29, 254
Napoleonic Wars, 214, 242
national missile defense, 227–228
Nixon, Richard, 4, 52–53, 61, 81, 114
nonsurrender agreement, 104
North American Free Trade Agreement, 119, 155, 188, 253
North Atlantic Treaty Organization, 9, 17, 30, 40, 44, 55, 66–67, 70, 72, 78, 80, 91–92, 94, 100, 119, 122, 128–129, 160, 166–167, 188, 213, 231, 243, 253
nuclear deal, 23, 218, 239, 244–245
Nuclear Nonproliferation Treaty, 171
Obama, Barack, 23, 84, 116, 119, 157, 188, 203, 236
offshore balancer, 70
Operation Barbarossa, 4
Operation Desert Storm, 64, 242
Operation Iraqi Freedom, 61, 191, 243
opportunity cost, 7

pacta (pactum) de contrahendo, 71, 227
Panama Canal Treaty, 244
Paris accord, 119, 188, 253
Permanent Court of Arbitration, 192, 226
pivot to Asia, 26, 53, 55, 127, 236
policy cycling, 119–120
Powell, Colin, 82, 131
power shift, 28
power-cycle theory, 106
power-transition theory, 28, 55, 68, 101, 108–109, 127, 131, 133, 210–214, 223, 248
Powers, Francis Gary, 81
preventive war, 61–62, 91, 102, 106–108, 126–127, 131, 136, 191, 210, 214, 224, 243, 248
prisoners' dilemma, 13, 135–137, 160
prophecy
    self-denying, 9–10
    self-fulfilling, 9
prospect theory, 94, 102–103, 107, 131
proximity, 66, 72, 198, 239
Putin, Vladimir, 254
Rabin, Yitzhak, 200
Reagan, Ronald, 6, 39, 82, 94, 128
reactive assertiveness, 226
reciprocity, 3, 21, 25, 176, 178–179, 215, 245
    diffuse, 16–17, 41, 136, 155, 160, 204
    specific, 16, 137, 155, 160, 204
regime change, 23, 26, 53–54, 67, 168, 213, 243, 246
reputation, 8–9, 16–17, 24, 28–29, 40, 43, 62, 75, 79–80, 82, 87–89, 95, 111, 117, 125, 135–137, 139, 144, 150, 155–156, 158–159,

reputation (*continued*), 162–163,
    168–169, 173–174, 176, 216, 249,
    255
responsible stakeholder, 62, 185,
    188
restrictive normative order, 224,
    242, 247
retrievability bias, 216
revisionism, 48, 51–55, 62, 101, 127,
    179, 181, 185, 196, 212–213, 243
Roosevelt, Franklin D., 84, 113, 116,
    132
Roy, J. Stapleton, 80
Russo-Japanese War, 213
Rwandan genocide, 49
Sadat, Anwar, 114, 198, 200
Sanders, Bernie, 157
scapegoating, 114, 125, 235
second face of security, 32, 45, 142
security community, 17, 29, 31, 137,
    183, 190, 195, 203–204, 219, 246
security dilemma, 5, 13, 39–40, 90
security externality, 141, 143
selectorate, 119–120
self-enforcing agreements, 149, 178
self-selection, 29, 160
Senkaku/Diaoyu Islands, 226, 233
shadow of the future, 28, 137, 165
sphere of influence, 22, 25, 33,
    66–67, 197, 230–231, 239, 247
Shah, 4
Sino-Soviet Treaty of Friendship,
    Alliance and Mutual Assistance,
    4
Snowden, Edward, 82, 189
South China Sea, 55, 58–59, 63, 75,
    192, 226, 249
Spanish-American War, 213
spiral model of conflict, 7, 13
status-quo orientation, 53–55, 100,
    127, 212

Stevenson, Adlai, 81
Stockholm International Peace
    Research Institute, 67, 92
strategic ambiguity, 118, 129, 229
Strategic Arms Reduction Treaty,
    244
strategic restraint, 4, 24–26, 33, 43,
    196, 202, 204, 209, 222–224, 231,
    234–235, 239
stuxnet, 189
Summers, Lawrence, 158, 178
superfusion, 32, 45, 152, 178, 197
Taiwan Relations Act, 24, 115
threat inflation, 84–85, 91, 249, 251
Thucydides trap, 43, 248
Tiananmen Square, 74
Trans-Pacific Partnership, 119, 155,
    157, 188, 235, 245, 253
transparency, 23, 83–84, 127, 157,
    255
Truman Doctrine, 52
Trump, Donald, 42, 100, 102, 119,
    145, 153, 156–157, 188, 238, 245,
    253
trust, 2, 4–5, 9–12, 18–22, 26, 32, 35,
    37–39, 42–43, 47–48, 51, 57–58,
    60, 62, 65–66, 68, 77–78, 80, 83,
    85–87, 89–91, 93, 99–100, 104,
    107, 109–110, 121, 126–127, 131,
    133, 136, 143, 146, 149, 153–154,
    156–157, 163, 168, 172, 174,
    177–179, 191, 195, 200–201,
    210, 214, 216, 224, 230, 233, 238,
    240–241, 247, 261
    generalized, 13, 15–16, 40–41,
        125, 138, 160–162, 183, 194,
        203, 219, 246
    particularistic, 13, 16, 161, 183,
        194
    semi-strong form, 17, 28–30,
        135, 137, 160, 222, 242

trust (*continued*)
  instrumental, 59, 137, 139, 142,
    161, 167, 219, 245
  strategic, 6–7, 16–17, 24–25,
    27, 33, 103, 128–129, 137,
    139, 161, 167, 196, 198, 202,
    204, 219, 222–223, 229, 231,
    234–236, 239, 243–246
  strong form, 3, 14, 17, 25, 28–31,
    34, 36, 50, 56, 103, 105–106,
    135, 137, 139, 159–160,
    162, 165, 173, 183, 193–194,
    204, 215, 218–223, 227, 236,
    242–246
  weak form, 14, 17, 27–30, 73,
    97–98, 105–106, 113, 124,
    128–129, 135, 142, 159, 169,
    199, 218, 242, 255
Tsai Ing-wen, 197, 254
Tsipras, Alexis, 154
two-level games, 19, 42, 115, 141
tying hands, 94, 112, 117, 229
United Nations, 16, 53, 58, 64,
  81–82, 100, 160, 162, 168, 171,
  184, 186–187, 192, 224, 226, 242
  General Assembly, 166,
    169–170, 181, 185
  Security Council, 167, 169–170,
    180–181, 191, 193, 243

United Nations Convention on the
  Law of the Sea, 192, 226
United Nations Educational,
  Scientific and Cultural
  Organization, 169
U.S.-China Strategic and Economic
  Dialogue, 203
U.S. National Security Agency, 189
USS Greer, 84
USS Liberty, 11
USS Maddox, 84
USS Vincennes, 11
veil of ignorance, 37, 57, 72
veto groups, 24, 99, 114, 118, 128
Vietnam War, 53, 63, 81, 84, 87, 94,
  113, 115, 123
Watergate scandal, 81, 124
Wilson, Woodrow, 4, 116
win set, 24, 128
World Bank, 68, 92, 162
World War I, 4, 7, 21, 35, 88, 93,
  107–108, 173, 211, 220
World War II, 3, 41, 52, 71, 74, 84,
  108, 123, 132, 211, 220
Xi Jinping, 77, 254
Yanukovych, Viktor, 48
Yinhe, 80
Zollverein, 197

Rapid Communications in Conflict and Security

Utilizing its unique capability to combine speed of publication with high-production values, Cambria Press is proud to announce a new series, Rapid Communications in Conflict and Security (RCCS), to bring to market in a timely manner books on a range of pressing aspects of global and national conflict—from foreign policy and diplomacy to the projection of both inter- and intrastate hard power. The series is headed by general editor Dr. Geoffrey R. H. Burn, a former army officer with a doctorate in organization theory and strategy as well as thirty years of experience as the chief executive of book and journal publishing companies.

The RCCS series will provide policy makers, practitioners, analysts, and academics with in-depth analysis of fast-moving topics that require urgent yet informed debate. Wherever possible, arguments will be set within an appropriate theoretical and/or historical context—but all books will have practical application.

Since its launch in October 2015, the RCCS series has published the following books:

- *A New Strategy for Complex Warfare: Combined Effects in East Asia* by Thomas A. Drohan
- *US National Security: New Threats, Old Realities* by Paul R. Viotti
- *Security Forces in African States: Cases and Assessment* edited by Paul Shemella and Nicholas Tomb
- *Trust and Distrust in Sino-American Relations: Challenge and Opportunity* by Steve Chan

For more information or questions on the RCCS series, please contact editor@cambriapress.com.

ABOUT THE AUTHOR

Steve Chan is College Professor of Distinction at the University of Colorado. His recent publications include *China's Troubled Waters: Maritime Disputes in Theoretical Perspective* (Cambridge University Press, 2016), *Enduring Rivalries in the Asia Pacific* (Cambridge University Press, 2013), and *Looking for Balance: China, the United States, and Power Balancing in East Asia* (Stanford University Press, 2012).